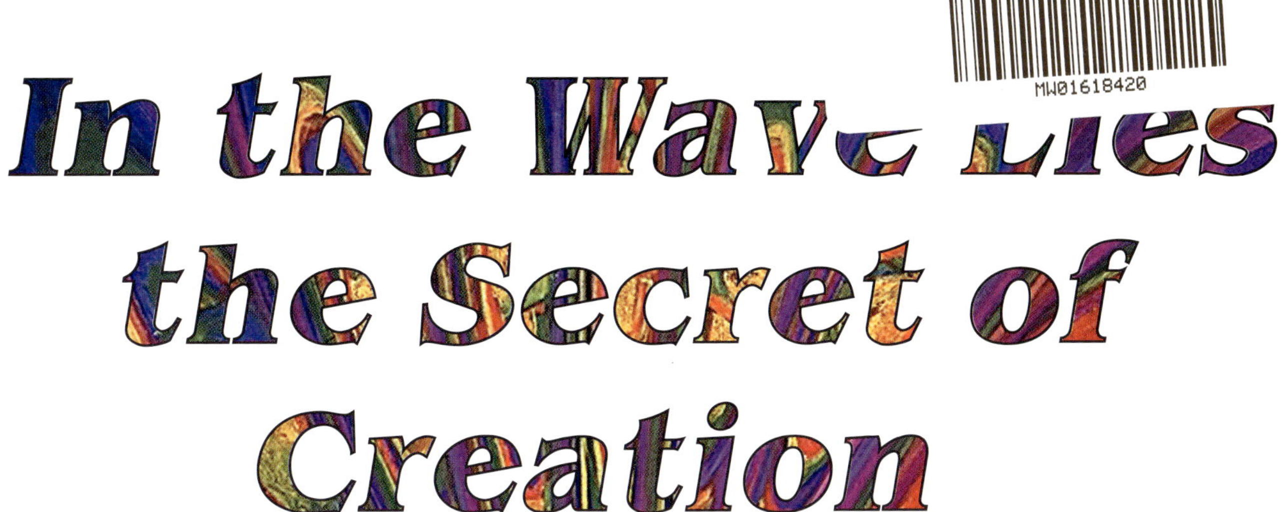

Scientific Paintings and Charts
of Walter Russell

with commentaries and an outline of
the Russell Cosmogony

by

Dr. Timothy A. Binder
President
University of Science and Philosophy

ISBN 1-879605-45-7
Printed in Waynesboro, Virginia 22980

Table of Contents

List of Diagrams

WALTER RUSSELL

PREFACE

Walter Russell said,

In the Wave lies the secret of Creation.

If this is true, then the wave is the basis of the Russellian scientific structure. With an understanding of the wave, one can see all of his principles in each of these pictorial representations of his scientific vision of the universe. It is my belief that each and every one of Dr. Russell's paintings and charts included in this volume contains every principle of the Russell Cosmogony either explicitly or implicitly.

I have organized the paintings and charts in a way that seems logical to me in the hope that it will assist students to better comprehend the Russell Cosmogony. My commentary is directed at those students who have already studied the bulk of the Russellian science writing in *The Home Study Course, Atomic Suicide?, A New Concept of the Universe, The Secret of Light,* and *The Universal One.* It is designed to be especially helpful to those students who are applying the Russellian science of the cosmos to create a new, sustainable, pollution-free technology for the coming millennium. This was one of the most important goals of both Walter and Lao Russell as a demonstration of the love principle in science and technology.

While my explanations are primarily addressed to scientists and students who have studied the Russellian science and terminology in depth and wish to approach the material both intellectually and intuitively, it is also true that paintings access our understanding on levels other than that of the intellect. Therefore, students and artists of all backgrounds can bypass the commentary and study these paintings in whatever way seems most appropriate to them.

For students interested in the intellectual approach who are new to Russellian science and terminology, I have included an introduction which outlines the Russell Cosmogony and compares it to the science of his time. I have also presented a universal systems model and an outline of language mechanics based on this model since I believe it to be an extension of the Russells' message. They used this model for universal processes, presenting the lever or seesaw as a simple analogy. By enlarging on the universal systems model and applying it to language and other symbols, I hope to make it easier for more people to understand the Russellian writings and scientific paintings.

The Russells hoped that by helping a sufficient number of self-realized souls to attain a full understanding of this unique cosmogony, they would ensure a peaceful, sustainable civilization for many future generations. I offer this book as a fervent continuation of that effort.

There is evidence, in fact, that Dr. Russell contemplated publishing a book such as this over fifty years ago. Dr. H. H. Sheldon of the Washington Square College Department of Physics at New York

NEW YORK UNIVERSITY
WASHINGTON SQUARE COLLEGE
WASHINGTON SQUARE EAST, NEW YORK

DEPARTMENT OF PHYSICS

January 30, 1931.

Mr. Walter Russell,
450 East 50th Street,
New York, N. Y.

Dear Mr. Russell:

Having expressed my appreciation of the painting which you showed to me in person, it has occurred to me that further encouragement might be given your work if I reduced to writing briefly my opinion on the value of the work you are undertaking. For some time as you know I have been urging you to reproduce your theories in concrete experiments which would either confirm or disapprove your ideas. To prove your concepts experimentally is a handicap to you that might defeat your purpose because of its attendant great expense which you admit to be beyond your means, and also because you have not been trained in experimental work.

If through painting you can express your ideas, which you explained to me briefly in words, I am inclined to think that you have found the basis of a new art, an art which is best fitted to interpret inanimate nature rather than animate nature. I believe that anyone capable of understanding your painting will have a much clearer conception of universal waves than he would through any textbook description. I sincerely hope that you will find it possible to complete the series of sixty or more paintings which you have in mind. I wish you every success.

Yours sincerely,

H H Sheldon

H. H. Sheldon.

University wrote Dr. Russell the following letter on January 30, 1931.

The fact that Dr. Russell completed the paintings as he was encouraged to do by H. H. Sheldon implies that he would be extremely pleased to see their long-awaited publication.

With heartfelt thanks to Walter and Lao Russell, I commend this book to you.

Faithfully yours,

Dr. Timothy A. Binder

Dr. Timothy A. Binder
Winter 1994

Early Walter Russell

Walter Russell planning a civic center for Coconut Grove, Florida, adjacent to Biscayne Bay

WALTER RUSSELL, THE MAN

Walter Russell was born in Boston on May 19, 1871. With only a fifth-grade education and five years of art school, he went on to excel in writing, sculpting, painting, architecture, ice skating, science and many other fields. He certainly deserved the titles "Most Versatile Man in America," "Modern Leonardo," and "The Man Who Tapped the Secrets of the Universe."

As a members of the Twilight Club, Walter Russell, Ralph Waldo Emerson, Mark Twain, Walt Whitman, Oliver Wendell Holmes, Sophie Irene Loeb, and many other notable figures worked for the betterment of humankind. Their efforts resulted in such notable service organizations as the Rotary Club, the Lions Club, the Boy Scouts of America, and the University of Science and Philosophy.

Starting at the age of seven, Walter Russell experienced annual periods of illumination. During the 39-day period of illumination in 1921, he believed he received the secrets of the universe from God, which he was asked to share with the world through his writings and lectures. In 1948, he married Lao Russell, and together they founded the University of Science and Philosophy for the purpose of spreading these teachings throughout the world.

Though Dr. Russell refolded in 1963, the work was continued by Lao until her refolding in 1988 and is now carried on by the University of Science and Philosophy.

During his dynamic lifetime, Dr. Russell described the fundamentals of purposeful living in dozens of different contexts. They are found in his scientific books, his speeches and articles, and in the profound lessons of *The Home Study Course* which he and Lao wrote together. More impressively, however, they are demonstrated by his abilities as a portrait painter, sculptor, architect, philosopher, composer, author and Doctor of Science.

In *The Fifth Kingdom Man*, edited by Emelia Lee Lombardi, Dr. Russell explains his vision in his own words.

I come to give that comprehension, to build a new universe, so that the eyes of the Spirit see rather than the eyes of the body. I say to man, to scientists, to mathematicians:

> *You have been seeing with the eyes of the body. Your laws of gravitation, your theories of chemistry, metallurgy, of the construction of the atom, of the expanding universe in which you have condemned God to die by a disease called entropy — the expanding universe — from your observation your eyes have told you things that are not so. Come with me, and with the eyes of the Spirit let us see what the universe is really like, not what it is not like.*

We must build a new universe with the eyes of the Spirit. That is why God took me behind the scenes, away from the illusion of the senses into the universe of knowing, so that with the eyes of the Spirit I could see what the universe and man really are; so that I could see the illusions by means of which man has built up wrongful theories; and so that I could see the senselessness and the waste of man building materially from empirical knowledge based upon the observations of his sensed body, with illusions that have deceived him so completely that his text books of today on science are to me as though they were written by the sages of King Arthur's time wherein they said the earth was flat and upheld on its four corners by wild elephants.

That is what it seemed to me when I came out of the universe of all-knowing where God kept me for 39 days and nights, that I might not only know these things but write them down in the words of *The Divine Iliad* for you and the world.

And during those 39 days, of every word I wrote down in *The Divine Iliad* there has never been an erasure nor a word changed in all of those 30,000 words. Ask any literary man or woman what that means. Ask if they have ever written 500 words without an erasure. Ask if they have ever written 500 masterly words that would endure through all time with 10,000 erasures.

These 30,000 words of *The Divine Iliad* will last through all time. They are God's words, not mine, written through me. They are the essence of all-knowing, for which I have been prepared to translate in the words of man, for the books which will form the foundation for the new civilization, the first of those books being *The Secret of Light*. Man has waited for that secret for long ages. Jesus said, "God is Light," but no one knew what He meant. And nobody knows today what He meant. They have been waiting.

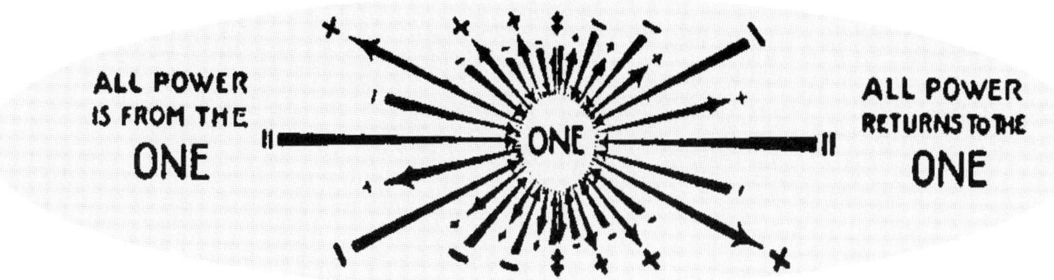

Sir Oliver Lodge wrote in a book some years ago — the book called *The Ether of Light* — and this is what he said:

> *We know the how of many things, but we do not know the why of anything. We do not know what magnetism is, nor gravitation, electricity, energy, light. If we knew the secret of light, we would have all knowledge. If the coming centuries ever give us that secret of light, it will not come through the scientific mind; it will come through the inspiration of a poet, painter, philosopher or saint.*

I will qualify for the first three of those, but not the last. And the secret of Light is coming to the world now from God through me; and it will make another world; it will make another civilization; it will give man a new comprehension of the universe, of man himself, man's relation to man and man's relation to God.

It is as much your duty to your fellow men to become messengers of the Light as it is mine. Study that book. Study all of the books that will come from this, and spread the word.

Many people say, "I'm not of a scientific turn of mind." I do not wonder from the way science is dished up to you that you are not of a scientific turn of mind. In *The Secret of Light*, you would become as great a chemist in two weeks as you would in a four-year university study, with the exception of the laboratory experience and the skills which of necessity one must have. But the underlying principles of chemistry, electricity, magnetism, gravitation, light, power — all of those things you will have because you will know the secret of Light, and you will know what lies behind it; and you will be able to apply it to your own life and multiply your own power and spread that power into the world — and thus sow the seed that is in the Light, the seed of Love, throughout the world to counteract the seeds of fear and hate and greed which have brought us to the pass that we are now in, the seed which will lift mankind out of this into a one world, into a one religion, which is the destiny of this new age, and into a knowledge of God which is the inheritance of this new age.

That is your responsibility. I will fulfill mine. I call upon you to fulfill yours.

RUSSELLIAN

SCIENCE

OVERVIEW

INTRODUCTION

The Russell Cosmogony is founded on a universal systems model, which is a model for everything in the universe from human beings, animals, processes and atoms to solar systems and galaxies. Such a model allows us to understand the fundamental nature and operation of all things. We can use it both to break down and analyze a system into parts as well as to combine seemingly separate parts into wholes.

The Russells used science's simplest machine, the lever, as a basic symbol in their teachings. A lever can be conceptualized as having three fundamental aspects:

Diagram 1. Aspects of the Lever

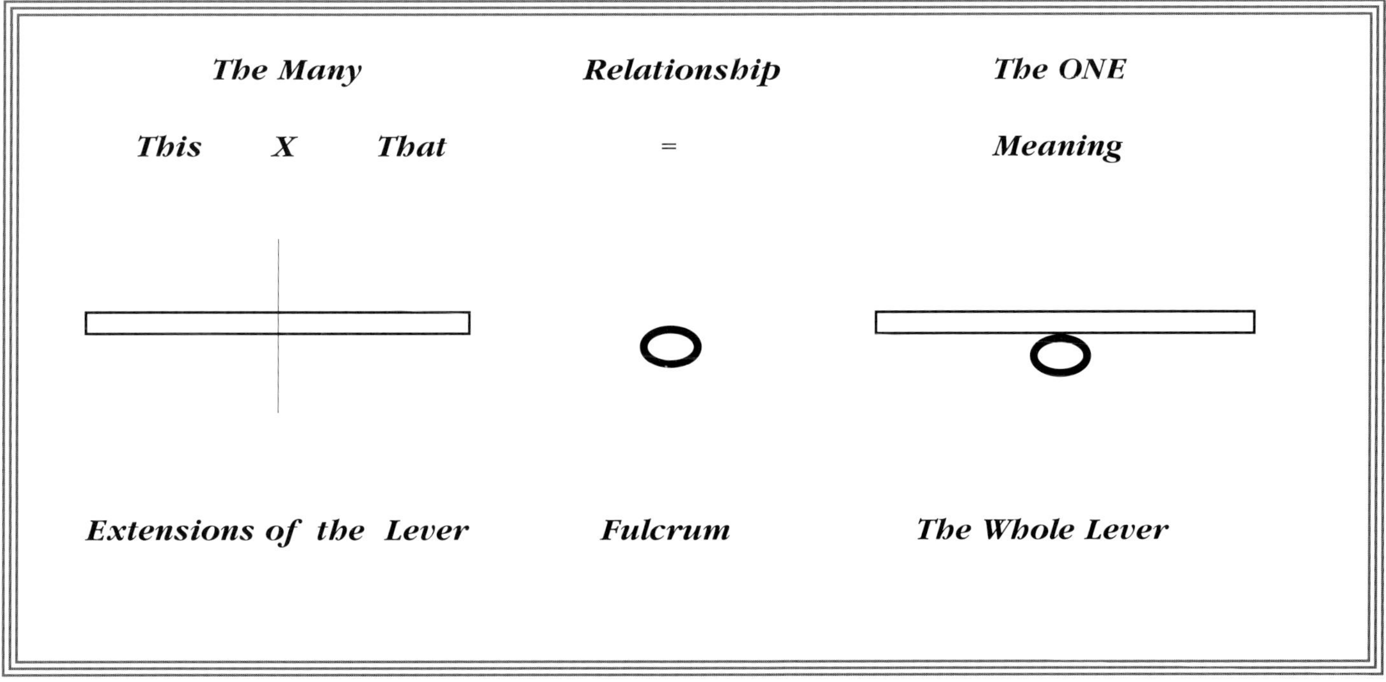

1. The ONE: the lever as a whole unit.

2. The MANY: both extensions of the lever.

3. The RELATIONSHIP between the MANY or the two archetypal parts of the lever (the male and female polarities of yang and yin) reveals unity. The fulcrum on which the lever rests and which unites the two extensions of the lever symbolizes relationship and the ultimate unity of related parts.

Language Mechanics

Overview

A universal systems model applies to everything, including language. Language is not only a basic tool for communication; it is also the main tool we use to think and to conceptualize. Understanding the essential nature of this language tool enables us to communicate more effectively. This, alone, can contribute to a more peaceful civilization since many disagreements arise because people are unaware that every word can be used in three different essential senses.

For example, one of the continuing problems in reconciling religious mysticism with science has been the conflict in terminology. Each has, quite naturally, incorporated the word, 'reality,' to describe its own world view. Religious mysticism uses the word, 'reality,' to describe an existence that includes and yet extends beyond the realm of the ordinary senses. Thus religion sees wholes and emphasizes the One; that is its reality. Science, on the other hand, uses the same word, 'reality,' to describe a world which can be experienced and measured using only the senses of touch, sight, hearing, smelling and tasting. Thus science sees parts and emphasizes the MANY; that is its reality. As we explore the Russell Cosmogony, we will establish a commonly agreed upon language.

Like the lever, language can be analyzed as having three different essential meanings or senses for which there are ultimately three different types of words. These correspond to the three possible essential meanings of any word as explained below.

1. ONE words express the concept of unity, wholeness, absolutes, an absence of division into parts, and an absence of opposition. Examples include Omnipresent, Omnipotent and Omniscient. One words are frequently, but not always, capitalized throughout this book to identify them.

2. MANY words express the concept of individuality, diversity and the presence of opposition. Examples include this, that, you and me.

3. RELATIONSHIP words express the dividing or connecting lines that relate apparently separate parts to each other. They reconcile opposites into the harmony of rhythmic balanced interchange by linking individuality in diversity with unity and wholeness and linking division or multiplication with a balanced whole. Examples include love, plus, minus, equals, force and facilitate.

Walter Russell's architectural office in New York City

The following table provides additional examples of these three basic types of words.

ONE WORDS	MANY WORDS	RELATIONSHIP WORDS
Brahma	Shiva and Vishnu, yin-yang	prana, energy
God the Father	God the Son, Jesus Christ	God, the Holy Ghost
Creator	sons and daughters of God	Spirit (of God or any being)
Universe	suns, planets, asteroids	, space and time
Zero and Infinity	all numbers but zero and infinity	'x,' '+,' '-,' '=,' '÷'
The Cube-Sphere	the cube, the sphere	crystallization, amorphous unfolding, refolding, freezing-melting forms
Humanity	you, me, man, woman	humane
Love	love, hate	universal relationship is love
Stillness, Void	centripetal motion centrifugal motion	friction, synchronization, simultaneous movement in opposing or in uniting
Circle, Sphere	right or left hemisphere	dividing/connecting line - circumference, diameter, inertial plane, cubic boundary wall, centering zero point
Wave	wave crest, wave trough	wave axis
Meaning	this, that	times, equals
Inertial Plane and Amplitude Zero Point	cuboids, spheroids	centripetal and centrifugal motion to and from planes and zero-point centers

ONE WORDS	MANY WORDS	RELATIONSHIP WORDS
Gravity (the entire balanced cycle of contracting and expanding mass)	implosion as contrasted with radiative explosion, generation as contrasted with radiation, compressive movement toward center of density in mass as contrasted with expansive movement toward equipotential boundary in tenuity	inward compressive motion
Radiation (the entire balanced cycle of expanding and contracting mass)	explosion as contrasted with gravitative implosion, radiation as contrasted with gravitation, expansive movement toward tenuity in mass at the wave field boundary as contrasted with compressive movement toward density in mass at the wave field center	outward expansive motion
Magnetism (the universal power behind all light-electric phenomena seen as the power of expansion and separation, the void battery)	electric expansion as contrasted with electric compression	according to Russell, the point of rest between electric current cycles and the centering zero point of stillness in all things
Electricity (the universal power behind all light-electric phenomena seen as the power of compression and cohesion, the infinite battery)	electric compression as contrasted with electric expansion	both inward compressive and outward expansive current cycles commonly called electricity and magnetism respectively

As can be seen from this list, each of the three types of words can also be used as either of the other two types. Each sentence or paragraph also can refer to any one of the three senses, as can the viewpoint for a book or a cultural norm. A One word can be used as a many or relationship word and vice versa. This potential source of confusion needs to be understood since the meaning or sense in which any word is used must be ascertained by its context.

An example from the list is the word, 'love.' Love can be, and frequently is, used in all three senses. Sometimes it is even used in all three senses in the same sentence such as: "My universal unconditional Love for you is not compromised by my paucity of relative love and excess of hate for your shortcomings, as I love to feel the energy of my Love expressed in all ways."

In summary, One words assert unity; Many words assert diversity; and relationship words assert that the many or diversity are ultimately and inseparably related, and are, in fact, the One. In other words, relationship words assert that the expression of the One and the expression of the Many by the same word are valid; both the One and the Many are real.

The (Non) Paradox of the Reality of the One and the Many

I feel the essential question of philosophy for thousands of years has been: Is the One real, or is the many real? For mystics and monists, the One is real; for pluralists and scientists, the many is real. Western civilization as a whole has been conditioned to think in terms of either/or, incurable diseases, insoluble problems, no final exits, and linear thinking. Thus it regards this question as a paradox. For the Russells, the Zen Buddhists, the masters of all traditional-natural philosophies, and the mystic scientists who are able to comprehend unity-in-diversity, both are real; they have no problem envisioning what others regard as a paradox.

Another useful distinction can be made for One words. The act of describing any object involves comparing it to and distinguishing it from other objects. If we were to describe anything accurately in an absolute sense, we would have to travel for infinite time over infinite space to actually observe and describe its infinite connections to every other thing. This would ultimately result in a description of the entire Universe. To know or describe anything absolutely is to know and describe the entire Universe.

As finite individuals, we do not have infinite time and space to do this; therefore, we tacitly assume what I will call a standard universe in our description for summing parts into wholes that is described by 'standard One' words. This means that we recognize our limitations, and select our descriptions of what is possible for us to experience and describe to the degree of practical accuracy needed. We then ignore the rest of the infinite regress of details required to give an absolute description.

In other words, in using standard One words we acknowledge our inability to actually describe the real ONE with our finite human consciousness. Nevertheless, we can know it abstractly in principle by understanding the universal systems model that the Russells taught and that has been part of all ancient traditions. In fact, all accurate descriptions of reality conform to this model. We can also use meditation to *experience* the absolute or God in mystical union as the Russells and mystics of all traditions have done.

An example of a standard One or a standard Universe would be to use the solar system as a description for the universe. Our solar system can be described as nine planets with their accompanying moons, a central sun, and the fields between them filled with varying amounts of asteroids and planetary dusts in an infinite regress of details. Expressed in simple mathematics, it could be:

$$(9+x)\ldots +10\ldots = 19+x\ldots$$

where 9 is the number of the planets,
x is the number of moons,
. . . is the infinite regress of asteroids, planetary dusts, and fields extending from and to the sun, planets and moons, and
10 is the central sun.

Therefore, the solar system is 19. . . + x. . . ,

or our solar system in the Universe is

This (19) . . . + That X . . . = the meaning.

Even with finite human consciousness, we can abstractly know the One or the absolute Universe in Principle. We can do that through understanding the unique principle of the universal systems model that the Russells revealed and that has been part of all ancient traditions and all accurate descriptions of reality. This universal systems model is congruent with all accurate descriptions of reality because it reveals that the One, the many, and relationship are all real.

We can also *experience* the absolute or God in mystical union as the Russells and mystics of all traditions have stated is our ultimate destiny. Virtually all mystics have shown through example as well as precept that the way to such experience is through meditation.

Another way to look at this (non) paradox is through the simplified language of mathematics. Mathematics uses three types of symbols which correspond to the three types of words. All symbols have these same three ultimate meanings. The three essential symbols of mathematics are the One, the many, and the relationship symbols of ordinary language.

The equation, 2+3 = 5, can symbolize any standard One divided into parts and summed into a whole, or it can symbolize the entire universe arbitrarily divided into 2 parts here and 3 parts there that really have no void space or discontinuity between them and thus are united into the Whole. Any division/multiplication or separation/unification of a whole bottom-line organic unit into ultimately divided/connected parts is arbitrary.

In the preceding case, both the 2 and the 3 are Many symbols or words; the + and the = are relationship symbols or words, and the 5 is a One symbol or word. When the 5 is meant to refer to the actual entire universe, it is a true abstract symbol for the Universal One. When the 2 and the 3 refer to peanuts or boys and girls, then the 5 peanuts or boys and girls are a standard One.

Ultimately all things — even standard Ones such as peanuts, boys and girls — are actually part of the Universal One since all things are united into ONE. Yet we do not usually think and speak in this ultimate sense, thus revealing our level of ordinary understanding and consciousness. As our consciousness of ourselves grows to encompass each other and all things, we will think, speak and otherwise act as the Universal One consciously.

When a word is used as a One word having no opposite meaning, it can be thought of as a Word Of God. The word, 'ecstasy,' is such a word which describes an emotional state with no opposite; this state is synonymous with Universal Love. Ordinary relative love is contrasted with ordinary relative hate just as ordinary relative good is contrasted with ordinary relative evil.

The background material for this description of language mechanics is derived chiefly from the work of Scudder Klyce, author of *Universe.* Additional insights accrued from study of the dialectic philosophy of the Far East as interpreted by George Ohsawa, Michio Kushi, Herman Aihara — all macrobiotic teachers — as well as others such as Jerome Canty, author of *Holoscene.*

Official bust of Mark Twain in the Victoria Embankment Gardens. London

A Universal Systems Model

Overview

These diagrams of a lever and the Tao illustrate the universal systems model that represents the essence of Dr. Russell's scientific paintings and charts.

Diagram 2. The Lever

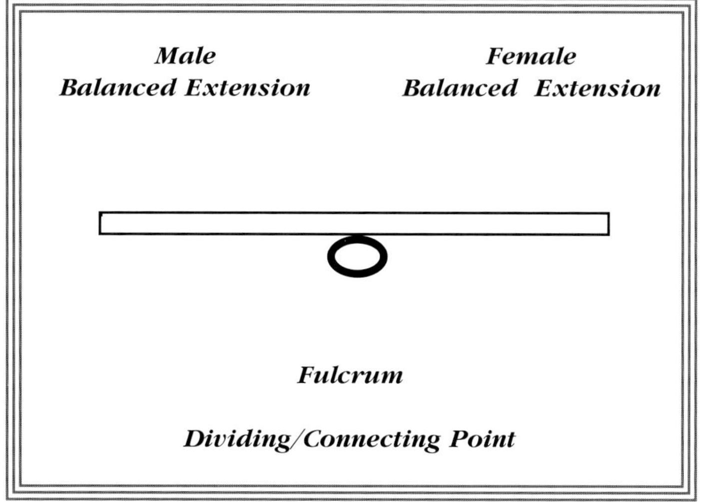

To be logically consistent with the model, a statement must conform to the following formula:

This times That equals Meaning, or

This... X That... = Meaning

where 'This' describes something close (the intensive, dense, hot, male center of the system) and

'That' describes something far out (the extensive, light, cool female periphery of the system).

'This' and 'That' are both 'many' symbols or words.

'X,' '.......,' and '=' are relationship symbols or words that assert that the 'This' and the 'That' are truly One — that they have their existence only together as One.

The series of dots '.......' are relationship symbols for the infinite regress of details that relate each thing in the Universe to every other thing. They explicitly assert that there is no void space or discontinuity in the Universe.

'Meaning' is another assertion, like an echo, of this bottom-line unity which is the basis of reality; thus it is used as a One symbol or word. The 'this' and the 'that' are unified as well as distinct; in other words, they are at the same time One and yet the distinctly separate parts of the many unified as One.

There is no meaning to any part of the formula— or to any part of the lever or the Tao — in itself alone. A 'this' without a 'that,' a '+' without a '-,' or a relationship without at least two things to relate to each other is meaningless. A lever

Diagram 3. The Tao

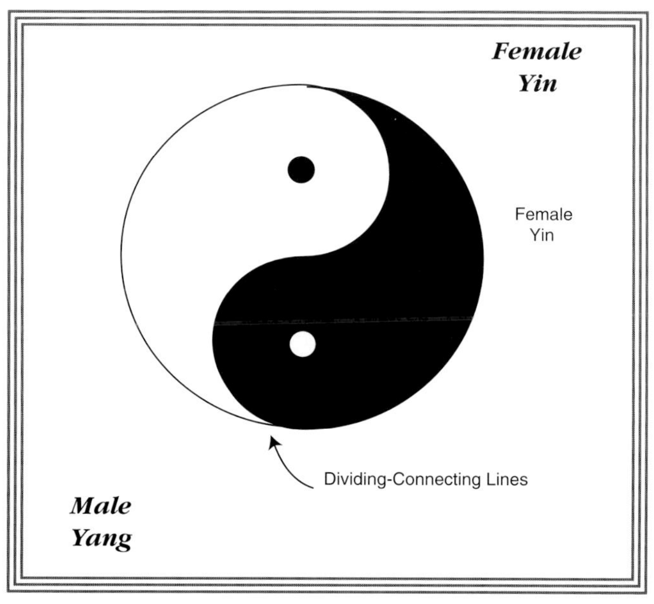

Diagram 4. Relationship between Male/Yang and Female/Yin

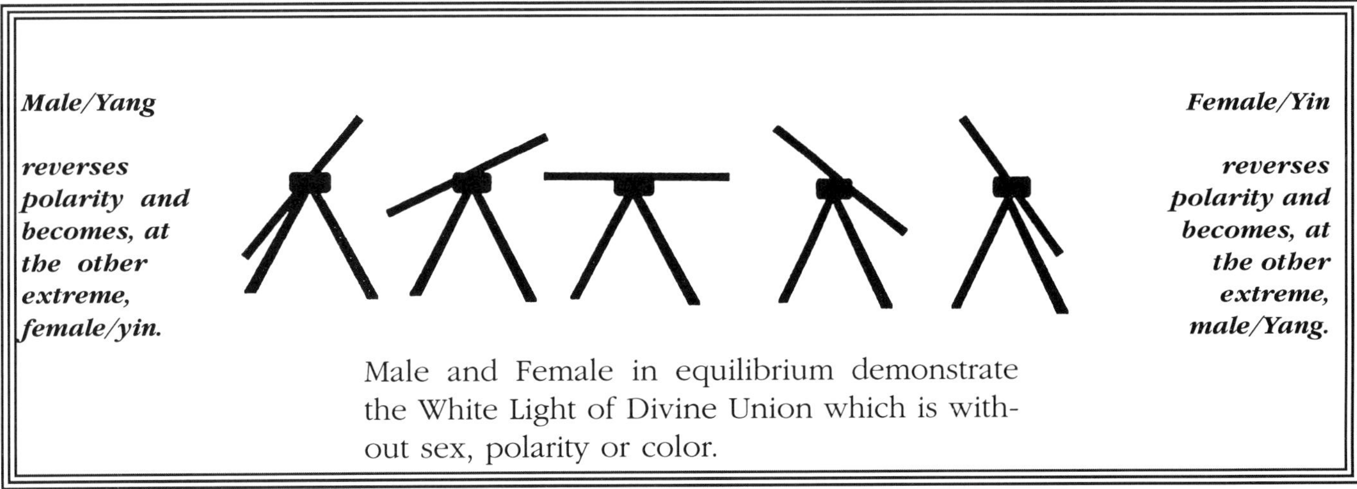

without a balancing opposite extension is as impossible and meaningless as night without day or yin without yang.

Even God evidently found no meaning in being a ONE alone, so human beings and all other things were created. Perhaps the only thing we can regive to God is our Love. We can demonstrate our Love for God by giving to and caring for all humanity, for all creatures of the earth, and for all things in God's Creation. The Russells gave us a formula to do this when they described rhythmic balanced interchange as giving for equal regiving. This expresses the same idea as the Biblical phrase "What ye sow, so also shall ye reap" and the common saying "What goes around comes around." This is the Creator's 'Way.' In following this way, we can 'follow the Tao' or follow the Creator by creating a peaceful and sustainable civilization.

Diagram 5. Relative Apparent Power to Attract and Repel

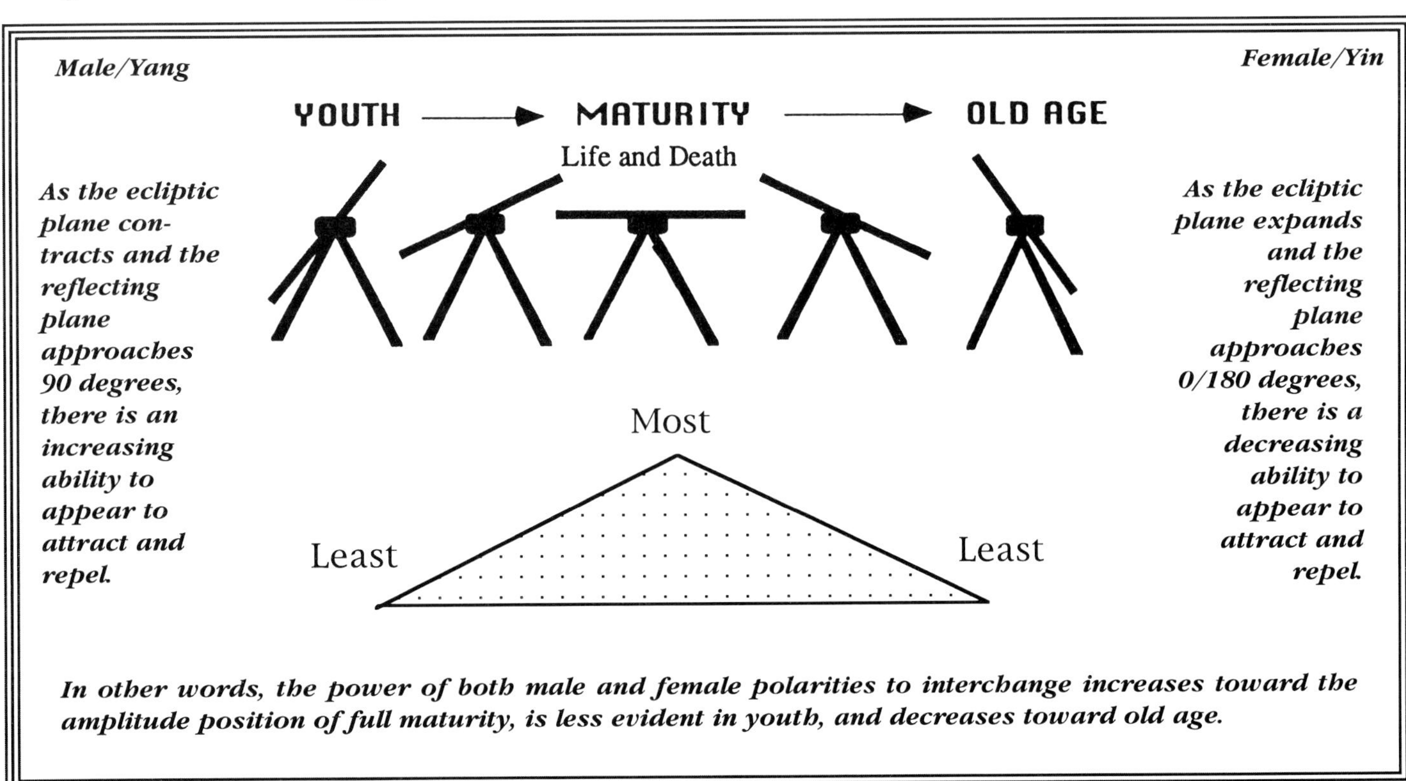

The following table provides a brief summary of the attributes of the opposing extremes of this universal systems model.

Attributes of the Yang/Male Dimension	**Attributes of the Yin/Female Dimension**
Space dimensions contract	Space dimensions expand
Day lengthens	Day shortens
Year shortens	Year lengthens
Male preponderance	Female preponderance
Temperature, potential, and pressure increase	Temperature, potential, and pressure decrease
Ionization decreases	Ionization increases
Hard simple crystallization	Soft amorphous crystallization
Valence increases from 1st to 4th locking point and desires union with the same female valence partner	Valence increases from 1st to 4th locking point and desires union with same male valence partner
Revolution increases	Revolution decreases
Rotation decreases	Rotation increases
Condensation and increasing mass	Evaporation and decreasing mass
Red ultraviolet to red to orange-red to orange to yellow	Blue ultraviolet to violet to blue to green to yellow
TO	TO

White incandescence

Diagram 6. Interrelationship of Male/Female Energies

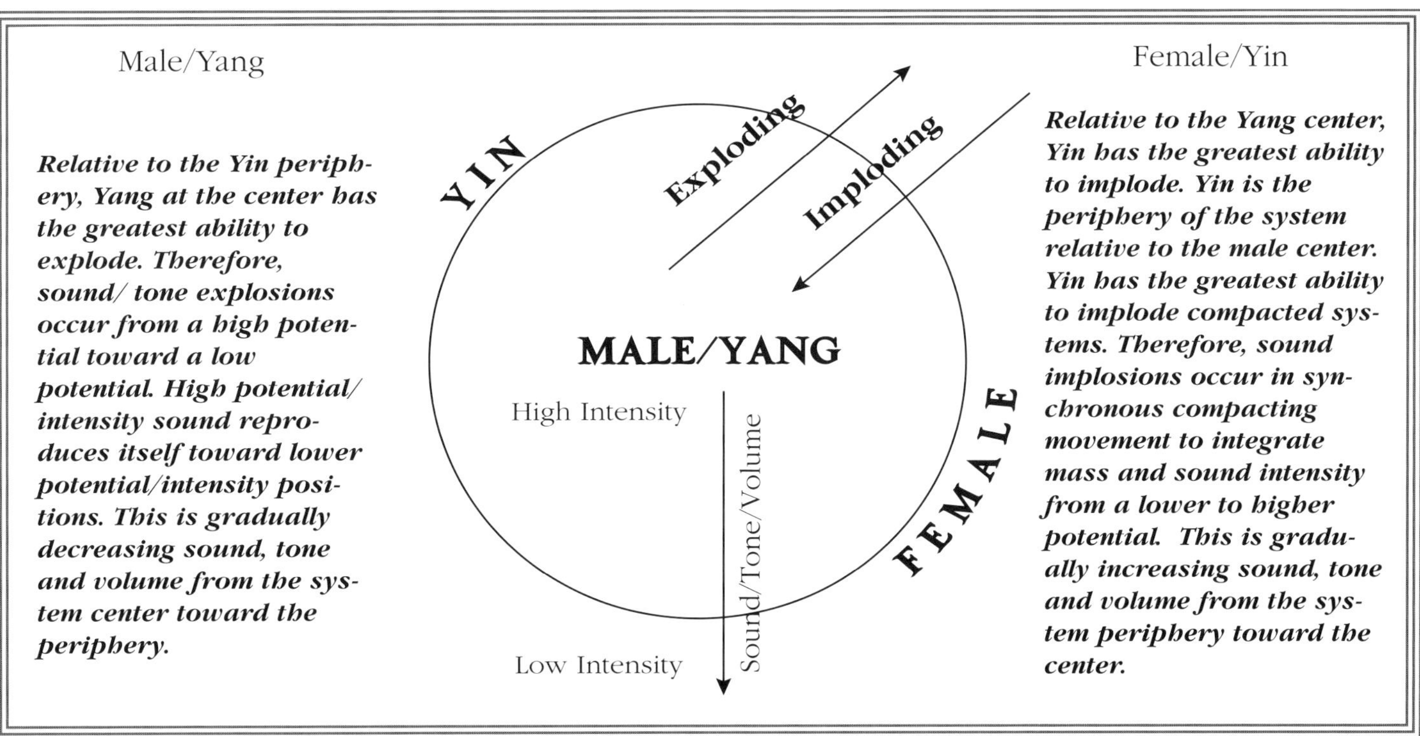

Sources of Confusion

Mistakes in communication occur when we confuse the three types of words as to their meanings since any word can be used in all three senses. To say that the One is only a many part confuses the One with the many; this is akin to idolatry.

One example of this confusion can be found in common interpretations of the Trinity. To say there is a God is to assert the One. To say there is only God the Son is to assert that there is only one part without a balancing harmonious part which is equivalent to saying that a lever has only one side. This confuses the many with the One. For the Trinity to make sense and conform to the model, it must represent God, God the sons and daughters of God (as the male-female/yin-yang archetypal symbols for the many), and the Holy Ghost as relationship.

Another example of confusion occurs when the lever is nonsensically asserted to have no parts. This denies the reality of the many since to say that the lever is only one side of the extension is to run one thing to infinity. To say, for example, that only the dividing/connecting line exists runs relationship to infinity.

Several common misunderstandings in daily life are caused by lack of understanding our universal systems model and language mechanics.

1. Confusing the many with the One. One good example is selfishness, where one person in a relationship feels more important than the other. As a result, that person can justify taking everything and leaving the other with nothing. This leads to slavery, rebellion and war.

2. Confusing the One with the many. A good example is self-deprecating unselfishness where one side of a relationship perceives that it is less important than the other. Thus it gives the other side everything, a self-

stunted expression of personal power. Ultimately this leads to stunting others through an eventual inability to give and regive.

3. Confusing relationship with the One or the many. What is commonly called a co-dependent relationship illustrates this. Two or more people in relationship may say and act as if that relationship is all there is, acting as if no one has any existence apart from it nor does anyone or anything outside of the relationship have any meaning. People in this type of relationship are non-functional when separated and selfish outside of the relationship — and ultimately within it too. This is the equivalent of describing the equation 2+3 = 5 using only the + or = signs. Alone they have no meaning except as abstractions. In groups it leads to clannishness, cults and group self-aggrandizement.

This universal model of the One, many and relationship is present throughout the Russell Cosmogony and is reflected in the paintings and charts. Understanding in which sense a word or symbol is being used will greatly simplify and enhance comprehension of the written material and reveal greater detail in the paintings and charts.

For example, in Unit 10 of *The Home Study Course*, the Russells use the word, 'cold,' in two different senses when discussing thermodynamics: they speak of cold as contrasted to heat in a many sense and also as the Absolute Zero of Cold in a One sense.

Used in the One sense, the temperature of the infinite universe could also be described as the Absolute Infinity of Heat. To do so would be to look at the other side of the coin in describing temperature as an absolute. The ultimate meanings of Zero and Infinity are the same; they are the limits of numbers and beyond measure. To consider the ultimate reality of the Universe as Absolute Cold reveals the viewpoint of compression into form with the appearance of relative heat. Considering it as Absolute Heat reveals the viewpoint of expansion out of form with the appearance of relative cold.

Another example of simplifying comprehension of the Russells' teaching through understanding the three senses in which words are used is to consider how these messages apply to good and evil. In Unit 1 of *The Home Study Course*, when the Russells say that there is only Good and no evil in God's universe of Love, they are using the words Good and Love as Words of God or One words which have no opposite. They also speak of the evil that humanity has created through ignorance of God's universal law of balance. In this case, they use the word, 'evil', as a many word that only has meaning in relation to something else which, in this case, is its opposite or relative good.

In light of the universal systems model we have established, we can now say that relative evil is an expression of God's balancing law of Love when seen in the context of the One; in this sense, there is only Good in the Universe. But it also means that God only creates relative evil by allowing us free will to take the unbalanced actions which create evil. God balances; humanity attempts to unbalance, but all relative imbalances are balanced in the One. All is Good in the One. We most closely and accurately demonstrate our knowing of God in us when we choose to express relative balance in thought and action.

Four Freedoms Monument: Freedom from Fear, Freedom from Want, Freedom of Speech, and Freedom of Religion. Based on concept of Franklin Delano Roosevelt as expressed to Thomas Watson. On view at Swannanoa near Waynesboro, Virginia, and at the Colin P. Kelley Memorial in Madison, Florida.

Overview of the Russell Cosmogony

Conventional Science Compared to Russellian Science

Comparing the Russell Cosmogony to the science of the early part of the twentieth century when Dr. Russell was writing (and which is still largely being taught today) is one way of grasping the truth of which is more accurate. The following comparisions of the Russell Cosmogony and conventional science illuminate the way to the science of the next millennium.

Conventional Science A Universe with No Creator	**Russellian Science** A Creator for the Universe
Dr. Russell said, *The cardinal error of science lies in shutting the Creator out of His Creation.* In effect, he asked, "How can there be a painting without a painter or a Universe without a Creator?" He was blessed with a conscious realization of the Creator, and this experience left no room for doubt or argument. In my opinion, a Universe without a Creator is synonymous with an inability to sum parts into wholes because of a materialistic focus on the many to the exclusion of the One. In my opinion, this materialism does not make sense in light of the Russell Cosmogony.	

Conventional Science No-unified-theory cosmogony	**Russellian Science** A unified-theory cosmogony
With no Creator and the inability to see the essential continuity of all things or to perceive the One, conventional science is handicapped with a vision of discontinuity. This discontinuous vision is the essence of the no-unified-theory cosmogony and the inability to relate all phenomena to a single mechanism. Conventional science confuses the three types of symbols as evidenced by scientific materialism attempting to make a One out of the many by having no unified cosmogony. The confusion can be seen in mathematics whenever zero and infinity are used as numbers rather than as limits of numbers. The latter confusion tries to use the One as the many.	Walter Russell unified all phenomena through his concept and description of the Gravity Cycle, the unity of the Cube-Sphere, and the description of all phenomena as the division of the One substance through concentrative and decentrative power of mind into the two archetypal male/female-yin/yang polarities by means of which all phenomena appear, disappear and reappear.

Conventional Science	Russellian Science
Electric current flow and magnetic fields	Electric two-way current/wave field in the relative (many) universe and a magnetic still white light in the absolute (One) universe

The Russells taught that all things in the relative universe manifest by and as motion in a spiral direction to the center of the system and dissolve in the same spiral direction from the center of the system.

Therefore, what science calls an electric field or current is motion to the center, and what science calls a magnetic field is motion from the center. Radiation is this same motion from the center, and gravitation is motion to the center, although Dr. Russell also spoke of gravitation as both inward and outward motions and in this way used gravitation as a One word.

The Russells speak of the still white light as magnetism. This magnetic still white light is beyond time and space, beyond motion and, as such, is a One word expression and concept. Their interpretation of the scientific concepts of electric currents and magnetic fields reveals a whole-cycle science and recognizes the Oneness of Universe as well as its separateness. This description of electric and magnetic effects is another aspect of the new whole-cycle science paradigm revealed by the Russell Cosmogony.

Both the cube wave boundaries and the wave axis connecting/dividing lines represent the still white 'magnetic' light in the relative universe of sensed illusion. Although the still white magnetic light of the mind at rest cannot be measured, it can be known through self-realization. This self-realization reveals the still light to be eternal and omnipresent.

Diagram 7: Relationship of the Still White Light to Form

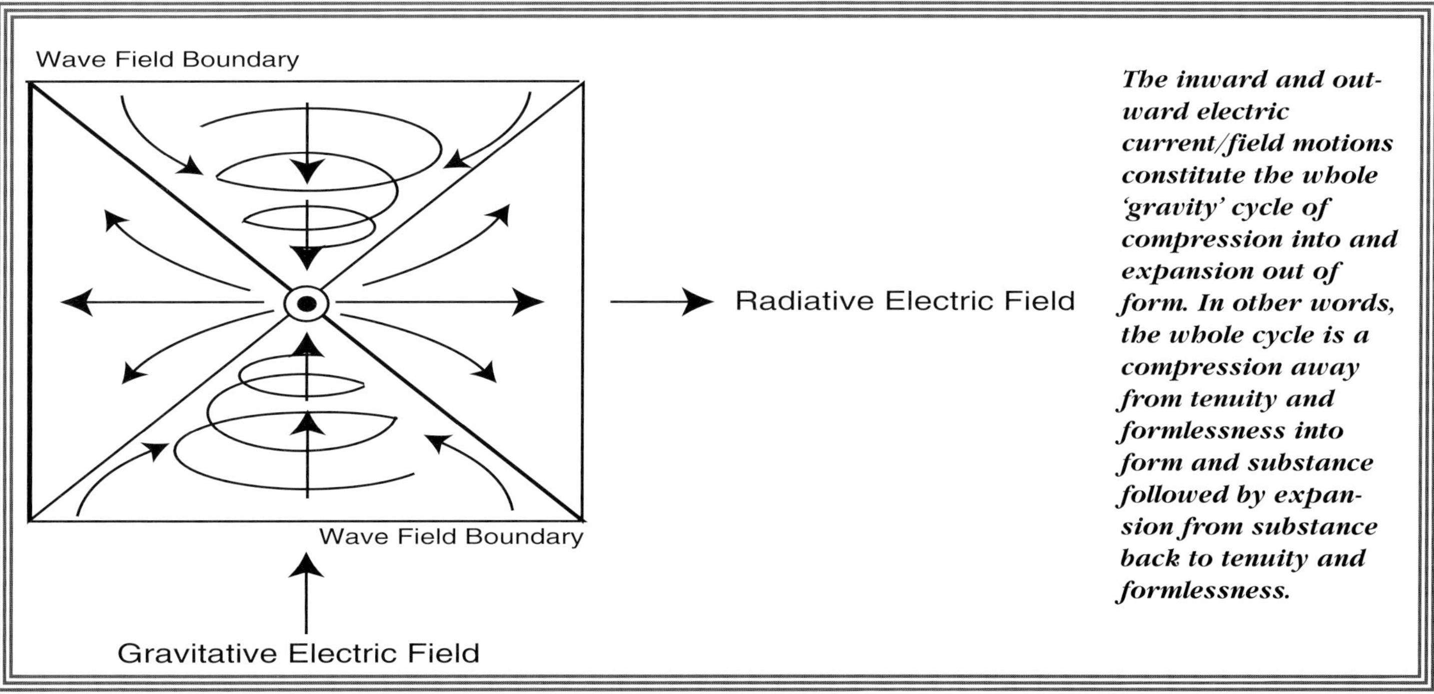

The inward and outward electric current/field motions constitute the whole 'gravity' cycle of compression into and expansion out of form. In other words, the whole cycle is a compression away from tenuity and formlessness into form and substance followed by expansion from substance back to tenuity and formlessness.

The whole Gravity cycle of electric compression (gravity or electric current) and electric expansion (radiation or magnetic field) is centered at the amplitude point or anode by the simulated still white 'magnetic' light and bounded by the still white 'magnetic' light cube wave field boundaries and wave axes at the cathode bases.

Diagram 8: 'Gravitation' Flow

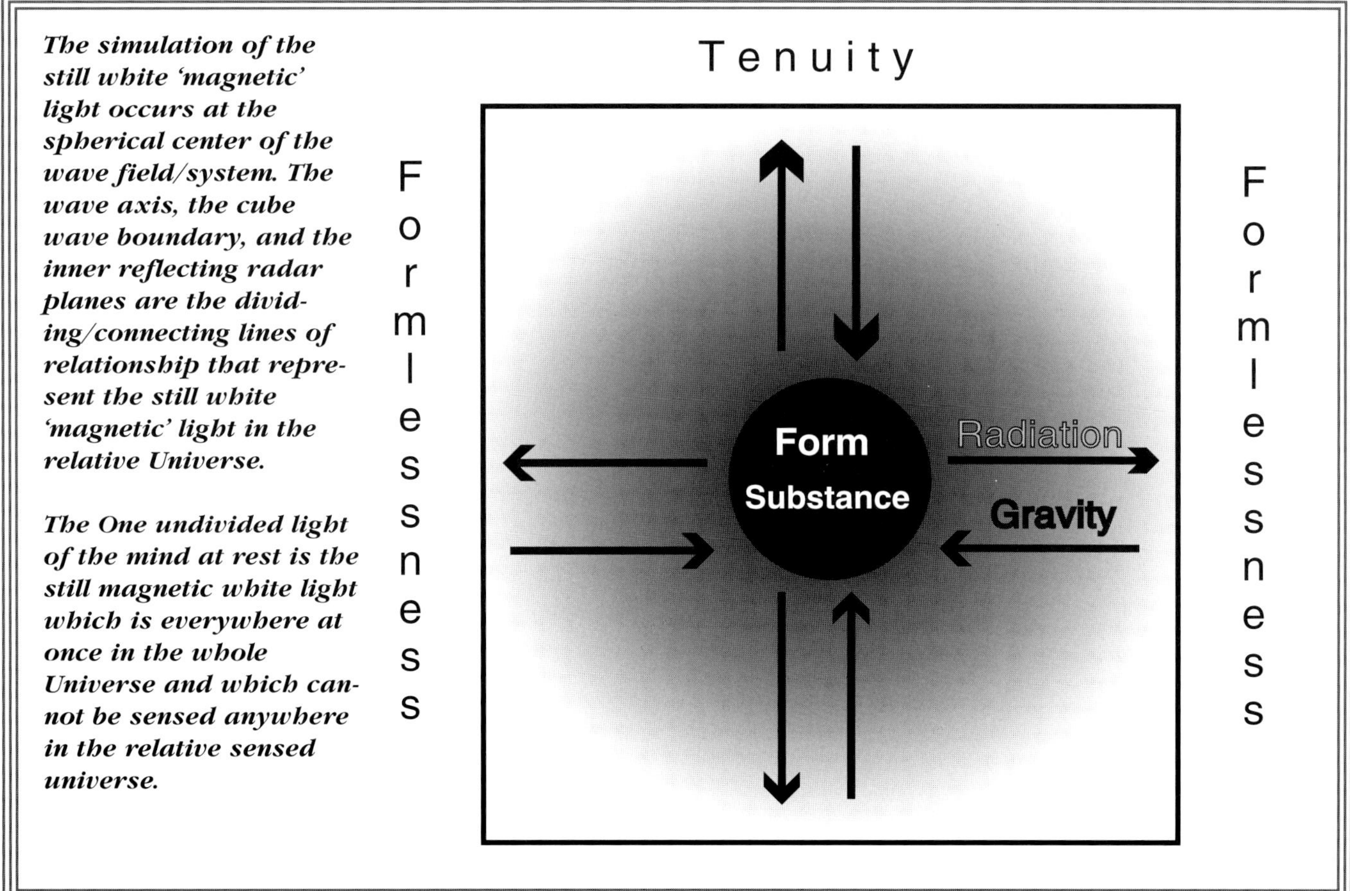

Conventional Science	Russellian Science
Gravitation occurs without radiation as an equal opposing force.	Radiation is an equal and opposing force to gravitation.

The interrelationship of gravitation and radiation is another aspect of the whole-cycle vision of the Russell Cosmogony which asserts that the One is divided into two basic archetypes that occur simultaneously and inseparably in every aspect of the relative Universe. Every part, thing, and motion occurs as two complementary opposite conditions.

Gravitation and radiation are other names for these two archetypes and are synonymous with electricity to and from the center of a system.

The still magnetic Universe is the One — the equilibrium condition out of which both opposites are manifested.

Conventional Science	Russellian Science
Gravity occurs without matter formation.	Matter always forms around gravity poles.

Space as a many concept is a condition of gravitation and radiation: the ceaselessly changing multicolored lights of God's universe of body sensing.

Space as a One concept is an equilibrium condition: the still white magnetic light of God's universe of mind knowing. Gravity, as the many concept is the centripetally inward-directed motion to compress into form in contrast to radiation as the centrifugally outward-directed motion to expand out of form. In this sense, gravity is the winding up of multicolored light waves to form ever more dense and more unstable matter. Radiation, in this sense, is the unwinding of this same light to form ever more tenuous and stable matter. Gravity as a One concept in Russell's use of the word represents both the inward- and outward-directed processes.

Conventional Science	Russellian Science
Time and Space are one in that they always occur together.	Space and Time are two of the 18 dimensions of matter, each of which is related to gravitation and radiation.

The Russell Cosmogony uses Time/Space in the One sense when it speaks of the Still White Light Universe of No Motion; in this sense, it is beyond relative measurable time and space.

The Russells also describe relative time and space as simultaneously occurring in all aspects of the Many universe of parts; in this sense, they are also One as they cannot exist separately or alone. In this case, the Russells are in agreement with conventional science.

Thus, time is measured by orbital revolution and axial rotation. Space is related to length, breadth, and width. A change in any of these dimensions simultaneously changes all the other dimensions, including an additional thirteen dimensions discussed later.

Diagram 9. The Relationship between Time and Space

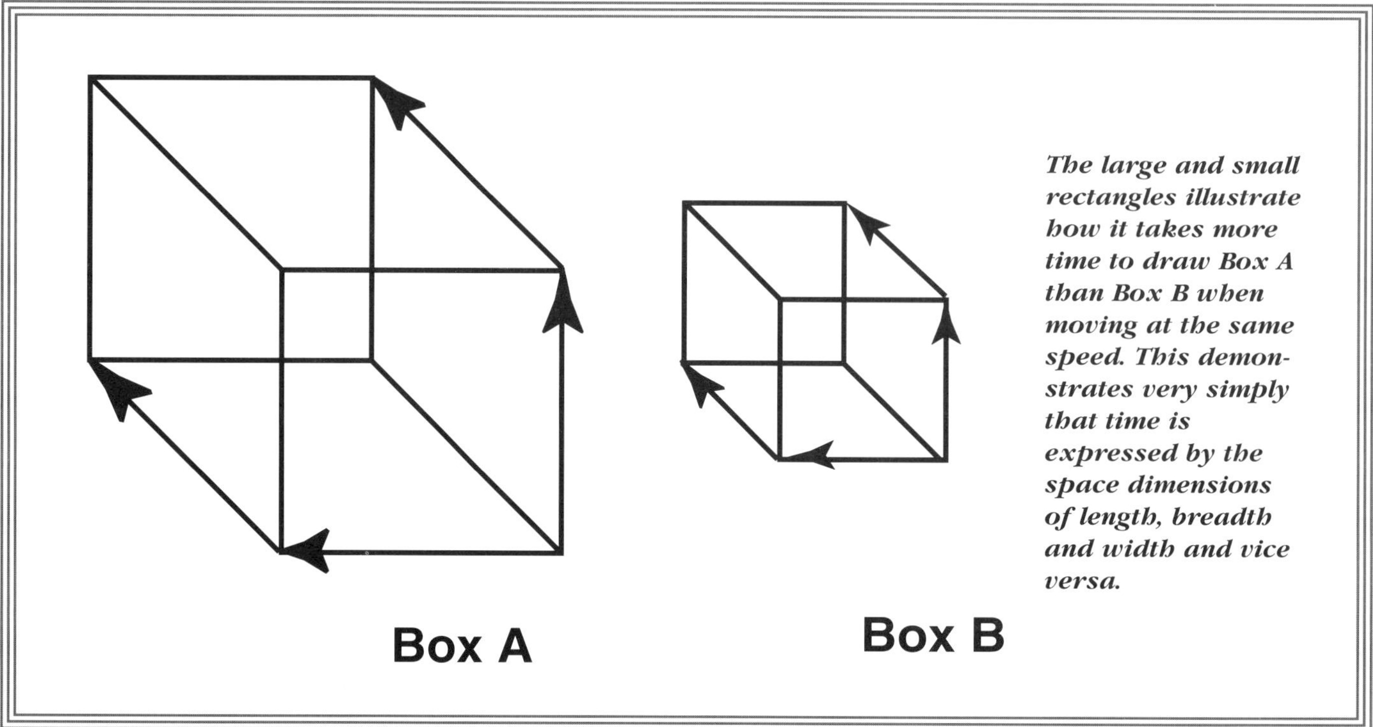

Diagram 10. Celestial Example of the Relationship between Time and Space

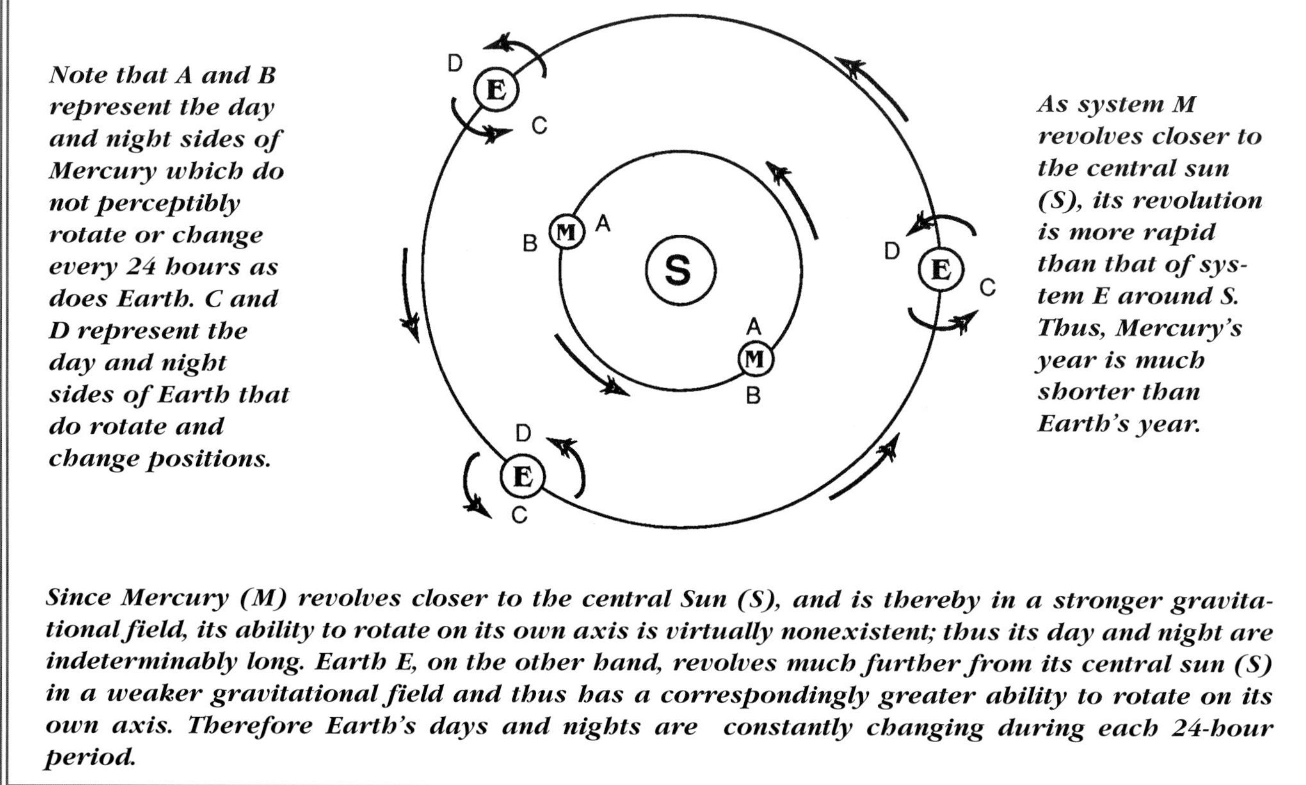

The diagram of Mercury and the Earth (planets M and E) orbiting a central sun (S) demonstrate how the distance traveled by a body around its central sun and its time dimensions (day/night cycle and year) are interrelated. Thus we see how the space and time dimensions expand and contract in relation to the distance of the body from its central sun.

Conventional Science	**Russellian Science**
Energy is within matter itself.	Energy is in desire of mind and is expressed in motion, which creates the appearance of matter.
The Russells identified themselves as true mystics by asserting the primacy of the One or the primacy of the Universal Mind in energy manifestation. They observe that all matter appears and disappears from the desire of the Universal Mind to express itself, which it does by winding and unwinding multicolored light waves.	

Conventional Science	**Russellian Science**
Energy is a condition like heat.	Energy is an attribute of the Mind.
The Russells believed that, in expressing itself, the energy of Mind manifests as heat when matter is compressed into form by the concentrative power of Mind and as cold when matter is expanded to formlessness by the decentrative power of Mind.	

Conventional Science	**Russellian Science**
Matter has power and the ability to attract and repel other matter.	Matter is electrically conditioned and controlled by the still magnetic light of the Creator's mind which creates an equal and opposite division of the universal equilibrium into two opposing conditions which appear to attract and repel other matter via the 18 dimensions of matter. Since all 18 dimensions are related' to gravitation and radiation, they are, in this sense, all One.

Conventional Science	Russellian Science
There are many different substances of matter.	The Universe has no substance; it is only an illusion based on motion.

The Russellian periodic chart of the elements has 121 elements: of these, 63 are full-toned elements; 49 are less than full-toned elements (the isotopes), and 9 are inert gases. An inert gas serves as the seed for each of the 9 octaves. The first and last octaves share common elements in tomium, alberton, blackton and boston. Tomium is the amplitude element for the last octave, and alberton, blackton and boston are the last unwindings of the 9-octave cycle and the beginnings of the cycle's winding up in the first octave. All of these elements are states of motion and can be considered illusory sound and light images of the Creator's imaginings. See the Periodic Charts created by Dr. Russell that were first presented to science in 1926 in *The Universal One* and then later revised to their present form as seen on pages 52-53.

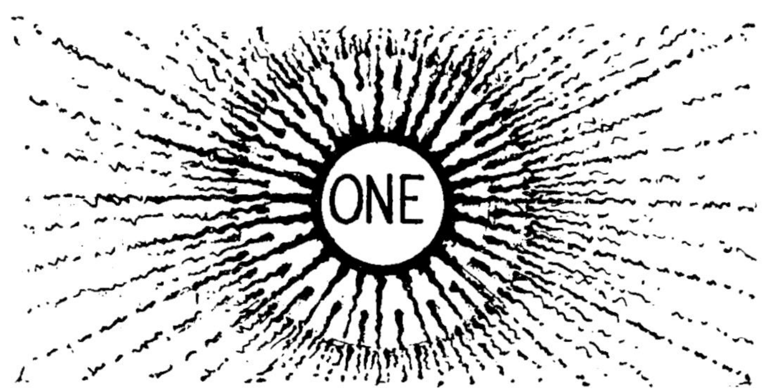

Secret of Light, p. 288.

Conventional Science	Russellian Science
Matter is reality and has qualities within itself.	Matter is an illusion and is but a mirror that reflects qualities outside itself to simulate those qualities within itself.

When we sense matter, we experience an illusion. Matter reflects the quality of the Creator's imaging like a cosmic sound-and-light wave cinema. We know the Creator of the cinema through our Mind when we are able to stop the mind from thinking. We sense the reflection through our senses. When we sense matter, it reflects qualities outside of itself. We sense ourselves and everything else as matter, not as eternal, infinite beings at one with the Creator. When we go beyond our physical senses to an inner knowing through meditation (which is beyond thinking) we understand the deep meaning of the reflection and we are beyond it, no longer believing in the illusion of the physical world. And yet this illusion is as real as we know it to be.

<table>
<tr><th>Conventional Science

Objective science and Universe</th><th>Russellian Science

Cyclic science and Universe</th></tr>
<tr><td>To see a thing as objective is to see it frozen at one moment of its life-death cycle where it reveals but a moment of its wholeness cycle.</td><td>The Russell Cosmogony reveals the constancy of change in all things and processes. All things are born, mature, age, die, rest and are reborn to repeat the cycle of their essential idea. The constancy of change is the universal polarization process of giving for equal regiving which in turn is the embodiment of Love.</td></tr>
</table>

<table>
<tr><th>Conventional Science

A beginning and an end to the Universe. The Universe begins with a big bang and ends by running down to entropy.</th><th>Russellian Science

An Eternal Universe. The Universe is eternal because the big bang/ implosion runs up as it runs down.</th></tr>
<tr><td colspan="2">The universe is, was, and always will be in a state of constant equilibrium that we sense as an expansive big bang and compressive big implosion process of living and dying things. When we know the One or the Creator, we know infinity and eternity, space without emptiness, and time without hurry or waiting.</td></tr>
</table>

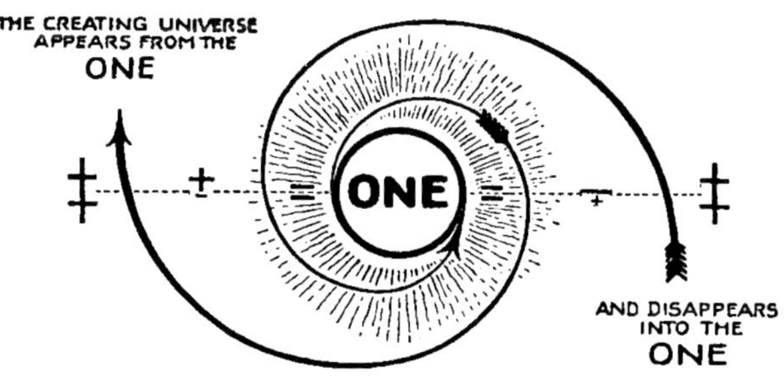

Secret of Light, p.91.

<table>
<tr><th>Conventional Science

Every particle in the Universe has a single charge.</th><th>Russellian Science

Every particle in the Universe is double charged.</th></tr>
<tr><td colspan="2">Each component of the Universe, be it particle or person, has both polarities or charges in varying proportions unto the One. There are balancing opposing forces or mates for all charges, conditions and beings in the relative Universe of ever changing polarities. Each cathode must have an anode and vice versa as depicted in the following diagrams.</td></tr>
</table>

Diagram 11. Double-Charged Particles

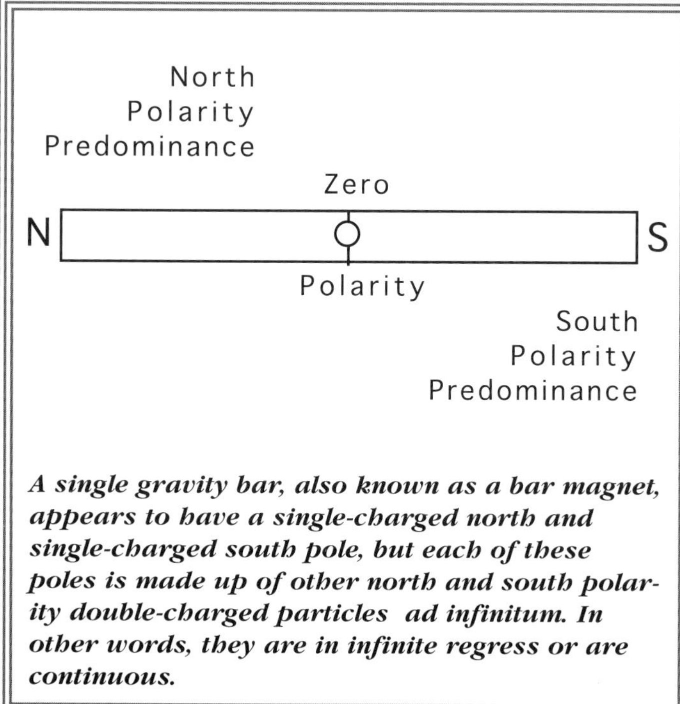

A single gravity bar, also known as a bar magnet, appears to have a single-charged north and single-charged south pole, but each of these poles is made up of other north and south polarity double-charged particles ad infinitum. In other words, they are in infinite regress or are continuous.

Therefore, a gravity bar can be diagrammed as an infinite series of gravity bars placed with north and south poles together as in the next diagram. When these oppositely-sexed charging poles unite, they void opposition at the union point and extend their greatest opposition through each other to the opposite poles at the other ends of the bar as in the previous diagram. Nevertheless, every particle on either side of the union point has both north and south poles within it as shown in the next two diagrams.

The anode apex points of north and south opposition on union become a cathode point so that when they unite, the two bars appear as a single bar as depicted in Diagrams 11 and 13.

Diagram 13. Two Gravity Bars Immediately after Union into a Single Gravity Bar

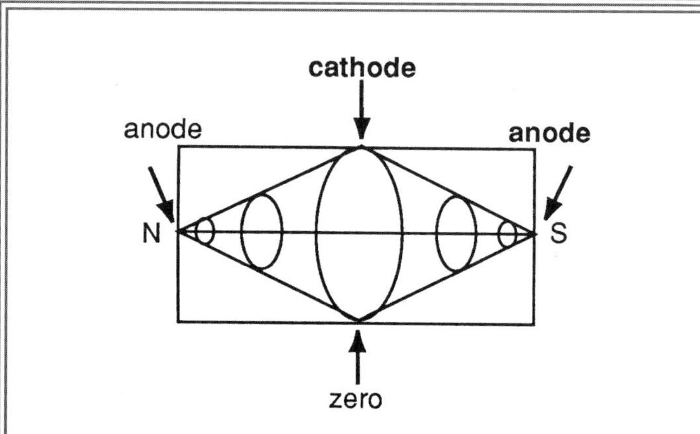

All cathodes must have anodes and vice versa since all charges are double-charged. Essentially everything in the universe is a series of polarized opposites in infinite regress.

Therefore, a single gravity bar is an infinite regress of double-charged gravity bars.

Diagram 12. Infinite Regress of Polarized Parts of a Gravity Bar

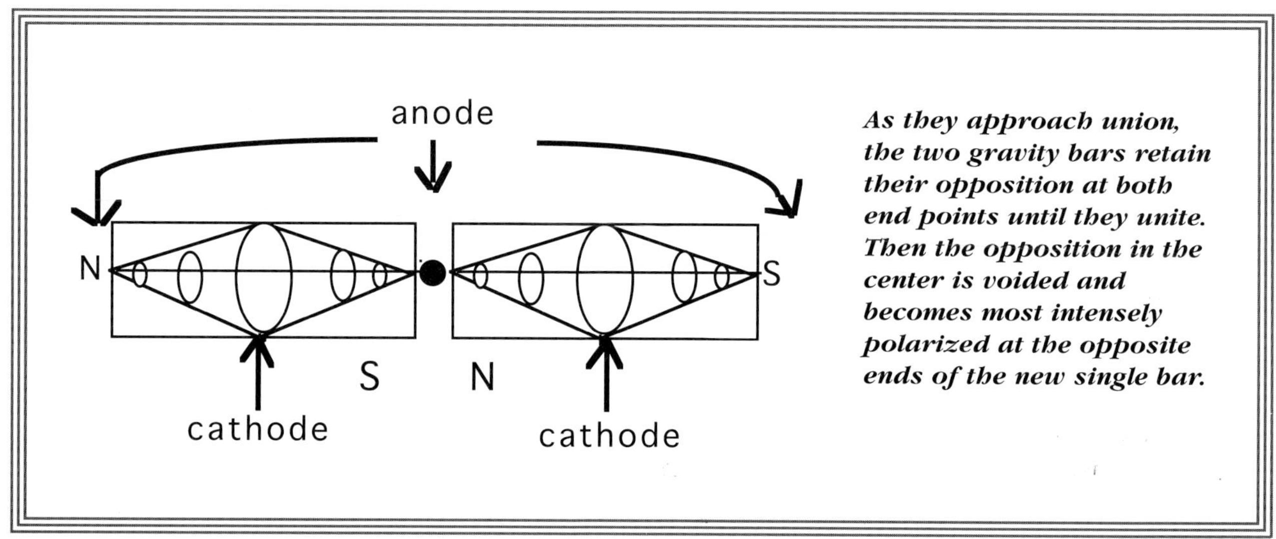

As they approach union, the two gravity bars retain their opposition at both end points until they unite. Then the opposition in the center is voided and becomes most intensely polarized at the opposite ends of the new single bar.

Conventional Science	Russellian Science
Cold is less heat.	Cold is the one unchanging eternal reality.

To the Russells, cold, in the sense of One, is static, unchanging and unconditioned. Cold Light is the essence of the universe. It is the substance from which everything is made. To distinguish this primary substance from cold used as a many word, we will capitalize the word, 'Cold,' when using in the One sense. Heat waves are dynamic, forever changing, and dually conditioned. Yet static Cold and dynamic heat express their opposite energies at angles of 90 degrees from their axes of rotation. Cold compresses to multiply itself into heat, and heat expands to divide itself into cold.

In this case, cold is used as both a One word and as a many word. As a One word, it stands for the equilibrium condition from which the two opposite conditions that we know as cold and heat (in the many sense) emerge. Motion simultaneously compresses toward the center of a system to create increasing temperature/heat and expands to the wave field cube wall boundaries creating decreasing temperature/cold. The equilibrium condition from which cold and heat each appear is beyond measure as the One.

This viewpoint of Omnipresent Cold as the absolute unchanging eternal reality is a One viewpoint. This viewpoint focuses our attention on compressing in an absolute cold vacuum to create heat from Omnipresent Cold. The reverse is equally valid. Heat can also be used as a One word to express the equilibrium condition, but that would change the viewpoint to seeing expansion out of an infinitely hot, dense, compressed state to create cold from Omnipresent Heat. In both cases, the cause is desire of Mind.

The heat waves that the Russells say are forever changing, dynamic and *dually conditioned,* are what we normally call both relative cold and heat. 'Dually conditioned' refers to both the centrifugally directed (cooling) motion and the centripetally directed (heating) motion. In this way the Russells use the word, 'heat,' as a One word to describe the entire compressing/heating and expanding/cooling process.

Secret of Light, p.241.

Conventional Science	Russellian Science
Coulomb law: Opposites attract and likes repel.	Like conditions seek like conditions, and opposite polarities void each other at point of contact. Matter moves to seek rest, balance and similar potential, pressure and condition.

If opposites did attract, we would find both polarities at the center of contact between two magnets rather than the voidance or zero of polarity that actually exists there. Both charging vortexes seek the high potential condition at the center of the system; those that are discharging seek the low potential condition in the cube wave field boundary of tenuous space surrounding the center. A high potential will become invaginated or be swallowed up by a low potential as both polarity predominances turn inside out by becoming one and reproducing themselves in reversed potential and polarity. (See Diagrams 14 and 15.)

Diagram 14. Charging Centripetal Vortex Whirl

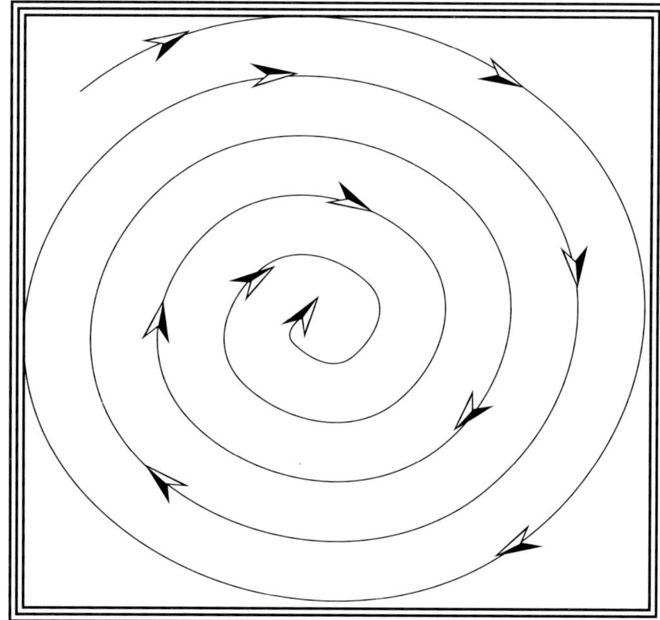

Charging, condensing, coalescing potentials seek like potential at the high-potential gravity centers.

Diagram 15. Discharging Centrifugal Vortex Whirl

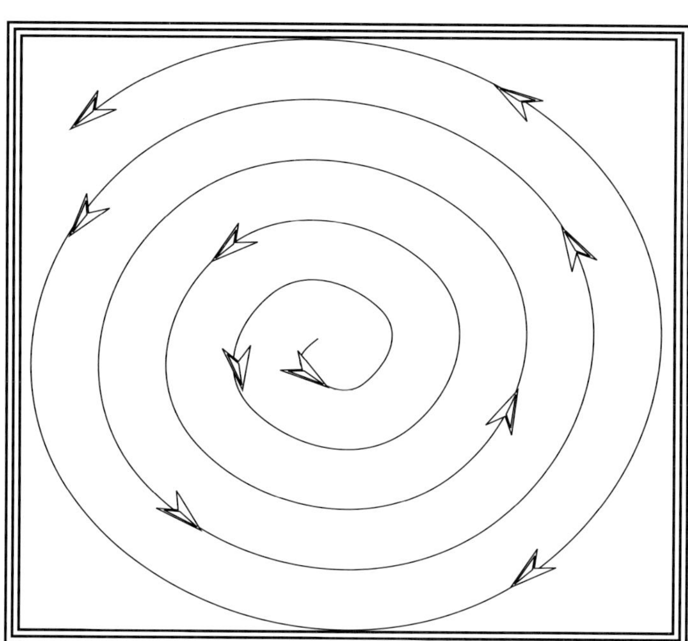

Discharging, evaporating, dispersing potentials seek like potentials at the low potential cube wave field boundary.

Conventional Science	Russellian Science
Conventional science seeks and sees the life principle or underlying basic cause in matter and motion.	Russell's wholistic cyclic science realizes the life principle in the zero light of universal equilibrium as manifested in thinking Mind.

Life as the ONE is the basis of Creation; it is the only thing there is. All matter is a reflection of the Creator's thinking, and, as such, each part is endowed with the life principle. The cause lies behind the matter/motion in the knowing Mind that thinks the form.

In *The Universal One*, Dr. Russell explained it this way on page 20.

> *Light, as man knows light, is but an unstable simulation of the real light of the Universal One. Man's concept of light is luminosity, an illusion of the universal light of inertia, sustained in its appearance as an illusion of light by the pressures generated through motion. The inner mind of ecstatic man knows the real light and that he is One with the light. He is not deceived by its illusion.*

Secret of Light, p. 244.

Conventional Science	Russellian Science
The amount of energy in the Universe is constant; as energy appears in one form it must disappear from another in a corresponding amount.	Russell sees energy as unchanging in the undivided light at rest. As energy is extended from its fulcrum zero of rest, the simulation of energy manifests as two opposing forces of compression/expansion that balance exactly.

Energy as the ONE simply is. Energy is expressed in the relative ever-changing universe through two-way motion: compression into form and expansion into tenuity. In other words, what science thinks of as energy is measured and expressed as matter appears and disappears.

Conventional Science	Russellian Science
Gravity is a force that pulls from within.	Gravity (as a One) is both the thrusting inward centripetal force from without to the mass center and the thrusting outward centrifugal force to the wave field boundary; it is also motionless and changeless: the magnetic zero center. As a many concept, gravity is simply a push from without to within.

Russell spoke of gravity in two senses. One was a counterpoint to the accepted Newtonian gravity seen as an inward pull or force of attraction. Russell's gravity (as a many concept with an opposite) is expressed as the inward-directed, compressing force of matter formation. In this sense there is no pull of gravity. This idea was expressed on page 135 of *Atomic Suicide?* as:

> *There is no force of any nature which holds it (an atom) together by an inward pull. Nature does not attract nor does it repel. It compresses within a vacuum.*

Russell's view of gravity as the force of compressing mass into form was novel at the time. He taught that nature moves and, in moving, creates a compression that simultaneously creates a vacuum; thus it compresses within a vacuum. The matter formation manifests by and at the compression end of the movement. The Russells call this gravity. Matter dissolution manifests by and at the expansion end of the movement. The Russells call this radiation.

Diagram 16. Piston Pump in Equilibrium

Absolute ONE in Equilibrium	

Zero Gravity

In other contexts, the Russells also use the word, 'gravity,' to mean the whole cycle of gravitation and radiation. The Russells never specified when they were using the word in a many sense and when in a One sense, so I am using the word, Gravity, when I believe they are talking about the whole cycle and the word, gravity, when I believe they are referring to the inward compression. As a One, Gravity is the whole process of gravitation/radiation while gravity as a Many is the opposite of radiation.

Diagram 17. Piston Pump Compression/ Expansion Creates Gravity

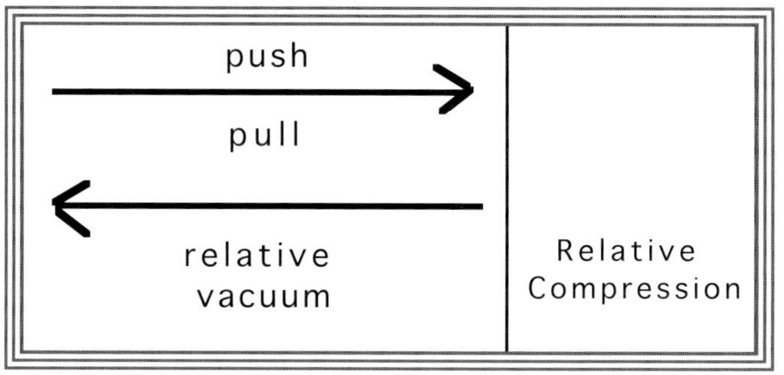

The idea of Gravity was expressed loosely by the Russells on page 139 of *Atomic Suicide?* as:

> *Gravity exerts no force, whatsoever, to either attract or repel.*

Diagram 18. Zero Gravity System

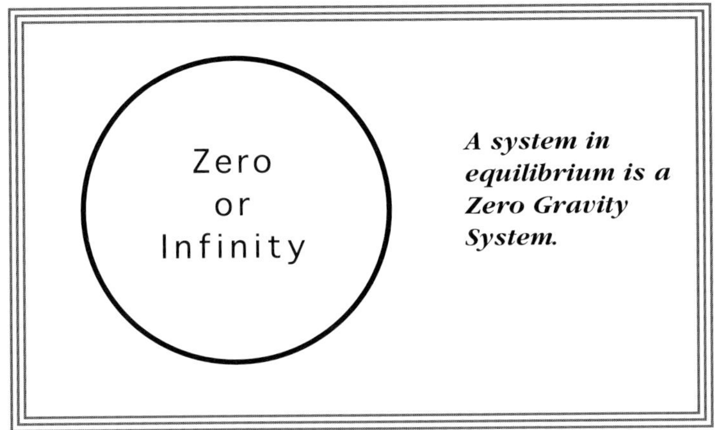

In this sense, the Russells use the word, 'Gravity,' as a One concept or a word having no opposite.

To be verbally and conceptually accurate, this usage of the word, 'Gravity,' must include the concept of the entire two-way, universal, push-pull motion that the Russells use to describe the basic-motion of the universe and to describe Gravity in *The Home Study Course.*

Diagram 19. Expansion/Compression Gravity System

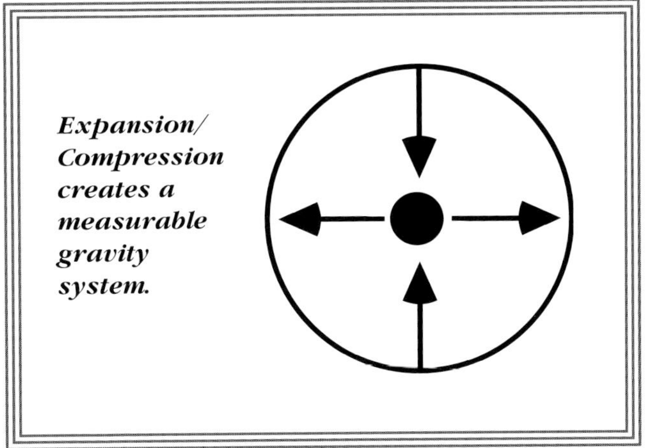

On page 719 of that course the Russells say,

> *. . . gravity both multiplies and divides by thrusting inward from without to compress and outward from within to expand.*

In this description, gravity means the whole process of compression into and expansion out of form. It is this definition of gravity as a whole process which best corresponds to Russell's whole-cycle science. See Diagram 19.

Conventional Science	Russellian Science
The universe has 4 dimensions: length, breadth, width and time.	The universe has 18 dimensions: the 4 of conventional science plus sex, potential, pressure, ecliptic, axial rotation, mass, tone, color, crystallization, ionization, valence, temperature, orbital revolution and plane of gyroscopic rotation. (These dimensions are described in more detail in the next section.)

Eighteen Dimensions of the Relative Universe

Eighteen Dimensions of the Relative Universe

Each component of the Universe and each element will exhibit or can be described by each of the 18 dimensions of matter. Each of these dimensions is briefly described below.

Dimensions 1, 2 and 3.

Length/Distance,
Breadth/Area,
Thickness/Volume

Each dimension is born from inertia (also known as the ONE, the unified field, and the universal equilibrium condition) as the basic two-way polarization motion process or, stated in another way, as opposition of gravitation and radiation.

Diagram 20. A Point in Equilibrium

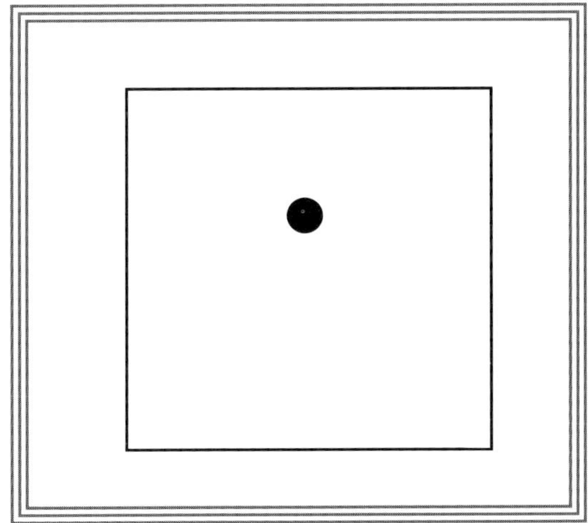

Motion begins with a simultaneous compression to an anode at the center in mass and expansion toward a cathode at the wave field boundary in tenuity. The motion to compress is resisted by the motion to expand. The resistance of both is greatest at the system center at an angle of 90 degrees. The motion to expand is resisted by the adjoining wave-field boundaries and by the inward-bound compressing motion and vice versa.

Diagram 21. A Moving Point Becomes a Line

All motion is simultaneous, forming centripetal cones toward a system center and centrifugal cones away from a center.

Diagram 22. All Lines Are Three-Dimensional

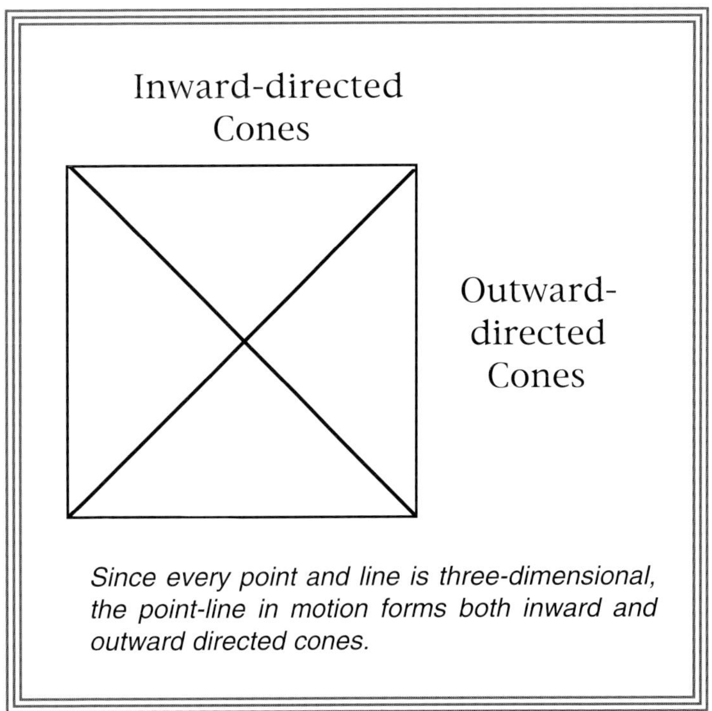

Since every point and line is three-dimensional, the point-line in motion forms both inward and outward directed cones.

Diagram 23. Cathode/Anode Positions

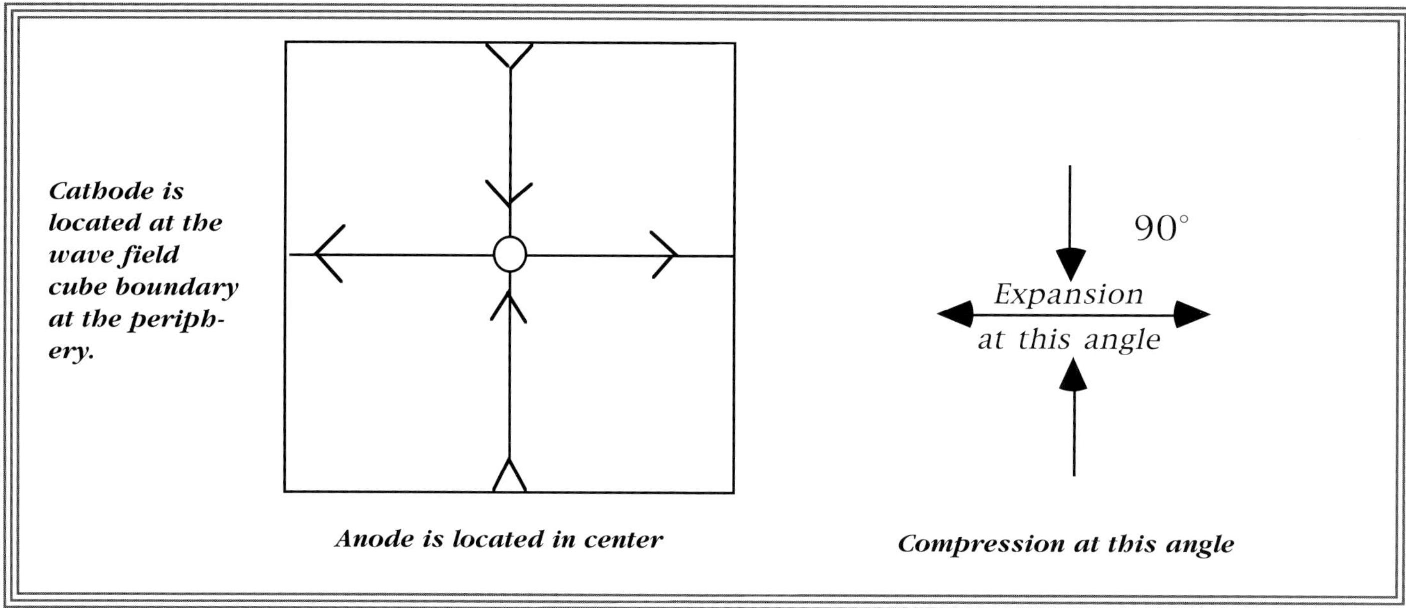

Thus, there are no straight lines in the Universe; all motion is curved. Motion begins at, or emerges from, an inertial plane and ends at an inertial plane. This two-way motion produces expanding and contracting cones and toroid donut-shaped vortex whirls which produce the length, breadth and width of the first three dimensions formed out of inertia or the One.

Gravity measures in mass accumulation the limits of the inward motion at the system center; radiation measures in mass tenuity the limits of the outward bound motion at the system periphery. These two opposing movements create the first three dimensions; thus length, breadth, and width are related to gravitation and radiation. To change any of these three dimensions changes gravitation and radiation. For example, reducing these first three dimensions results in moving toward the system center with its greater gravity and vice versa.

Dimension 4. Time/Duration

All dimensions are simultaneous in inertia and are sequentially transferred in (degree of) expression to the wave which records sequences of motion; thus time is born out of inertia. All dimensions change simultaneously in all parts of the Universe. All changes are changes in degree. Changes in degree mark the passage of time. Deceleration contracts time. Acceleration expands time by an accumulation of the speed/time constraint transformed into power and vice versa.

Time-power appears by lengthening the day and shortening the year and disappears by reversal of these effects. In other words, greater time/power results in longer days and shorter years, while less time/power results in shorter days and longer years. Therefore accelerated revolution and decreased rotation of planets is found at the center of the system.

On the other hand, speed/power appears by shortening the day and lengthening the year and disappears by reversal of these effects. Thus it appears at the periphery of the system by accelerated rotation and decreased speed of revolution. The day is shortened by decreased revolution and increased rotation, by lower potential position or gravity, and vice versa.

In other words, greater speed/power results in shorter days and longer years, while less speed/power results in longer days and shorter years. Therefore, the periphery of the system experiences accelerated rotation and decreased speed of revolution. Thus increased revolution and decreased rotation bring longer days because of the higher potential position or gravity, and vice versa.

Thus variations of the time dimension change the ability of mass to appear to attract and repel, making it related, as are all dimensions, to gravitation and radiation. Time in the One is eternity. Time in the relative Many universe is ever changing; in fact, it is change itself.

Dimension 5. Sex

Male and female are the essence of the polarization process that exhibits sex by expression of concept in opposing cones of inward- and outward-directed pressure predominance. With any movement, the male (inward, compressive, gravitative) and the female (outward, expansive, radiative) expressions of motion are born out of inertia and demonstrate the apparent ability of sex to appear to attract and repel. Thus is sex, too, related to gravitation and radiation as are all dimensions.

Dimensions 6 and 7. Pressure and Potential

Each of these dimensions occur within the opposing cones of sex energy. High potential pressure occurs at gravitative centers, and low potential pressure occurs at peripheral cube wall boundaries. Potential is energy wound up ready to be released and to penetrate its opposing cone of energy which is unwound and ready to accept and incorporate its opposite. Pressure can be measured by position relative to the center or periphery of a cyclone, the greatest pressure being at the center. By reproduction through sex union exerted in sequence and in and through opposing pressures and potentials, they are thus born out of inertia. By appearing to attract and repel, they, too, are related to gravitation and radiation.

Dimension 8. Temperature

Temperature is born out of inertia by resistance to the gravitative, centripetal, electric flow of motion from its opposite electric radiative, centrifugal motion flow. Heat increases in the direction of gravitative compression and decreases in the direction of radiative expansion. Variation of temperature correlates with the apparent ability of mass to attract and repel; thus is it, too, related to gravitation and radiation.

Dimension 9. Ionization

This dimension is an abnormal replacement of that which gravity/electricity has displaced/integrated/compacted. Radiation is the normal replacement. Ionization is, in this sense, an intensification of normal radiation. Separate substances under varying conditions (pressure zones) have a relative power of disintegration through ionization or intensified radiation. The power of repulsion (disintegration) is relative to the potential of the substance and its position; therefore ionization, too, is related to gravitation/radiation. Ionization decreases as generation increases, and vice versa.

For example, under normal conditions the potential of our environment is high enough to support a very low radiation for the metal, silver. When placed in nitric acid, which is a much lower potential environment, silver ions (particles or mass units) fly away from the mass much like our bodies would explode in the vacuous suction of deep space if suddenly placed there.

Since this phenomenon varies with the apparent ability of mass to attract or repel, it, too, is related to gravitation and radiation.

Dimension 10. Crystallization

The crystallization of mass is a frozen record in the form of the generoactive effort of accumulating potential. Greater gravity produces hard simple crystals; less gravity produces soft amorphous ones. Crystallization occurs according to the potential position of the crystallizing masses.

All accumulating mass is governed by gravity. More gravity means more mass which yields

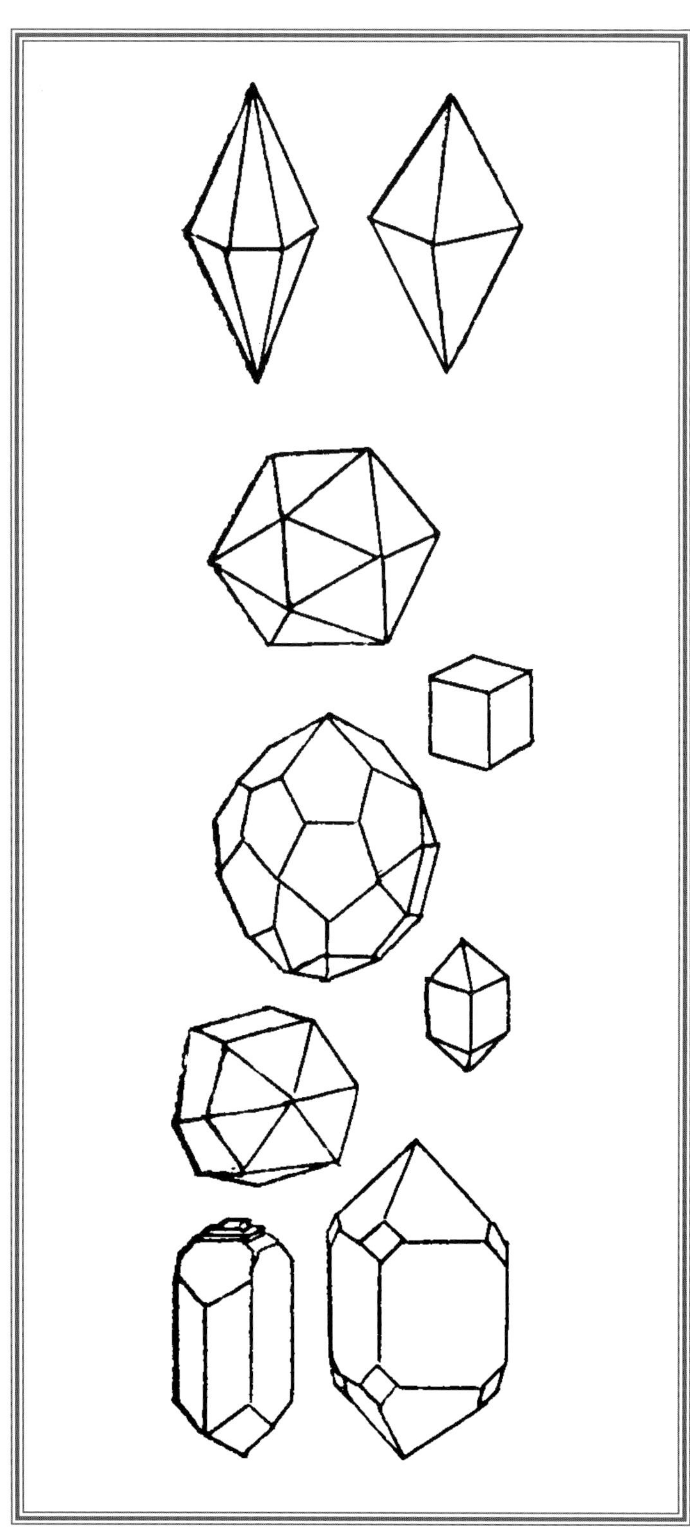

All crystals are cube sections. *Secret of Light*, p.224.

simple hard crystals. The cube is the hardest and simplest crystal, like diamonds which are formed at the center of the system. Redistributing mass is governed by radiation. Greater radiation means more tenuous mass which yields amorphous soft crystals; these are found at the system periphery.

As radiation increases, crystallization becomes more and more complex, and the cube is transformed toward a sphere. Urium — which was predicted by Dr. Russell in 1926 and later detected and named plutonium by conventional science — has a very complex crystal according to the Russell Cosmogony.

As the effort to compress relaxes and heat dissipates, all accumulating mass freezes in its potential position as the crystal shape appropriate to that potential position. As mass reaches the archetypal carbon amplitude position of the nine-octave cycle, it approaches cubic hardness and simplicity. As it approaches the end of the nine-octave cycle as in urium, it recedes into spherical softness.

Since the crystal shape is related to the apparent ability of any mass to attract and repel, it, too, is related to gravitation and radiation.

Dimension 11. Valence

Valence is a standard unit of tonal relations measuring the willingness or unwillingness of various elemental tones to unite. Elements of different valences have different powers to attract and repel and therefore are related to gravitation and radiation, e.g., carbon with a valence of +4 and -4 and sodium and chlorine with a valence of +1 and -1 respectively.

Carbon's greater valence gives it a greater apparent ability to attract and repel and thus greater powers of gravitation/radiation. The valence of an element is in accordance with and can be determined by the formula of the locked potentials. Valence of all elements is in accordance with the formula of the locked potentials. The farther up the scale of 1 to 4 (first locking point position to fourth locking point position), the greater the ability to appear to attract and repel as in the previous example of carbon, sodium and chlorine. (See pages 51 + 99 for an overview of locking points.)

See page 54 for diagram and text on the Cosmic Clock.

Male and female elements, such as male sodium and female chlorine, unite more readily with those of equal valence (and pressure, potential, and octave position) than with those of higher or lower valence (and pressure, potential and octave position). For example, sodium and chlorine preferentially unite more readily and with more stability than, for example, sodium and bromine which are in different octaves but have the same valence, or sodium and sulfur which have different valences but are in the same octave. See the Russell Periodic Charts on pages 52-53.

Again, valence thus appears to affect the ability to attract and repel and is thus also related to gravitation/radiation.

Dimensions 12 and 13. Axial Rotation (speed/time) and Orbital Revolution (power/time)

These dimensions influence the ability of any mass to attract or repel and therefore are related to gravitation/radiation. Slow rotation and fast revolution, such as exhibited by the planet Mercury close to the solar system's intense fourth locking point amplitude position of high potential and high gravity, is related to gravitation. Fast rotation and slow revolution, as demonstrated by the outer planets such as Jupiter, Neptune, Uranus and Pluto, demonstrate higher radiation. Thus these factors are related to gravitation/radiation.

Dimension 14. Mass

Mass demonstrates an apparent ability to attract and repel depending on factors such as potential position, density and tone and is therefore related to gravitation and radiation. All mass contracts and becomes more dense on the inward, compressive, generative, gravitative, centripetal journey to the accumulation of mass at the system center; thus, it demonstrates greater gravity. All mass expands and becomes less dense on the outward, expansive, degenerative, radiative, centrifugal journey to

The Formula of the Locked Potentials

This formula measures dimensions just as time is measured by hour, minutes and seconds. Periodicity is an absolute characteristic of all effects of motion. With the exceptions of mass and tone, the dimensions of all effects of motion are of the same, orderly, octave periodicity expressed as:

$$\ddagger\ 4 + 3 + 2 + 1 + 0 \ = \ - 1 - 2 - 3 - 4\ \ddagger$$

or

$$0 + 1 + 2 + 3 + 4\ \ddagger - 4 - 3 - 2 - 1 - 0$$

Zero represents inertial energy, and the numerals represent the orderly progressions in locked potentials, pressures, and orbits.

Octave periodicity is an orderly progression to and from the maximum effect of each octave. The two exceptions to octave periodicity – mass and tone – vary in that mass accumulates from the first to the ninth octave, and tone lowers from the ninth octave to the first octave.

The numerals in this formula are the hours of the Cosmic Clock. They are in the relative positions of the atoms of the elements and in the order of their respective varying dimensions. The seconds of the Cosmic Clock are the corpuscles or light units which make up the atom's structures.

The hands of the clock are the indicating line of charging and discharging potential. The main spring is the nine-octave cycle, half of which are decelerating time dimensions transformed by accumulation into power, and half of which are power dimensions released into accelerating time. The winding of the clock is the sublime $4\ ^1/_2$-octave inhalation (to carbon) and its unwinding is the $4\ ^1/_2$-octave exhalation.

The cosmic pendulum ticks off the varying dimensions of all motion forever and ever with unfailing accuracy, but never departs from this simple formula.

the redistribution of mass in plane at the system periphery; thus it demonstrates increasing radiation.

Mass is stored energy bound into form as potential. Density and tone are the two cyclic exceptions to the octave periodicity formula of the locked potentials. Density of mass and frequency of tone increase with each of the nine octaves of light wave motion.

Dimension 15. Color

Color is nature's recording in light of the effects of gravitation/radiation in her octave wave volume coloring book. The color spectrum springs from the white, colorless, inertial plane in both directions of sex charging as ultraviolet. On the male end, it begins as the first locking point red-ultraviolet to infrared, to the second locking point as red, to the third locking point as orange-red to orange, to the fourth amplitude position as yellow to white incandescence in the zero of union.

From the female end, it progresses from the first locking point as blue-ultraviolet to violet, to the second as blue, to the third as blue-green to green, and to the fourth as the yellow to white incandescence of union.

The apparent ability to attract and repel varies with the color of a tone as it progresses from one stage to the next and is thus also related to gravitation/radiation.

Dimension 16. Plane of Gyroscopic Rotation

The apparent ability of an element to attract and repel varies with speed. A faster spinning gyroscope approaching the amplitude position (plane of 90 degrees) demonstrates a greater apparent ability to attract and repel, while a slower spinning gyroscope approaching the 180-degree plane demonstrates a lesser ability to attract and repel. Mass devolves in four opposing radiative, expansive, centrifugal exhalations and stages to return to its inertial plane of rest. Mass evolves in four opposing gravitative compressive centripetal inhalations and stages to simulate stillness at the amplitude point of union.

The gyroscopic plane angle of elemental rotation is expressed as the degree of angle of an element as expressed by a gyroscope rotating with the force necessary to determine its shape and angle. The first locking point of the cycle of elements for the carbon octave is at 42 degrees, the second at

Diagram 24. Cycle of the Elements from Rest to Rest

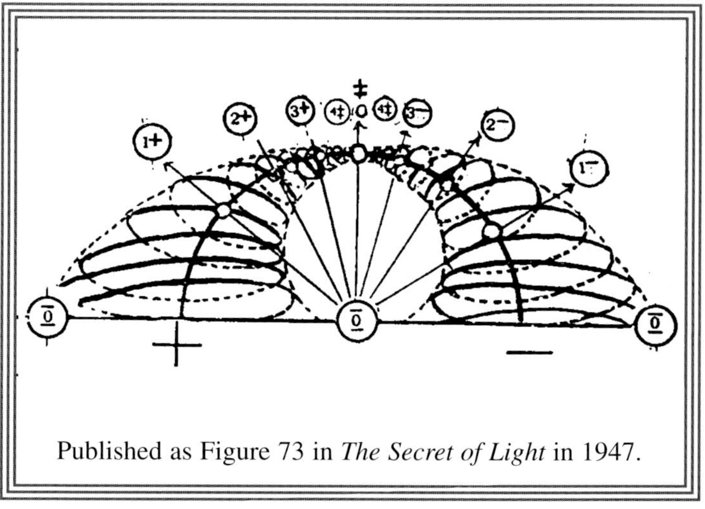

Published as Figure 73 in *The Secret of Light* in 1947.

72 degrees, the third at 86 degrees, and the fourth or amplitude point at 90 degrees. These angles are important in engineering the transmutation of elements using magnetic field controls along with temperature, pressure and time as depicted in the following diagrams.

The apparent ability of mass to attract and repel increases or decreases as the reflecting plane approaches and recedes from 90 degrees and is therefore also related to gravitation/radiation.

Diagram 25. Octave Gyroscopic Principle

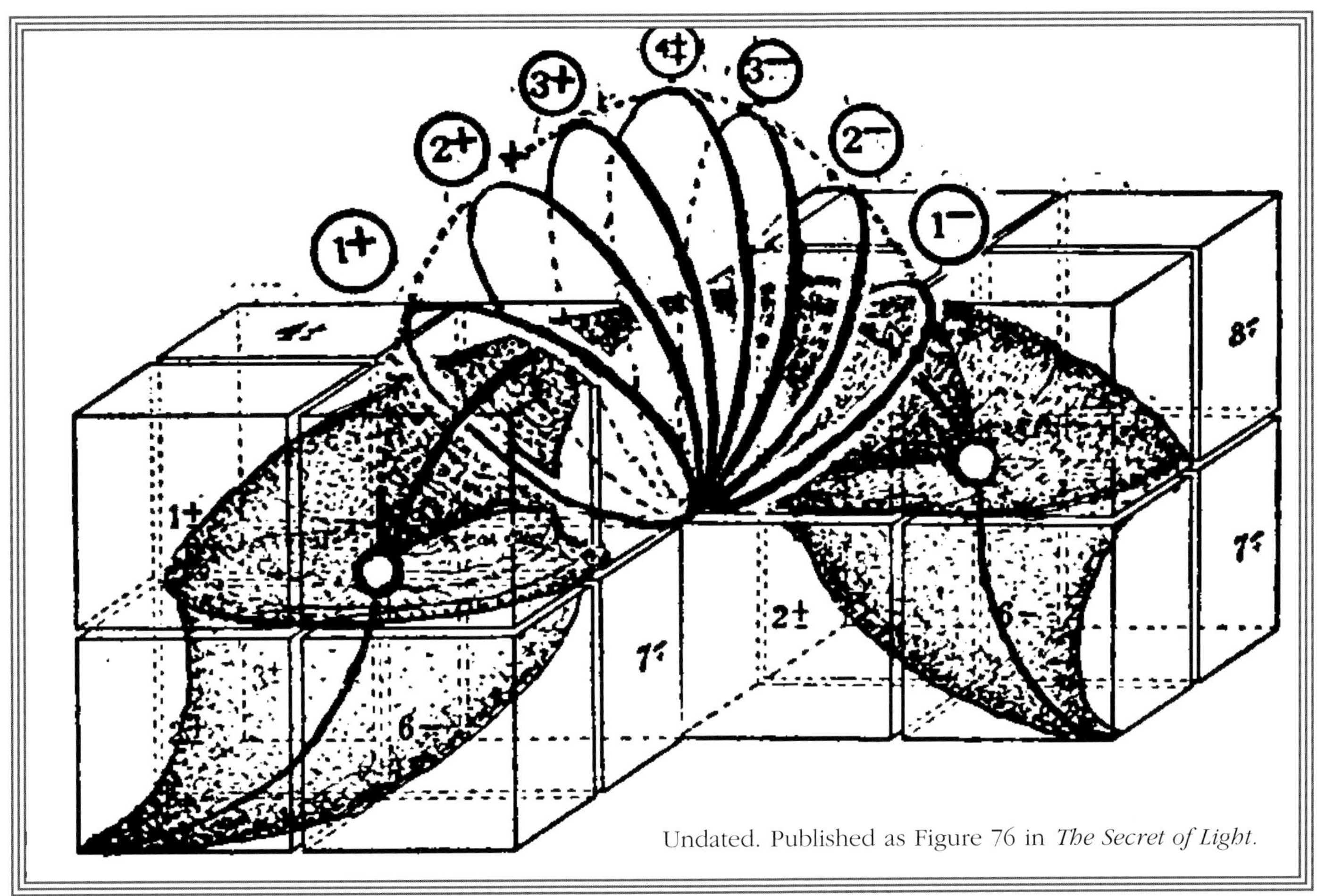

Undated. Published as Figure 76 in *The Secret of Light.*

Dimension 17. Ecliptic

The ecliptic of all mass is that equatorial plane area and beyond toward the polar axis that demonstrates the centrifugal expansive discharge of mass. There are charging polar vortexes that centripetally wind motion/matter into form, and there are discharging equatorial vortexes that centrifugally unwind motion/matter into tenuity and plane.

These two sets of vortexes, two charging and two discharging, change their shapes at each locking position in the wave. They both contract as the amplitude position is reached, and they expand as the first position is reached. Since they both achieve maximum apparent ability to attract and repel at the amplitude position, they are related to gravitation/radiation.

Again, the ecliptic of all mass increases with increasing expansion, thus decreasing the power of attraction/repulsion. Likewise the ecliptic decreases with increasing contraction/compression and thus the increasing power of attraction/repulsion. The gyroscopic plane angle of rotation rises from 180 degrees to 90 degrees as the ecliptic decreases and vice versa. As mass progresses from the first locking point to the fourth locking point (which is the amplitude position), the ecliptic contracts; from the fourth to the first locking point position, the ecliptic expands. Thus the ecliptic, too, is related to the apparent ability of mass to attract and repel.

Dimension 18. Tone and Sound

Tone or sound is caused by any motion, which is either by potential impacting against potential (gravitation or fusion) or by separating from potential (radiation or fission). Tone/sound is the result of implosions and explosions of accumulating or redistributing mass. Each form in the universe has its own particular tone or sound.

Sound frequency increases in ever shorter waves as the center of the system (fourth locking point amplitude position) is approached. Likewise, sound frequency decreases in ever longer waves toward the system periphery and first locking point to the inertial plane of birth and rest. Since the tone/sound frequency is related to potential and position, and these are related to the apparent ability of mass to appear to attract and repel, then tone/sound is also related to gravitation/radiation.

A more complete description of the 18 dimensions of matter can be found in *The Universal One,* written by Walter Russell in 1926 – six years after his 39-day period of illumination. Dr. Russell believed that the 18 dimensions of matter held the key to the age of transmutation and to new pollution-free sustainable energy sources.

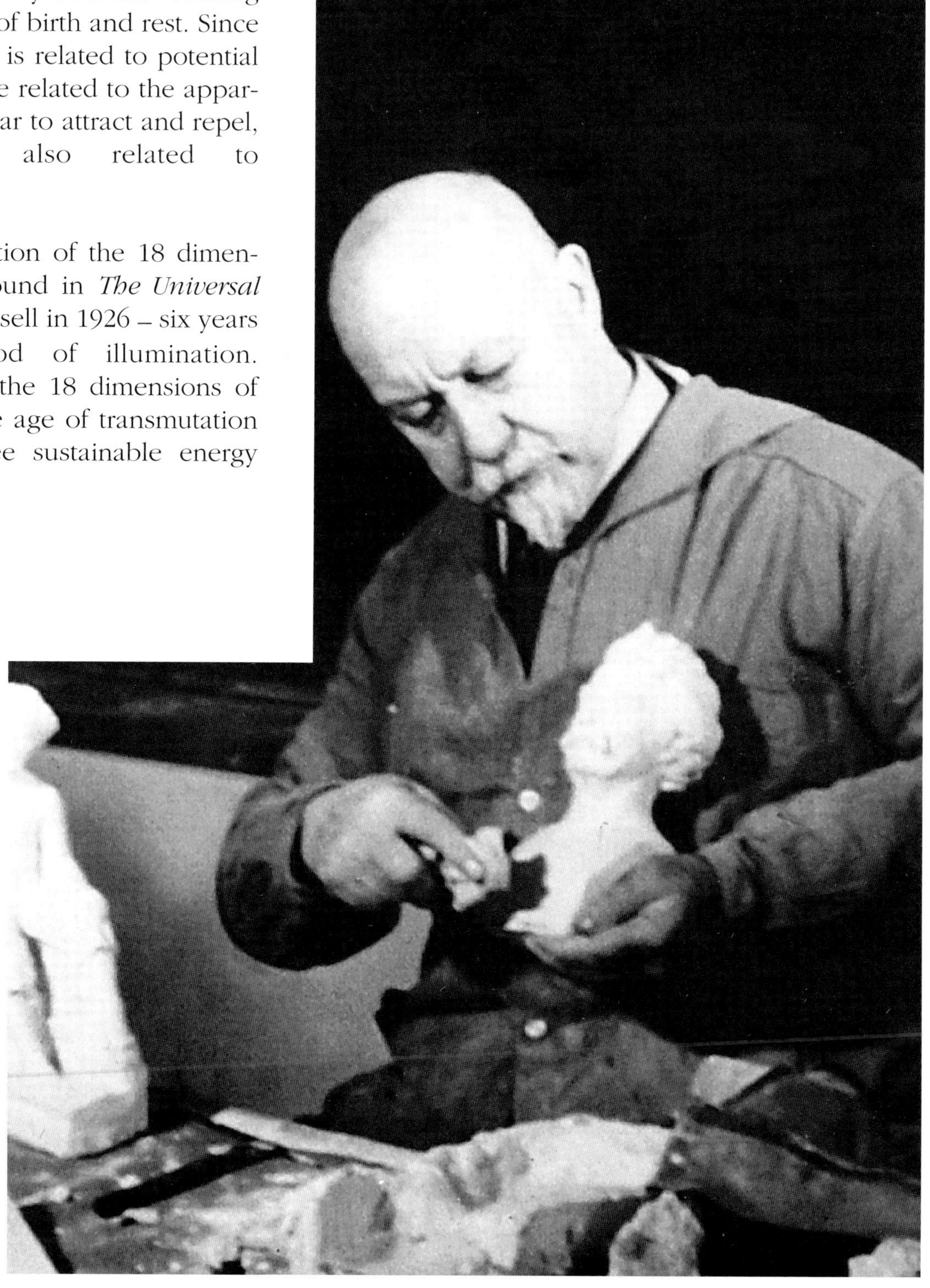

Walter Russell sculpting the Mark Twain Memorial in 1934.

Current and Potential Applications of Russellian Science

Dr. Russell demonstrated the truth of this assertion at the Westinghouse Lamp Laboratories in 1927. With the World Balance through Free Energy project, the Russell Science Research team re-verified this principle in the early 1990s.

It also appears that the 18 dimensions of matter may provide the key to developing new transportation systems and to Gravity control, in the sense of controlling the entire gravitation/radiation process, since changing one dimension simultaneously changes all the others, resulting in the apparent ability to attract and repel.

The Russell Cosmogony places the Einstein equation in a new perspective. Energy is not in mass, but is expressed by Mind in accumulation and redistribution of motion/matter into and out of mass.

Conventional Cosmogonies Objective science and Universe	**Russellian Cosmogony** Cyclic science and Universe
Three cosmogonies seem to dominate conventional science. First, the big bang claims that creation started as an explosion, and the universe is expanding and running down as entropy to non-existence. Second, continuous creation claims that matter is produced from nothing all the time in the form of hydrogen atoms from which galaxies grow so that the density of the universe remains the same. Third, initial impulse and steady state theories believe that the universe has always existed pretty much the same as it does today; in this cosmogony matter appears to fill the space left by the expansion of the universe.	Russell posits a steady explosion and implosion state of eternal creation, a continuous life-and-death cycling. Matter is created out of space, and space out of matter, via gravitation/radiation. It is a two-way, continuous-creation, eternally living-dying universe. Hydrogen atoms are created out of the three octaves of prehydrogen elements which are given life from the death of the ninth octave elements.

In light of the Russell Cosmogony and logical thought, I pose the following rhetorical questions to conventional science.

What is nothing?

Nothing is ultimately only a change of state and place as both happen simultaneously. There is something, and, since it changes its state and its place, we think there is now nothing.

How can an explosion, which is a release of wound-up and bound-up potential and accumulation of mass, occur if there is no winding, binding and accumulation also occurring?

It cannot occur unless there is such a generative process. There can be no big bang without an equal big implosion. The universe is exactly balanced between expansion and contraction, and, in that sense, it is in a steady state. There was no initial impulse in eternity. In eternity there is no motion-now. The relative universe has always been moving in all ways, in all directions and in all dimensions.

How can hydrogen atoms appear out of nothing?

They can only appear out of nothing if nothing is a change of state and place. Hydrogen atoms can appear from the lower potential octaves that Russell claims must exist, although we have yet to discover them. As mass expands out of form in the ninth octave, it reverses direction and potential and begins to compress into form in the pre-hydrogen octaves with an equal amount of generative energy as the higher octaves express degenerative energy. These pre-hydrogen octaves may be the source of a new energy.

Conventional Cosmogonies	Russellian Cosmogony
Science more or less accepts the general and special theories of relativity. The special theory states that mass can be changed into energy and vice versa and that nothing can move faster than the speed of light. The general theory states that gravity is a bending or curving of space/time caused by the presence of matter.	The Russell Cosmogony states that mass is an expression of the generoactive cycle of energy accumulation. As mass accumulates in universal ratios according to the theory of the formula of the locked potentials, it acquires greater ability to appear to attract and repel. The ultimate form of creation is the cube/sphere. They are the archetypes for all geometric forms. The ultimate energy expression as an apparent ability to attract and repel appears at the carbon line, fourth locking point amplitude position (See Figure 13 for an in-depth explanation). Mass expresses energy as it accumulates and redistributes. Light reproduces itself at the 'speed of light,' the ultimate speed in matter, but conceptually it is expressed universally and simultaneously beyond time and space and thus beyond speed. In matter, the 'speed of light' is the universal generoactive speed of the highest octave of the lowest *perceptible* potential, i.e., the hydrogen octave. The generoactive gravitative speed is gradually appropriated by radiation and applied to the radioactive speed from mass toward plane. The generoactive speed of light is appropriately the lowest potential octave, and on up to the midpoint of the fourth octave in this generoactive speed of accumulating mass from plane. The radioactive speed of light is appropriately the highest potential octave up from the midpoint of the fourth octave in this radioactive speed of redistributing mass toward plane. In this way, the speed of light varies from octave to octave. Gravity is the centripetally-directed, spiral-motion force of compression to accumulate mass and is caused by the concentrative power of Mind. Radiation is gravitation's opposite in all ways.

Light does not travel, but simply reproduces itself from one wave field to the other. All motion is balanced by an equal and opposite motion, so whatever happens is simultaneously unhappening.

Gravity is expressed by centripetally-directed motion/matter into mass accumulation. Radiation is expressed by centrifugally directed motion/matter toward dissipation in plane. All motion is curved motion since any movement is resisted by its opposing force. Space and time dimensions change as mass accumulates and redistributes while approaching or exiting a system center. The presence of solid matter represents a greater gravity center than less dense matter which demonstrates gravitative beginnings.

If Dr. Russell's postulate,

In the Wave lies the secret of Creation

is true, then the wave embodies every aspect of the Russell Cosmogony. The wave demonstrates the basic polarization process, the cube and the sphere, the 18 dimensions of motion/matter, the periodic chart of the elements, the Cosmic Clock, the Russellian laws of thermodynamics, and all of nature's other processes. A brief description of this polarization process, the cube/sphere, the periodic charts, the Cosmic Clock, the Russellian thermodynamic laws, and Newton's first and third laws and postulates completes this discussion of the Russell Cosmogony.

The essence of the wave can be expressed as the appearance and disappearance of motion/matter from the One in two directions: one direction from the inertial, cathode plane and its progression through four generating stages to maturity at the anode where it simulates stillness in the One by fast motion, and then from there in the other direction through four degenerating stages to dissolution where it again loses form in the inertial, cathode plane, stillness. The one aspect of motion common to both these directions is spiral motion. The lever and the Tao both express the idea of the wave as stated above. Refer to Diagrams 1 through 3.

A wave can form in two ways. It can form by the impact of radiative energy against an inertial plane where it reverses potential and becomes gravitative energy. It can also form by the impact of gravitative energy against an inertial plane, and it reverses to radiative energy. Each wave has an axis, harmonics, amplitude, crest and trough as illustrated in Diagrams 26 and 27.

The basic polarization process is the essence of the Russell Cosmogony. The One is, and the One is an equilibrium condition. The equilibrium divides itself into the two male-female archetypes of motion, form, and condition such as the lever or the Tao, and the infinite complexity of the Universe appears from this polarity. Each of the diagrams, paintings and charts in this book embody this process.

At the wave field boundary walls, the wave demonstrates the cube as one case of the two basic archetypes of form, the cubic feminine. At the center of the wave field, it demonstrates the sphere as the male archetype of form.

At each extreme — the cube boundary wall and the spherical center — the other polarity can be perceived in reverse image. A cube is an expanding sphere flattened as centrifugal, radial, outward-directed/reflected motion is resisted by the cube wave field boundary; this is the frozen image. A sphere is a compressed cube as gravitative, inward-directed motion is reflected/directed centripetally to the system anode center; this is the molten image. Each form becomes the other as they turn inside-out and outside-in in their life-death cycles. All other forms are special cases or variations of the basic cube-sphere.

All of the 18 dimensions of matter shift at each step along the wave from inertial plane and tenuity to the system center and solidity and back again to the system periphery and tenuity. Each element identifies itself at each point in the wave, with all 18 dimensions appropriate to its place in the wave. Thus each dimension varies in form, intensity and all other measurable quantities at each step in the wave. The dimensions manifest in a continuum of

Diagrams 26 and 27. The Essence of the Wave: Wave Mechanics

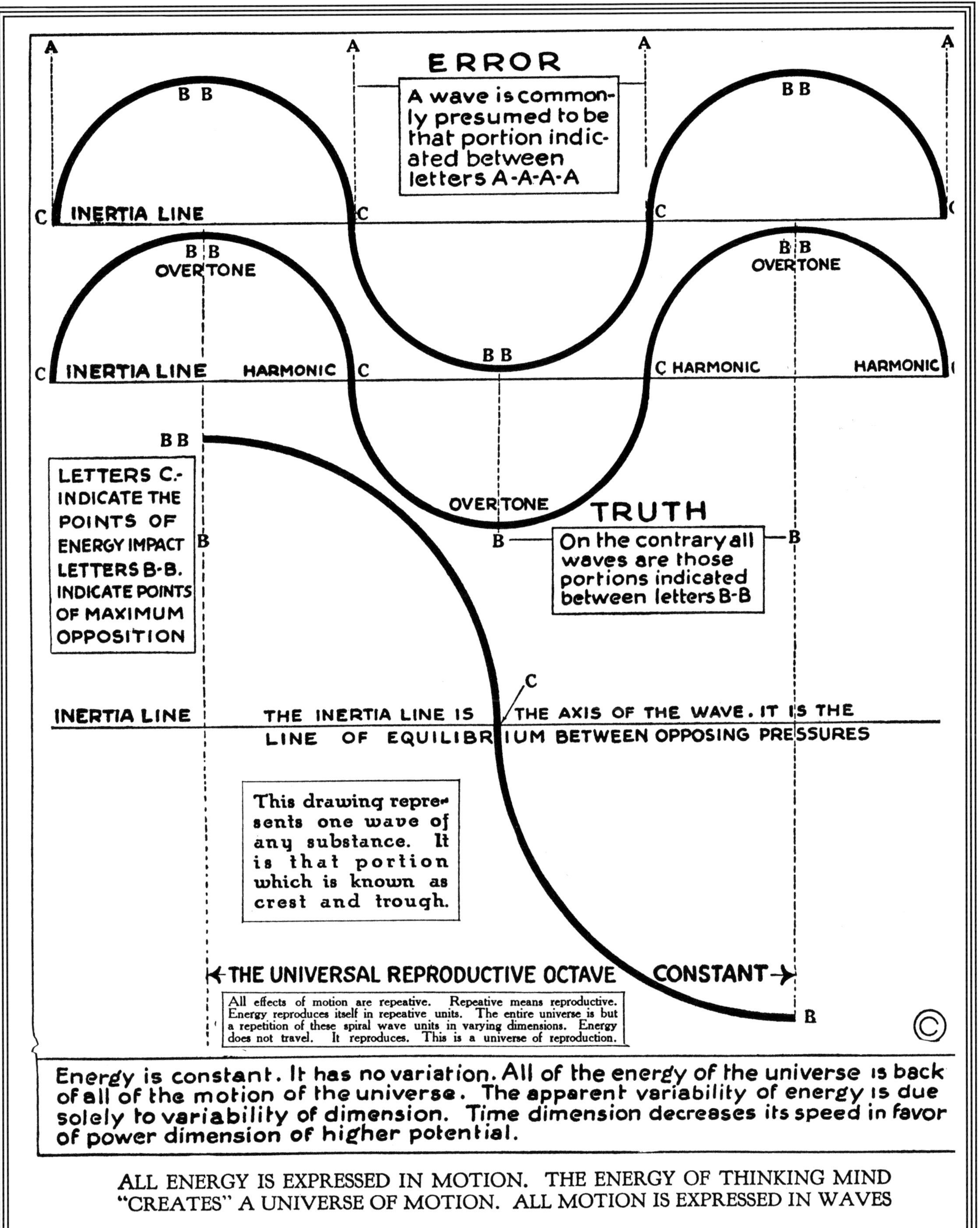

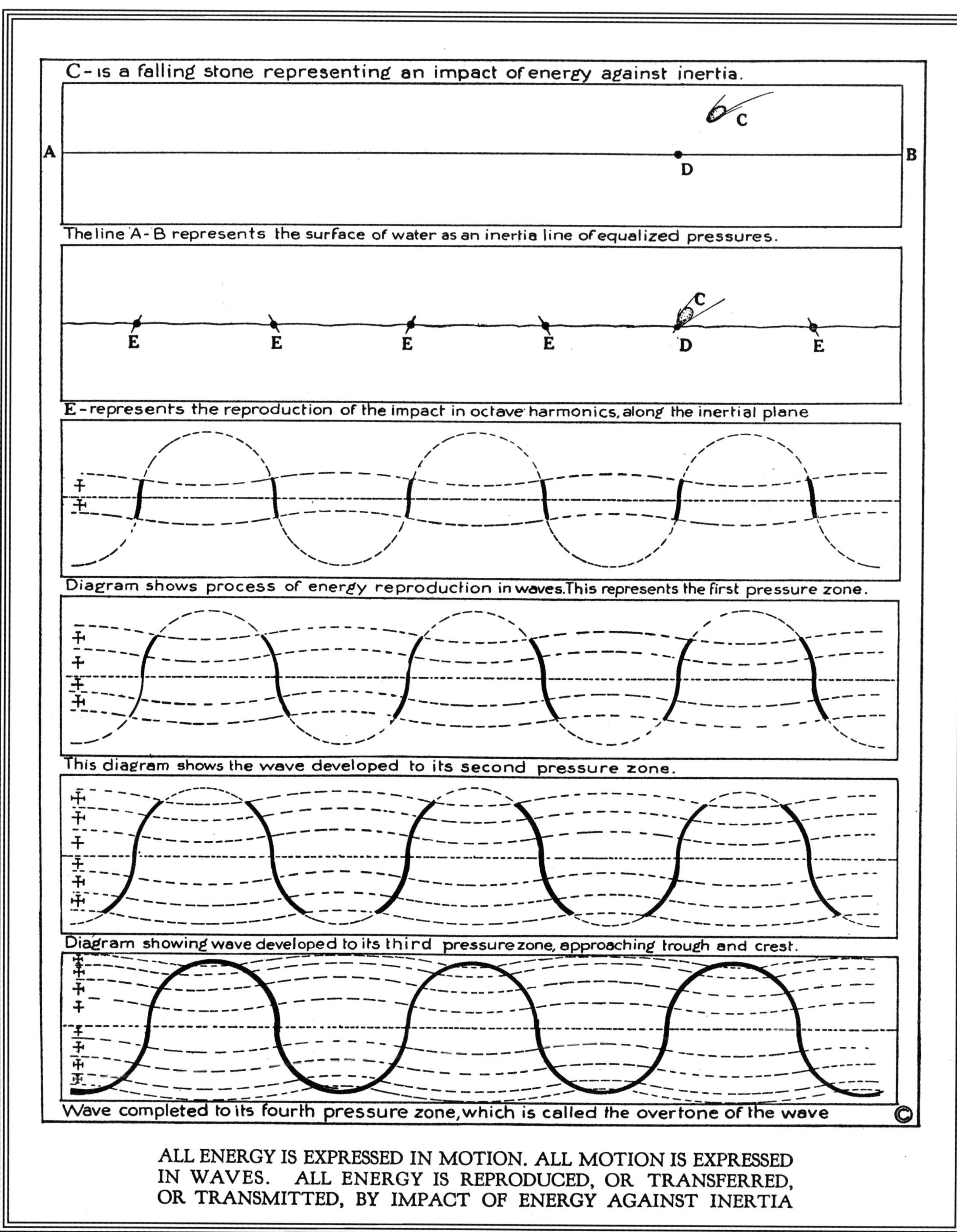

Both figures were originally completed in 1926 and published untitled in The Universal One*:181 and 179.*

Diagram 28. The Cube/Sphere: Female-Male Archetype for All Forms

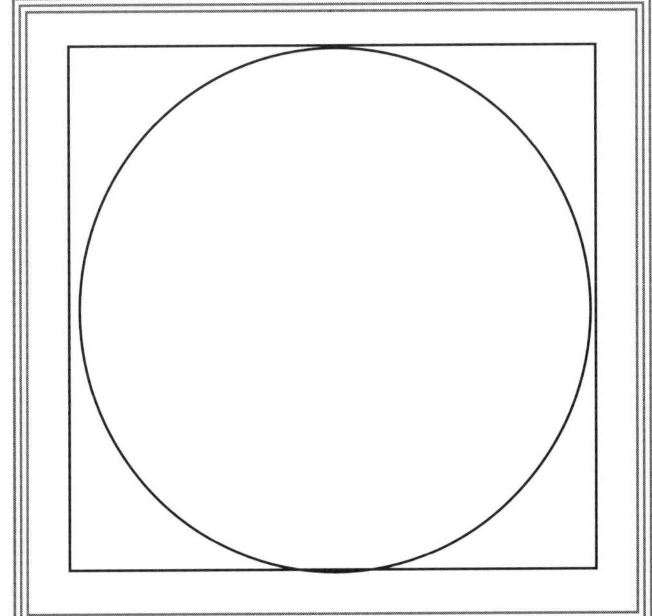

forms that are expressed at each step in the wave. *The Universal One* was the only book in which Dr. Russell described these 18 dimensions.

The Russell periodic chart of the elements is an octave wave chart of integrating and disintegrating motion/matter to and from the center of the chart. It contains within itself, explicitly or implicitly, all of the elements of the Russell Cosmogony.

Each of the nine octaves grows from an inert gas which is the seed for all the elements or isotopes in that octave. The idea for each octave is in the seed, and it is expressed in maturing and aging steps. The maturing stages of the idea are expressed from the inertial plane to the first locking point to the amplitude fourth locking point position within each octave. The aging stages of the idea are expressed from the amplitude position to the first locking point to the inertial plane again.

The mature point for the idea of the entire chart — the mature prototype for all elements or for the idea of solid elemental matter — is expressed at the amplitude point for the entire nine octaves. This mature point is at the amplitude position of the fourth octave and is expressed in carbon, the most vital of all elements. Accordingly, carbon is the basis for organic life on our planet.

The Russell's laws of thermodynamics are a wave-like expression of the appearance of increasing and decreasing temperature in octave wave progression from the eternal equilibrium of the One to motion/matter as compressed into form and higher potential and temperature, then to its expansion out of form to lower potential and tem-

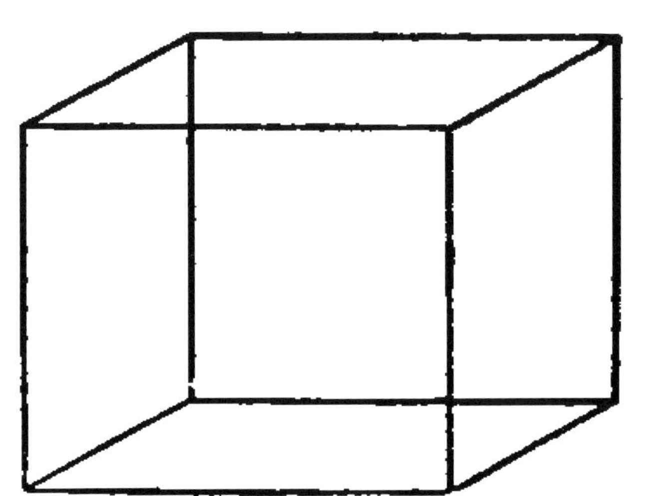

The cube and sphere are one, being two opposite phases of the same thing. The cube is the sphere extended to black coldness while the sphere is the cube contracted to white incandescence.

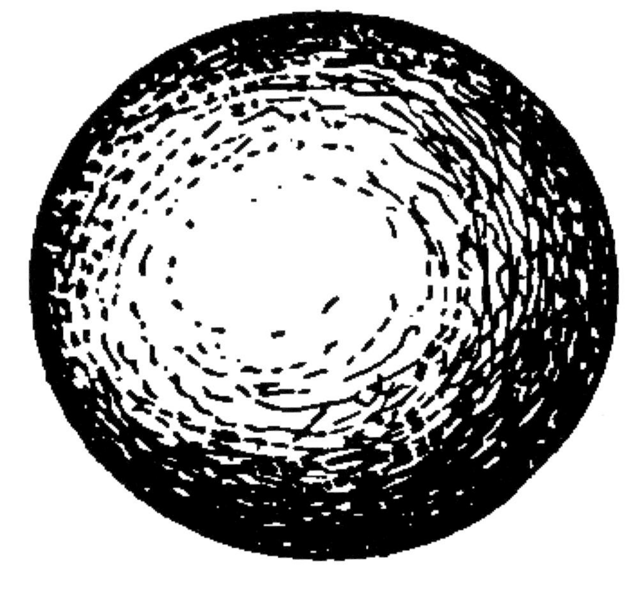

The Secret of Light, pp.22-23.

Diagram 29. The Russell Periodic Chart of the Elements, Number 2: Periodicity is a Characteristic of All Phenomena of Nature

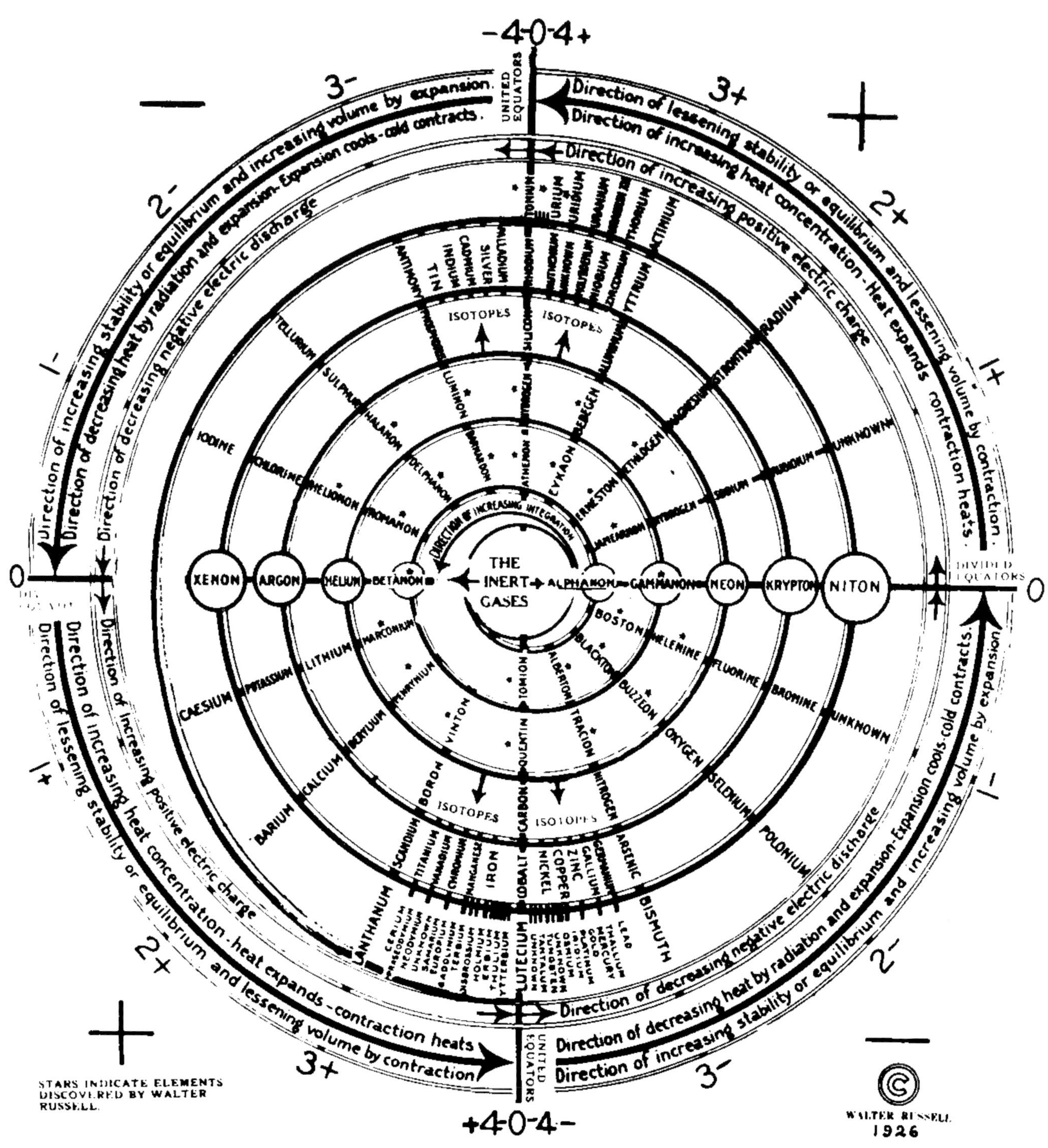

First published in this form as Figure 69 in *The Secret of Light* in 1947.

Diagram 31. The Russell Periodic Table of the Elements, No. 1

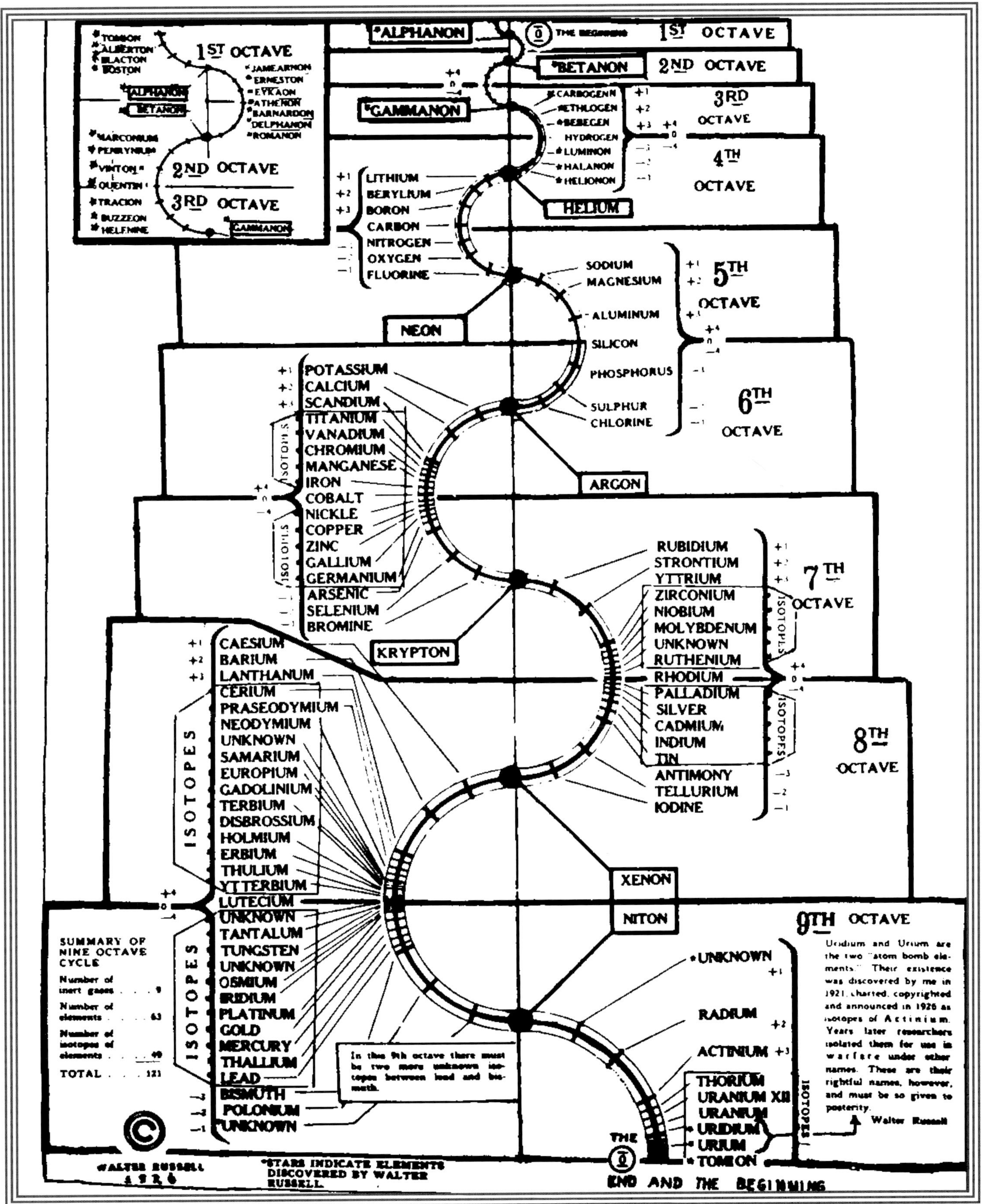

First published in this form as Figure 70 in *The Secret of Light* in 1947.

The Cosmic Clock expresses the wave as four increasing, generoactive, integrating efforts to express solidity and form and four decreasing efforts to express tenuity and dissolution of form. This wave action is common to all parts of the universe. See the discussion on the formula of the locked potentials on page 41.

Diagram 31. Cosmic Clock

First published in 1926 in *The Universal One: 58.*

The Secret of Light, Note 4. Editors' note regarding the nine octave periodic chart (as of 1994). Some of the elements Walter Russell thought were unknown when he prepared his 1926 periodic charts had actually been discovered prior to this date. These elements, including their discovery dates and octave positions, are enumerated below: Hafnium (1923) in the eighth octave at the third locking point, thirteenth isotopic position on the blue spectral side, and Rhenium (1925) in the eighth octave, third locking point, tenth isotopic position on the blue spectral side.

Protactinium was discovered in 1917 which Walter Russell had predicted and named as Uranium XII in his 1926 charts. This element occurs in the ninth octave, third locking point, second isotopic position on the red spectral side.

Other elements predicted by Walter Russell in 1926 were subsequently discovered after 1926 and before publication of *The Secret of Light* in 1947, again without his knowledge. These elements include: Technetium (1937), seventh octave, third locking point, fourth isotopic position on the red spectral side; Francium (1939), ninth octave, first locking point, on the red spectral side; and Astatine (1940), eighth octave wave, first locking point on the blue spectral side.

Note that each octave runs from inert gas keynote to the next inert gas keynote with the amplitude element at the center of each octave. For instance, gammanon is the keynote for the hydrogen octave with hydrogen as the amplitude element, so the octave runs from gammanon through carbogen and helionon to helium as the next carbon octave's keynote. The octaves are designated by the vertical brackets to the sides of the element names, and the amplitude elements are designated by their names and the horizontal lines running through these amplitude positions.

perature, and back to the eternal equilibrium of the One.

In Lesson 38 of *The Home Study Course*, Dr. Russell presents seven new laws:

WALTER RUSSELL'S NEW LAWS

FIRST LAW: Cold generates energy. Heat radiates energy. Cold multiplies. It cannot divide for it is the fulcrum of the universe which must extend to multiply. Heat divides. It cannot multiply but can be multiplied.

SECOND LAW: Every action must be preceded and followed by its equal and opposite reaction. Heat is the reaction of cold. Heat could not come into being save for the compressive action of cold, nor could it repeat itself without losing itself in basic cold.

THIRD LAW: Cold is static, unchanging and unconditioned. It eternally lives. Cold light is the basic ONE THING of this universe. Heat waves are dynamic, forever changing and dually conditioned. They are eternally living and dying to simulate life.

FOURTH LAW: Cold light is the omnipresent basis of universal intelligence and energy. Hot waves of light, which man calls matter, are a simulation of intelligence and energy. There is no intelligence or energy in matter.

FIFTH LAW: Static cold and dynamic heat express their opposite energies at angles of ninety degrees from their axes of rotation. Cold retains its static, motionless condition along wave axes where motion ceases at points of maximum heat, while heat extends along equators to again expand as cold. This balanced interchanging completes the wave cycle.

SIXTH LAW: Cold compresses. Cold multiplies cold to create heat. Heat expands to divide heat into cold. Varied pressures of heat constitute the octave color spectrum cycles and the octave chemical cycles of matter. Their varied wave lengths are the basis of our mathematics.

SEVENTH LAW: Long low waves of low potential and high frequencies constitute the invisible spectrum and low density gases, while short high waves of high potential and low frequencies constitute the basis for high density solids.

In the same fashion, all of nature's processes can be described in terms of the wave since all of nature's processes are wave actions. Every part of the Universe demonstrates wave mechanics.

Newton's Postulate and First and Third Laws Versus the Russellian Cosmogony

Newtonian Postulate	Russellian Cosmogony
Every body tends to continue in its state of rest or uniform motion in a straight line unless it is acted upon by an outside force.	All motion is curved and spiral in this polarized radial universe. Every body is the result of two opposing strains thrusting away from each other in opposite curved radial-spiral directions to condition its attributes and determine its motion. Every body is perpetually in motion until the strains of opposition which keep it in motion void each other in the universal zero of rest into which all bodies disappear for reappearance in reversed polarity. In the relative 'many' universe of illusion, there are no bodies at rest and no straight lines; all bodies are continually being acted upon by an outside and an inside force.

Newton's First & Third Laws	Russellian Cosmogony
To every action there is an equal and opposite reaction.	Every action is simultaneously balanced by an equal and opposite reaction and is repeated sequentially in reversed polarity.
Every particle of matter in the universe attracts every other particle with a force that varies directly with the product of the masses and inversely with the square of the distance between them.	Every light unit (mass) in the Universe has the relative apparent ability to attract *and repel* every other mass (light unit). Its relative ability is dependent upon its relative potential. In other words, every body appears to attract and repel every other body with a force which increases and decreases in universal ratios according to its potential position and according to whether its mass is moving toward the north (center of system) or toward the south (system periphery). All of this apparent increase and decrease in attraction and repulsion is dependent upon, and occurs with, an increase or decrease of all of the 18 dimensions of matter. Each dimension of matter simultaneously expands and contracts with its changing potential. All effects of motion are gravitational and radiational effects and thus are measurable dimensions.

WALTER RUSSELL'S SCIENCE PAINTINGS AND CHARTS

FIRST SERIES. The Science of the Future and An Analysis of the Harp String

Figure 1. The Science of the Future is Based upon God, The Creator God is Light — God is Mind.

With this chart, Walter Russell established himself as a true scientist of the future with roots in humanity's distant past. He reminds us that we are not alone because everything is connected to every other thing. He reiterates the teachings of mystics such as the ancient rishis who authored the Vedas, wherein he confirms that the illuminate alone can see all of the Creator's connections by using his inner seat of vision, the pineal gland.

The chart of Walter Russell on the following page conditions and prepares us to look with open minds, new eyes, and hopeful expectations at his charts and concepts. Dr. Russell also suggests that we use deep meditation as a tool for understanding his work.

Figure 2. The Nine-Octave Harp of the Universe

This later arrangement of the Russell periodic chart assists visualization of the preponderantly charging, red-orange (male, compressive polarity) and the preponderantly discharging blue-green (female, expansive polarity) sides of the spectrum of elements in each of the nine octaves. The inert gases are the seeds of each octave and are arranged at both ends of each vertically displayed octave.

The middle of the chart shows the midpoint of the wave center with +4 and -4 for the carbon position amplitude element of each octave. The red, male, positive (+) and the blue, female negative (-) elements are tonally arranged vertically in their first, second and third locking point positions on each side of the balanced centering element which is a plus four male (+4) and minus four female (-4) position centering amplitude element.

The womb side of the chart features the lighter, younger elements in the first four and one-half octaves of elements preceding carbon. The tomb side is the realm of the heavier, older elements in the last four and one-half octaves of elements following carbon. This chart clearly states that all the elements of matter are tonal in nature and therefore possess a sound. Elements that are states of motion open the possibility of transmuting one element/tone into another state of motion/sound and ultimately transforming any one thing into any other thing. Intimations of a living and dying Universe of constant being!

THE SCIENCE OF THE FUTURE IS BASED UPON GOD - THE CREATOR.
GOD IS LIGHT - GOD IS MIND
MIND IS ALONE OMNISCIENT AND OMNIPOTENT —— LIGHT IS ALONE OMNIPRESENT

THE UNDIVIDED WHITE LIGHT OF THE UNIVERSAL GOD-MIND

THE WHITE MIND-LIGHT DIVIDED INTO SPECTRUM PAIRS.

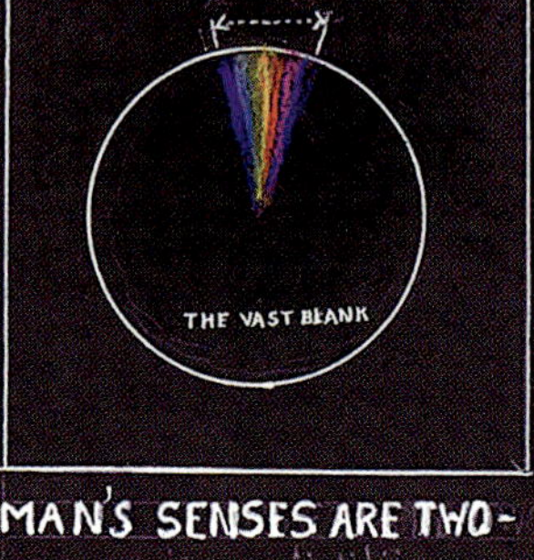

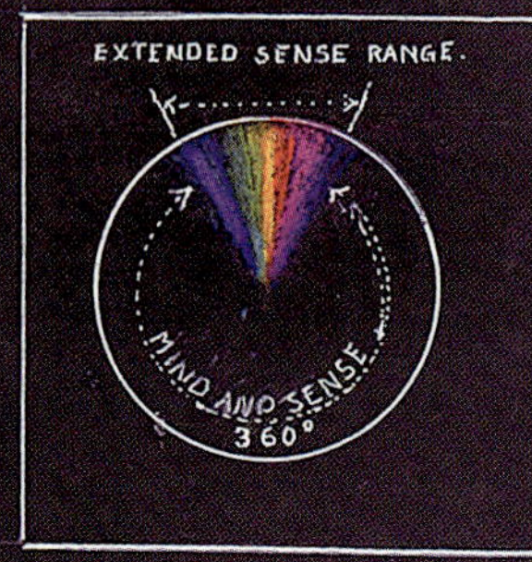

GOD'S UNIVERSE OF "SPACE" IS AN INTENSELY LUMINOUS BLINDING WHITE LIGHT WHICH NO EYES CAN SEE. ILLUMINATES ALONE CAN SEE THAT LIGHT THROUGH THEIR CENERS OF CONSIOUSNESS LOCATED IN THEIR PINEAL GLANDS.

GOD'S WHITE MIND-LIGHT IS DARK TO MAN UNTIL HE DIVIDES IT INTO SPECTRUM PAIRS OF RED AND BLUE LIGHTS TO SCREEN THE WHITE LIGHT OF GOD'S MIND WHICH CENTERS EVERY CREATING THING

MAN'S SENSES ARE TWO-WAY WAVES OF LIMITED FREQUENCIES. THEY DO NOT RESPOND TO VIBRATIONS BELOW OR ABOVE A VERY LIMITED RANGE

MAN CAN EXTEND HIS RANGE OF SENSE VISION BY TELESCOPE OR MICRO-SCOPE, BUT HIS SENSES CANNOT GO BEYOND SPECTRUM EFFECT INTO MIND CAUSE.

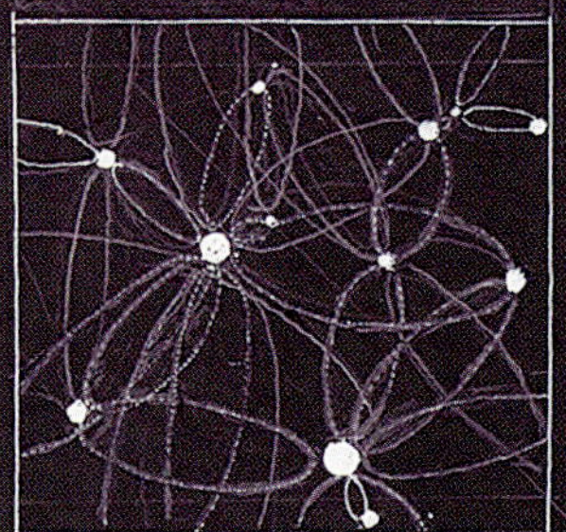

THE STONE

GRAVITY MATE OF THE STONE

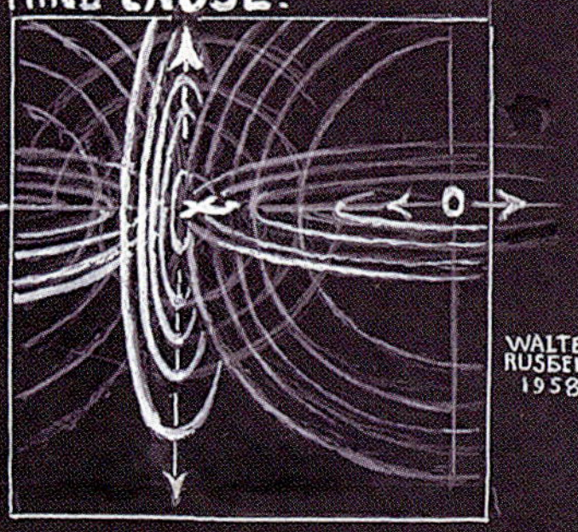

MAN'S LIMITED SENSE VISION HAS CAUSED HIM TO SEE AN OBJECTIVE UNIVERSE OF MANY SEPARATE DISUNITED THINGS. WHEN MIND-VISION UNFOLDS TO A HIGHER STAGE IN THE HUMAN RACE, BY INCREASING AWARENESS OF THE DIVINE LIGHT WHICH CENTERS MAN, HE WILL THEN SEE THAT EVERY THING IN THE UNIVERSE IS INSOLUBLY BOUND TO EVERY OTHER THING. SCIENCE WILL THEN KNOW THAT MATTER IS BUT MANY FOCAL POINS OF ONE BODY.

WHEN A MAN MULTIPLIES GRAVITY BY CASTING A STONE IN THE WATER HIS SENSES SEE ONLY WAVE-RIPPLES. THEY DO NOT TELL HIM THAT THOSE RIPPLES ARE EQUATORIAL RING SERIES OF EXPANDING SPHERES WHICH ARE DISSIPATING GRAVITY IN THE SAME RATIO AS IT IS BEING MULTIPLIED BY THE FALLING STONE. THE SAME PRINCIPEE APPLIES TO ALL ACTIONS. THIS IS, IN FACT, THIS IS THE VERY BASIS OF THE UNIVERSAL LIFE PRINCIPLE.

SCIENCE HAS BUILT A STRANGE UNIVERSE FROM SENSE EVIDENCE, AND HAS BEEN MIGHTILY DECEIVED.

Figure 1

Completed in 1958 and not previously published.

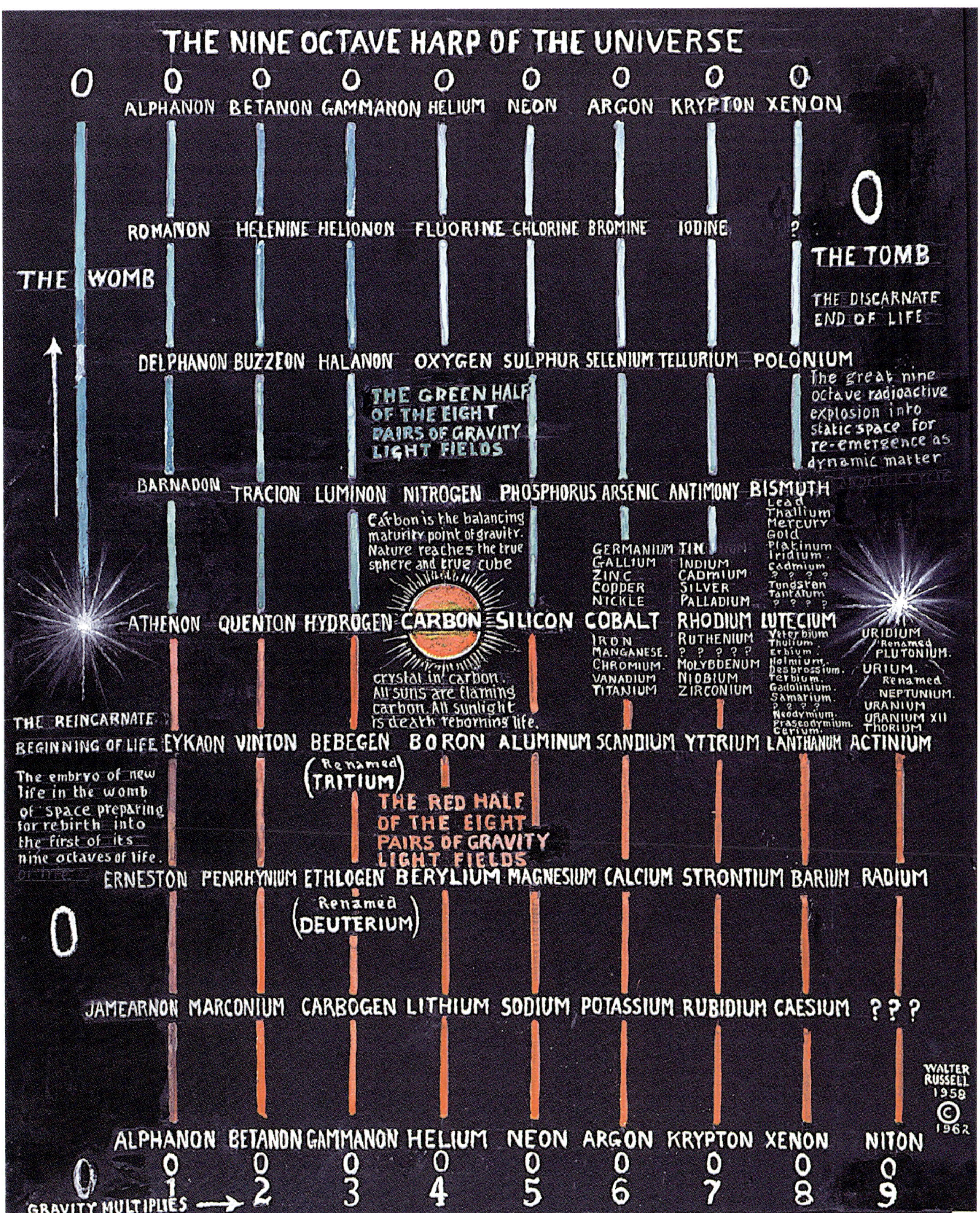

Figure 2

Completed in 1962 and published in *The Home Study Course*, XI: 830.

Figure 3. Analysis of the Harp String I
All Motion is Curved, and All Curvature is Spiral.

The special case, logarithmic spiral called Spiral Mirabilis (wondrous, miraculous) by the Romans and also known as the Golden Spiral is evident in this chart. The Spiral Mirabilis *is* a very special spiral that serves as a model for all possible spirals and thus for all possible types of motion. A model can be thought of as the simplest case or form of any number of different cases or forms. The Spiral Mirabilis serves as a model in that it expresses the simplest form of all spirals. It is the simplest because its ratio of expansion or contraction utilizes the only possible proportion of division containing only two terms.

As all motion is spiral, this spiral is also a model for all types of motion. Thus it represents the constancy within change. The logarithmic Spiral Mirabilis reveals that the ratio of a smaller part of the spiral curve (the length) to a proportionally larger part of the same spiral equals the ratio of the larger part to the sum of the smaller and larger parts. Expressed mathematically this is a:b::b:(a+b).

This same proportion or rate of change is evident in the squares representing cubes and also applies to the rate of change of all dimensions in any octave wave as change progresses to the center of a system or away from it.

For the Spiral Mirabilis, n equals 1.618 for an expanding spiral and 0.618 for a contracting spiral. Note that 1.618 is the Golden Proportion, and 0.618 is 1 ÷ 1.618. See *Sacred Geometry* by Robert Lawlor for a fascinating examination of the Golden Proportion.

The small diagrams to the left of the large center sphere/cube are shown again on the right side but rotated 90 degrees to reveal their other face. The diagram on the upper left shows the centrifugal spiral arms on edge, while the diagram on the upper right shows them in planar perspective. The cube wave field boundary cubic planes for each of the four stages of increasing and decreasing effort to compress matter into form via increasingly faster centripetal motion and then the decreasingly slower centrifugal motion are partially shown as squares in their tonal positions. Each square represents a slice of the cube and has its logarithmic spiral inside itself displaying the same curvature dimensions.

In this chart the spiral that is within cube 4 (the smallest cube) bears a relationship to the spiral that is within cube 3 (the next larger cube). It can be expressed as: the lesser spiral within cube 4 is to the greater spiral in cube 3, as the greater spiral

This proportional rate of change can be expressed mathematically as a form of

Log to the base n of a function of X = a function of Y.

A polar mathematical equation that expresses the logarithmic spiral is:

Log to the base n (i.e., n= 1.618 for the Spiral Mirabilis) times RHO (distance from reference point theta)

= a times the angle formed from the theta reference point (constant) and the line RHO as one side of the angle.

This proportional rate of change can also be expressed mathematically as

$\mathrm{Log}_n(f(x)) = f(y)$ or, in polar coordinates,
$\mathrm{Log}_n\rho = a\theta$

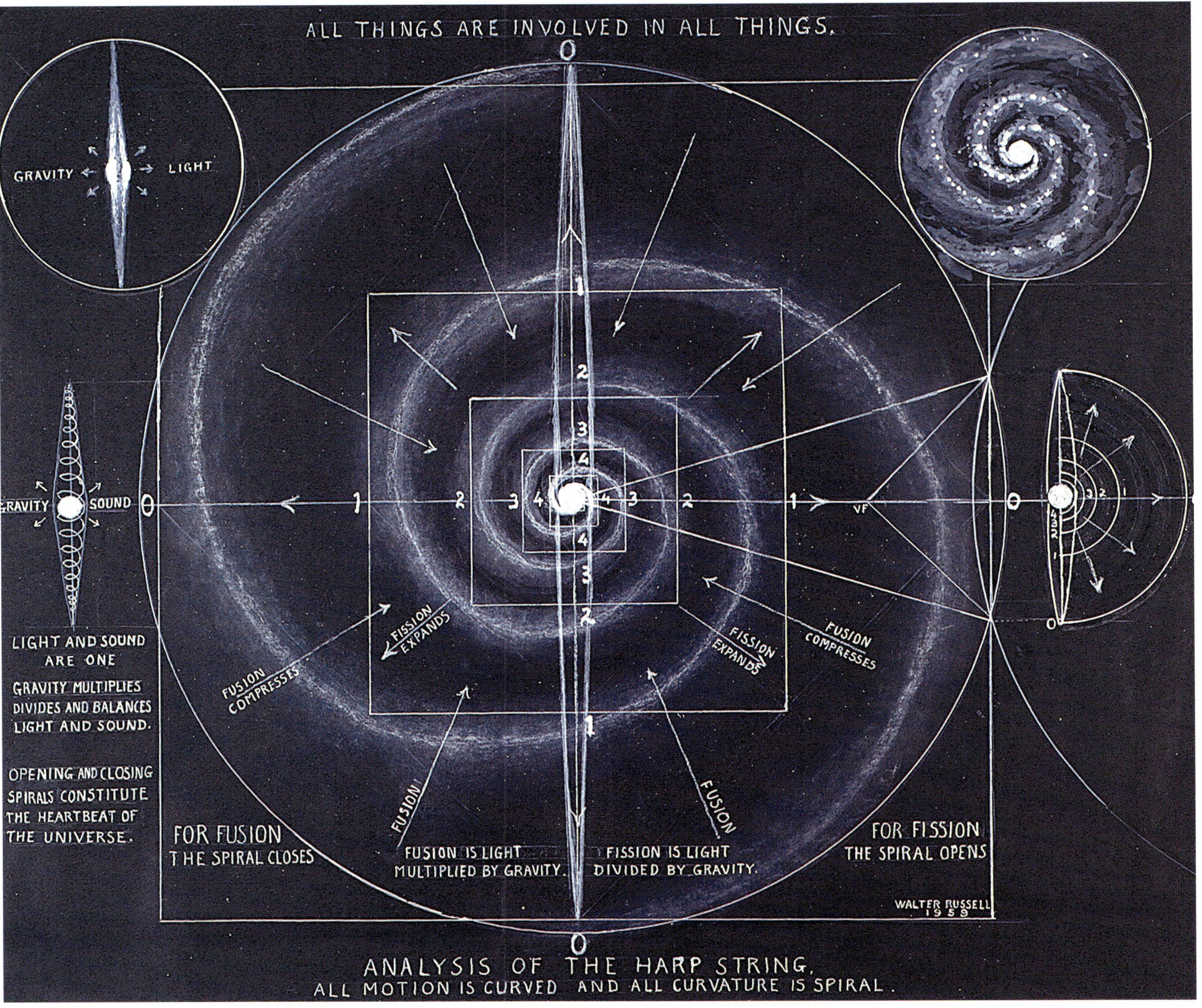

Figure 3 Completed in 1959 and published in *The Home Study Course*, X:770.

in cube 3 is to the spirals in both, or that within cubes 3 and 4.

This two-term proportion is the best way to approach the sense of unity or Oneness using proportional thinking; it is the minimum number of terms (two) to express any whole as its parts. Another way of stating this is that the relative or the divided light wave universe is polarized into two basic archetypes: male and female polarity.

The same proportion of rate of change of the lengths of the spirals that are within cubes 1, 2, 3 and 4 applies to all other rates of change of all dimensions within the entire octave wave. For example, the rate of change (in the area and length of the diagram's sides) of each cube surrounding each part of the spiral bears the same ratio. The area of cube 4 is to the area of cube 3 as the area of cube 3 is to the sum of the areas of cubes 3 and 4; the same is true for the lengths of the sides.

In the same way, all 18 dimensions of the octave wave will vary proportionally, even a dimension such as sex which varies its proportions of male to female. Take the case of the innermost cube-spiral sphere, which is the perfect cube-sphere amplitude position and has a balanced sex. We know all of its other dimensions will similarly be in balance and correspond to this position.

In the next cube-spiral sphere, which is the +3 or -3 position of less than perfect sex polarity balance, we also know that all of its other dimensions will vary in the same proportion. The Spiral Mirabilis formula says that there is a relationship between all the dimensions of cubes 3 and 4. The pressures of cube 3 are to cube 4 as the pressures of cube 4 are to the sum of the pressures of cubes 3 and 4. The same applies to planes of rotation and ecliptic, ionization, sex, valence, potentials, and all of the other 18 dimensions.

The square cross sections of the cubic wave field planes for each of the four stages of increasing and decreasing effort to create and de-create matter are shown in their tonal first, second, third and fourth locking point plane of rotation positions. The invisible dark spiral arms are the increasingly faster and increasingly more visible centripetal motion which compresses the formless into form. The visible white spiral arms are the decreasingly slower and decreasingly visible centrifugal motion which disintegrates form into the formless from whence it was born. Within each square are sections of the spiral which display the same increasing or decreasing proportions, one square to the other.

Light and sound are revealed as One, and indeed all other dimensions are implied as One; all are expressions of gravitation/radiation or closing and opening spirals.

Figure 4. Analysis of the Harp String II: The Winding of the Cosmic Clock Spring

According to Dr. Russell, this chart portrays the process of emergence of the dynamic universe from the static. The spiral cones shown on the left represent the spiral path on a conical surface of the centripetal motion that winds light into solids. These paths are responsible, along with their conical spiraled centrifugal motion mates, for the absence of straight-line motion in the universe. Together they mandate curved motion since all motion in any direction is resisted by its oppositely paired mate of motion.

The four steps to integration are symbolized in these cones, and in the numbered sequence on the cube's lateral borders. The numbered sequence on the top border goes from one to nine and thus symbolizes the four steps to integration and the four steps to disintegration, with a balanced unity at $4\ ^1/_2$.

The centripetal spirals are shown in planar view as if you were looking down the center of them in the

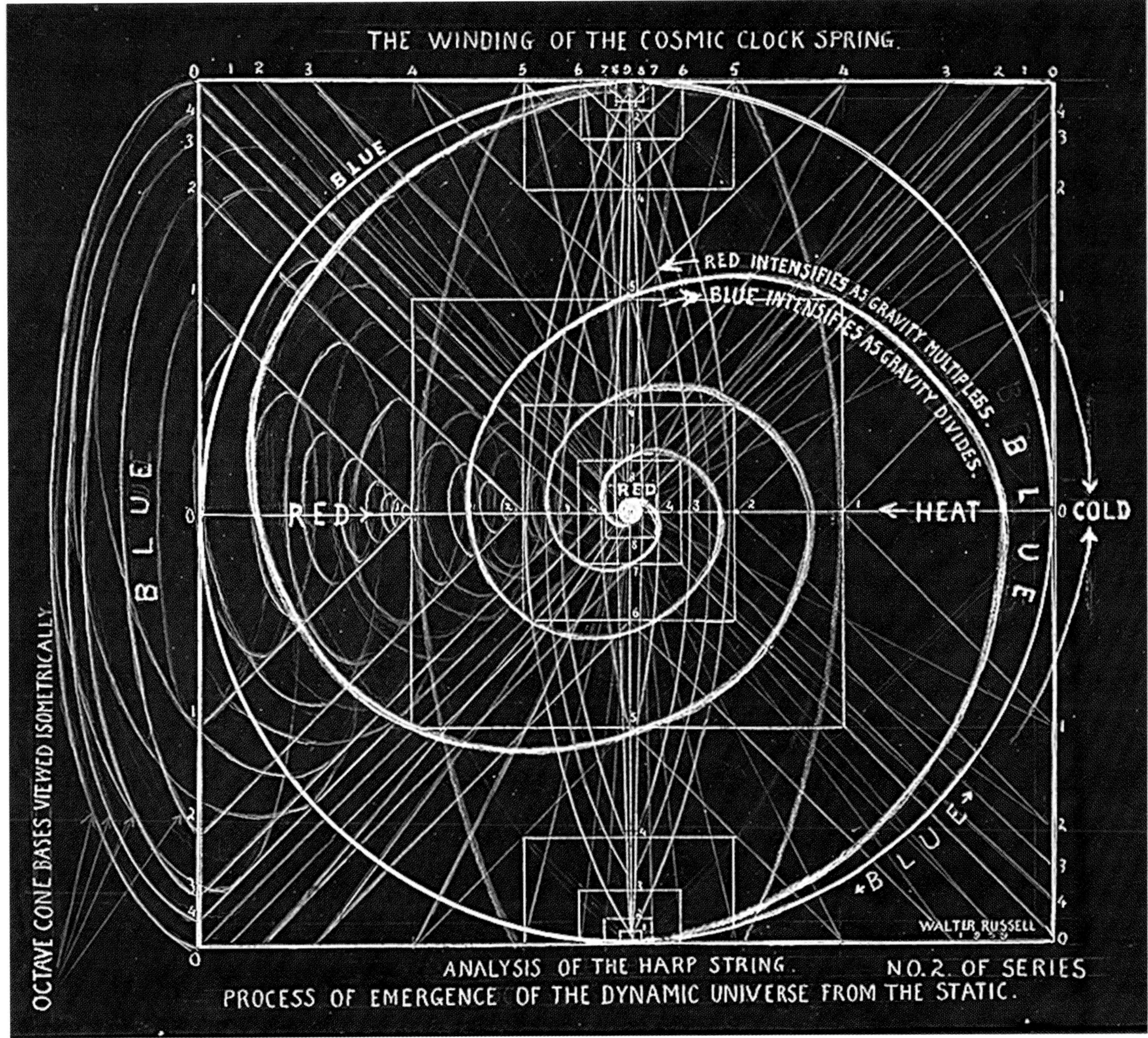

Figure 4

Completed in 1959 and not previously published.

heavily outlined spiral within the cube's wave field boundary planes. The blue and red areas of the spectrum are named and placed in the outer and inner portions of the spirals respectively, thus depicting a predominately charging or youthful system. An older system would have the colors reversed with red outside and blue inside. Maximum density, heat and the red color is on the inside of the system, and relative vacuity, cold and the blue color is on the outside in this relatively young, still mostly charging system.

Figure 5. The Unwinding of the Cosmic Clock Spring. The Dynamic Universe Disappears into the Static Zero

This chart suggests a pyramid with its apex at the center of expansion. The center of expansion is where the multiplication of cold into heat has reversed and has now created an expanding sphere that has a relative vacuum and coldness at its center. In time the expanding sphere flattens into a cube. The cube boundaries expand outward with ever greater space between each cube. The series of square-cube shapes correspond to the various locking points in the octave wave and represent the cube wave field boundary planes of the system at different stages of growth and decay, in different states of motion and for different aged elements.

The large central portion of the chart represents an aging system where the heat, density and red color are on the outside with the cool, vacuum, blue color on the inside.

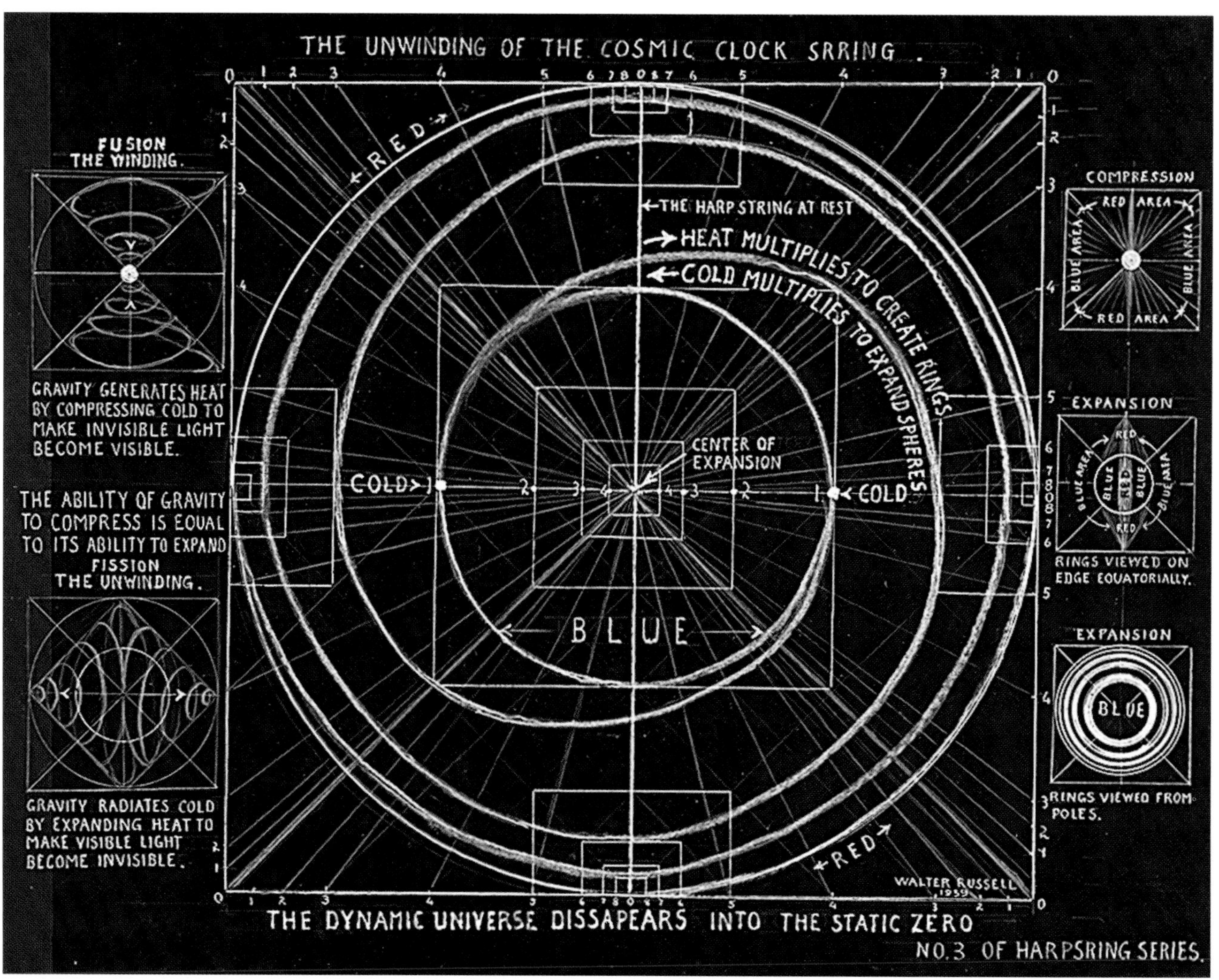

Figure 5

Completed in 1959 and not previously published

The smaller charts show the expanding direction of south cones and the contracting direction of north cones at 90-degree angles to each other; their respective color spectrum names are also noted. In the upper left-hand chart, the spiral centripetal north charging paths seek the system center, while in the lower left-hand chart the spiral centrifugal south discharging paths seek the system periphery.

There is lessening resistance and decreasing friction/increasing synchronization in centripetally imploding movement to the center of a system which generates increasing temperature, potential and pressure at this center as the two approaching spirals collide. Contrariwise, resistance and friction increase while synchronization decreases in centrifugally exploding movement to the periphery which lowers the temperature, potential, pressure, tone and density of a system at the periphery as the two receding spirals separate.

The chart on the upper right corresponds to the one on the upper left: it diagrams the colors related to the incoming and outgoing spirals as seen from a side equatorial view. The system is hot, dense and solid on the inside. If it were in a mostly degenerating mode, it would have a hole in the center of the system.

The upper two small side charts reveal the generating, compressing aspect of all systems even though this chart primarily focuses on fission, the degenerating expansive aspect of all systems.

The chart in the lower right corresponds to the left lower chart. The chart on the lower right shows the same system from a polar top or bottom view with an expansion series of rings (see Figure 30). These both reveal a system that is in a predominately radiating or aged mode.

The middle chart on the right shows the expansive discharge viewed on edge, but rotated with the plane of discharge perpendicular. The hot, red, expanding rings of discharge are mostly red at the system center; as they cool, they change to a blue color. The expansive discharge will still be mostly red at the center even though an aged system has a predominately blue center and red periphery. Both charging vortexes and discharging vortexes are mostly hot and red at the high gravitational center of a system.

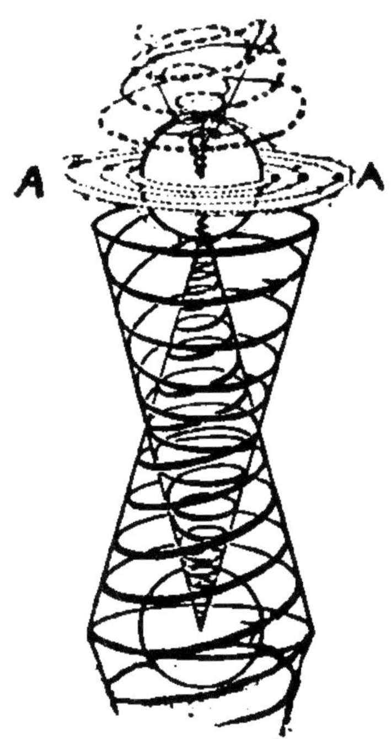

AA Birth of Electronic Systems *The Secret of Light*, p. 69

SECOND SERIES: Analysis of the Octave Wave Bar Magnet

Figure 6. Untitled

Figure 6 Undated. Not previously published.

This color painting depicts the red-orange male and blue-green female poles of a gravity bar (magnet). The color spectrum that corresponds to the octave wave steps and potential locking points in the wave is brilliantly visible.

Starting from the outside on the female side, the first potential locking point position is violet; the second is blue; the third is green, and the fourth, yellow.

The male side is illustrated similarly from infrared to red to orange to yellow at the midpoint of union in the wave. The point of least polarity — that of approaching zero polarity — is in the black space at the center of the gravity bar and/or where the two colored fields meet.

Figure 7. Untitled

Two gravity bars are shown approaching union in the center. In this position before union, polarity still strongly exists between the two approaching poles. After union, the two bars void their separateness in their union and become one bar. This painting vividly reveals the strong desire of the male and female polarities to void their polarity and separateness in union.

A + sign on both ends of each gravity bar draws attention to the fact that both male and female sexes are charging. It is neither one attracting and the other repelling nor opposites attracting. Both poles charge and discharge. The predominance of charge over discharge identifies a male, and the predominance of discharge over charge reveals a female.

Male and female poles appear to attract as each pole voids the other in union and removes itself as far from the other as possible in opposite polar relation again. They both act as giant screw vortexes that void friction as they are drawn to seek their like pole through their mate's opposite pole. Centripetal charging motion voids friction through synchronization or movement toward a common center in coming together. Centrifugal discharging motion results from friction or movement away from a common center in coming apart.

The space between the two approaching male and female poles is an anode equator, that amplitude point uniting equator where elements, planets, suns and galaxies become visible at maturity. The cathode base pole is whatever space exists between united male and female poles that have become two-dimensional in Russellian terms. This is the space where elements, planets, suns and galaxies are invisibly born at the beginning of the wave. When two gravity bars unite to become one gravity bar, the point of union is such a cathode base space.

Figure 7 Undated. Not previously published..

Figure 8. Untitled

Figure 8 Undated. Not previously published.

The third chart in this series shows the two gravity bars at a further stage of voiding separateness in a simulation of stillness at an eventual point of contact. As they approach this voidance, the color spectrum polarized male-female fields change shape from the preceding more nearly spherical fields to toroid or doughnut-shaped fields. It is between such approaching opposites that matter is formed.

The center field represents the center of any system where maximum gravity, pressure, heat and visible light exist. Once the contact is consummated and the contact point becomes a point of zero polarity, all polarization is voided as if it had never been.

As in the previous chart, both poles are represented with a plus (+) sign because both the male and the female poles are positively charged. Anything that is capable of uniting with another thing — such as an element with another element — does so because it has sex polarity.

An inert gas from this point of view does not have sufficient polarity to exhibit sex and therefore cannot unite with any other polarized element or any other inert gas. The inert gases are like young children without developed sexual characteristics and correspond to the close-to-center-point "bloch wall" of the magnet (also called gravity bar zero polarity point or a cathode base pole).

All elements, indeed all things, unite or exchange because of the basic law of sex interchange or polarity.

Figure 9. Untitled

This painting with its four separate images across the top appears to reveal the red-orange male and green-blue female spectral colors surrounding the ends of a gravity bar; these colors surround all polarized opposites.

Figure 9

Undated. Not previously published.

The upper right and left paintings reveal the male pole on the left of the pairs and the female on the right. The lower pair reveals the spectral fields of these paired bars/vortexes/poles as if the upper pairs were both rotated 90 degrees horizontally to a close-up side view. In the upper pairs, the poles are seen in end view and separated.

A possible reason for painting the left upper painting with smaller central gravity maximums than those on the upper right was to either give the view from closer up on the right or to depict the left as systems at the amplitude point in their cycle. If the latter was the case, then the more tightly wound central sun amplitude position is depicted with smaller yellow centers than those on the right in order to convey this idea.

The lower pair appears to be opposite in size from those directly above each of the pairs in order to convey the idea that the central field seen on side view in a more tightly wound amplitude position is more prolate on the left than that on the right. This might appear contradictory unless you consider that the upper and lower right sides of the pairs represent systems beyond the amplitude position on the aging expansive side of maturity. If they were on the more youthful contracted side, they would be more on the prolate side of maturity than the amplitude position.

These paintings depict the spectral colors around a gravity bar magnet; the upper pairs represent an end view, and the lower pair represents a side view approaching union and voidance of polarity in the lower pair. If the relative sizes simply denote close and far perspectives, then the upper and lower pairs are paired diagonally.

Figure 10. Untitled

This painting reveals a pair of gravity (magnet) bars side by side in parallel or with mirror image symmetry having male pole vortexes alongside male pole vortexes and female vortexes alongside female vortexes and thereby in a mutually repelling mode.

female poles appear to attract each other, but in reality they bore through each other and move to the farthest opposite pole of a gravity bar system, leaving in their wake a point of voidance or zero polarity at the bar's center point where they fleetingly experienced complete union. A female pole repels another female pole without boring through the other's center; likewise, a male pole repels another male pole without boring through the other's center.

Figure 10 Undated. Not previously published.

The lower half of the painting has male pole vortexes, and the upper half has female vortexes, each with their identifying spectral colors brilliantly painted.

This painting reveals that like-sexed poles repel, while Figures 7, 8 and 48 reveal male and female poles approaching union and eventual voidance of opposition and polarity in that union. Male and

In this sense, we can say that opposite-charging poles charge through each other, and like-charging poles charge away from each other. In other words, charging poles charge through each other away from a common cathode toward a common anode; repelling poles repel both each other and charging poles. Charging males charge through charging females. Charging females charge through charging males. Repelling males and females repel repelling or charging males and females. Repelling occurs by mutual radiation/repulsion.

A female system may become a male system in relation to a greater female than itself; likewise, a male system may become a female system in relation to a greater male than itself. All systems are only relatively or predominately male or female systems. All systems are relatively or preponderantly charging male or preponderantly discharging female systems, yet each is both charging and discharging.

An aging system is preponderantly discharging, while a youthful system is preponderantly charging; therefore sex must be something more than preponderance of charge or discharge. Sex is the polarity preponderance that determines structural form and function. A youthful system can be preponderantly charging in its life cycle and yet be a female system with the structure and form denoting that system, i.e., a female is an enveloping structure and functions to nurture and birth a new system.

Figure 11. Nature's Bar Magnet of Light

Figure 11 — Completed in 1960 and not previously published.

A single gravity bar (magnet) of light is revealed in this painting showing the male-female colored poles in octave progression. The four octave steps of male preponderance are shown from the center outward to the right from infrared to red to orange to yellow. The four octave steps of female preponderance are shown from the center to the left as violet to blue to green to yellow. Their maximum expression of male or female polarity is at the ends of the gravity bar as orange-yellow and green-yellow respectively.

Figure 12. High-Pressure Short Waves and Low-Pressure Long Waves

These waves are diagrammed in this chart by the octave wave placement of the lenses along the axis of a pair of gravity bars. The lenses formed by the high-pressure waves are proportionally wider relative to the lenses formed by low-pressure waves and appear as more expanded structures under greater pressure with lenses closer together and overlapping.

they are bisexual, as are all things, with a preponderance of one sex over the other defining which sex it is. At the point of union, the two bars simulate stillness and one pole in their apparent union. This illusion is created through increasingly fast centripetal motion which increases toward the center of the system and union.

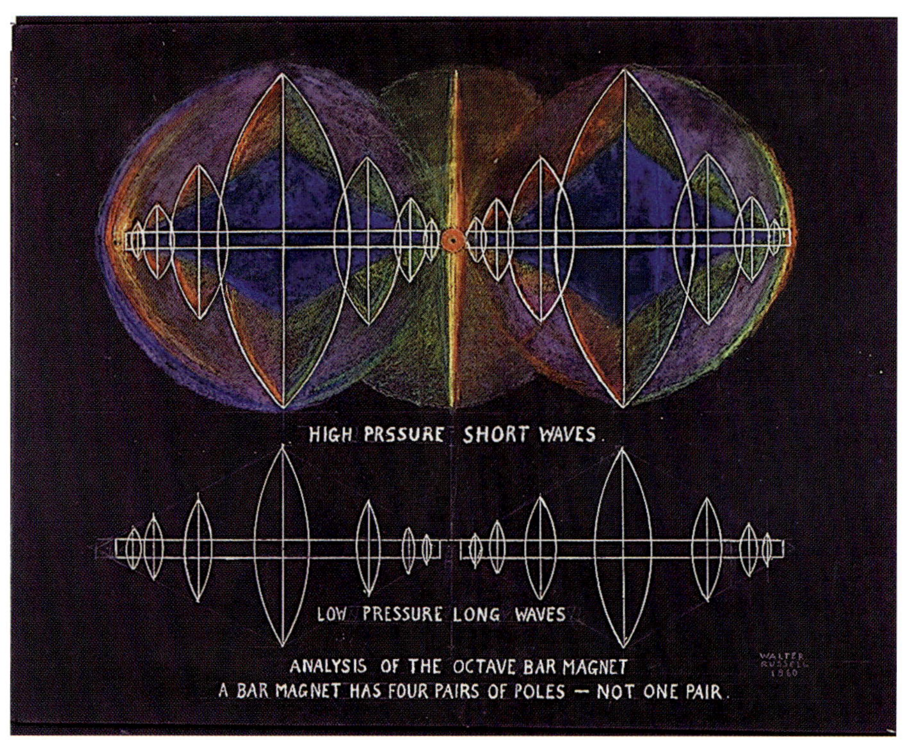

Figure 12 Completed in 1960 and published in *The Home Study Course*, XI:

The high-pressure waves represent and, in fact, produce the heavier elements and their isotopes. They create additional smaller lenses by interpenetrating interference patterns with the adjacent lenses that exist only in the high-pressure waves. These additional lenses which do not exist in the low-pressure waves both create and represent the isotopes.

The four poles of a gravity bar are visible and reveal their female-male spectrum colors in each gravity bar. Each gravity bar appears as two bars approaching union in the center. The bisexual nature of that newly forming system is illustrated by both its female-male colors. This shows that

The upper painting reveals color spectrum positions in the wave. For example, the large triangular-shaped blue is greatest in area at the center of each gravity bar where the cathode expansion is predominant or where the first locking point begins. The extreme polarized ends have the +3, -3 and ±4 colors in excess. While the preponderantly male and female poles are clearly distinguishable by their predominant color spectrum, the impossibility of absolute male or female polarity is clearly evident by the existence of female colors in the male pole and vice versa.

The new life that always appears when the two male-female polarities simulate balance, exchange, and, eventually, void separateness and polarity is shown in the upper color painting in the center of the gravity bar. The four centripetal steps that focus into and as the charging poles of any system are colored as red-orange male or blue-green female polarities. The mass that forms in the center of this system, like a sun, is shown on edge with its balancing, centrifugally directed, spiral arms emerging from the edge of its equatorial plane.

The beginning of a hole in the center of the system is depicted in the sun between the two bars; the red outside surface of its equatorial ring corresponds to the inner blue center spot to reveal a system just past the mature point. Likewise, both male and female gravity bars with high-pressure short waves have blue diamond tetrahedral shapes at the center that can be said to identify them as aged heavy elements-systems as well as identifying their cathode areas.

Figure 13. The Gravity Cycle is the Motovative (sic) Force of the Universal Heartbeat

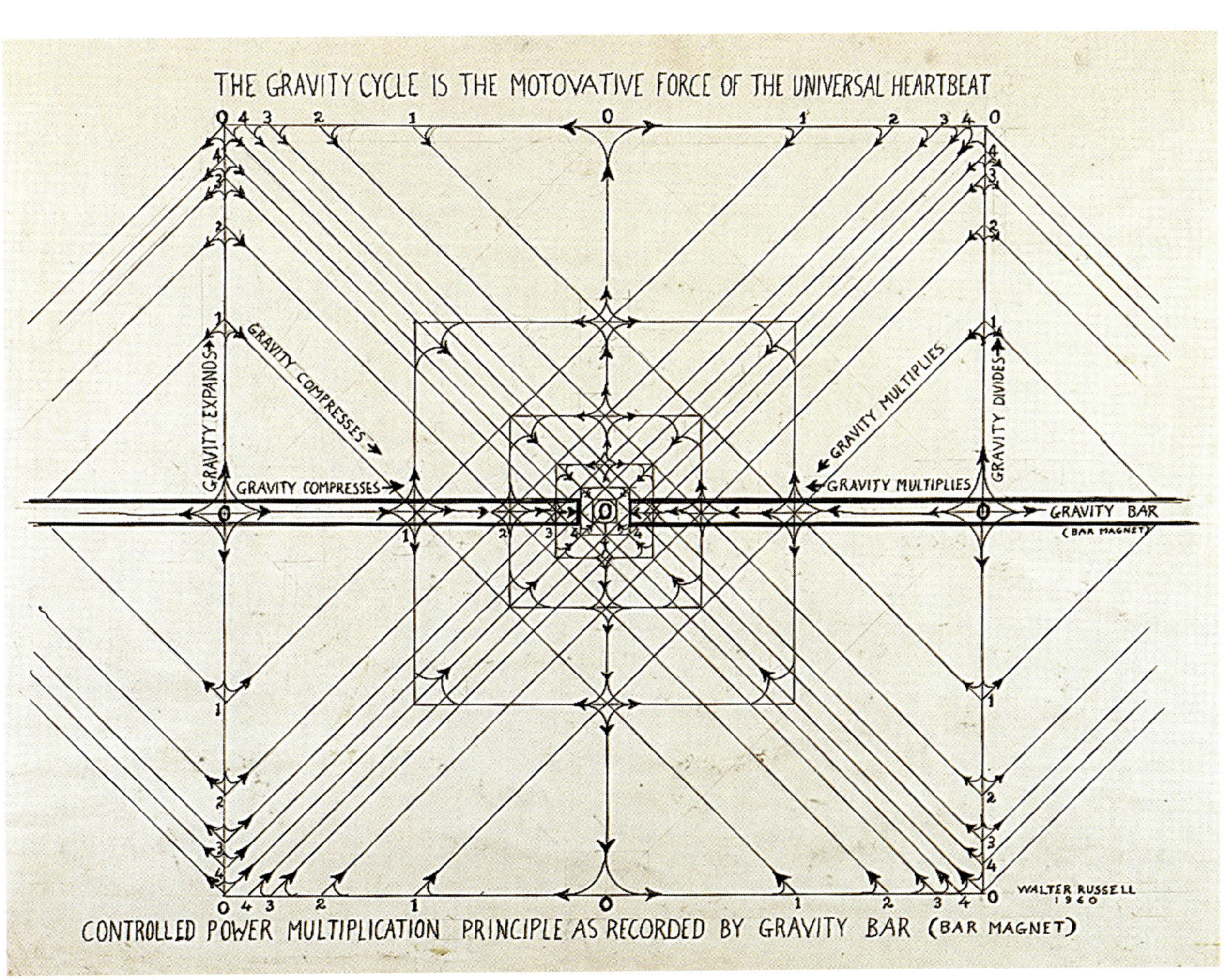

Figure 13

Completed in 1960. Not previously published.

This black and white chart shows the cube wave field boundaries around each step of the octave wave. It also delineates the path motion takes toward the center of the system by way of the poles seen from a side view as it expresses gravitation. The radiative path away from the center is seen on edge with arrows pointing in and out respectively. The biggest cube, identified by 0 at its side midpoints and corners, corresponds to the inertial plane wave field boundary of the fully matured system. Each succeeding smaller cube corresponds to the next position in the wave. If these two gravity bars were to touch, they would void each other and would void the geometry of creative power multiplication through the polarization evident here.

If you view all the squares within the biggest square, nine are visible, and each succeeding one is rotated 45 degrees from the adjacent squares. If another square were drawn in between the largest and next largest ones, there would be a total of ten squares.

The largest square is also divided into four additional squares. Two questions arise:

Why is the tenth one not depicted as well?

What is the significance of the squares that are rotated at 45 degrees to the level squares and that show the wave field boundary cubes for each locking point in the wave from the baseline inert gas through the first to the fourth amplitude position each side of the center?

The corner point of each succeedingly smaller square touches the midpoint of the sides of the next larger square.

A double pyramid structure is suggested by the squares rotated 45 degrees from level balance with their apexes on a line perpendicular to the center of the point of eventual union of the two gravity bars. Similar pyramid structures are shown on a line perpendicular to the center of each individual gravity bar with their apexes touching at the first, second, third and other octave wave locking-point positions. At contact of the poles, only one pyramid shape would appear instead of three since the polarization would be voided and cease at the center. The structure would then resemble Figure 11, rather than resembling Figure 12 as it does here.

The significance of this chart lies in its description and illustration of the entire gravity cycle as both multiplying compression and dividing expansion. Thus it expresses gravity as the whole cycle of gravitation/radiation.

The Mystery of Gravitation and Radiation

The Secret of Light, p. 277.

THIRD SERIES. Space Geometry, Wave Optics and Cycles of the Octave Wave

Figure 14. Basic Principle of Space Geometry

Figure 14 outlines the symbiotic relationship between cubes and spheres which is the basic principle of space geometry. The cube wave field boundaries that act as light mirrors to reflect light into the center of the system are shown in the series of tetrahedrons at the top. Spheres are created by implosion from the cathode cube wave field boundary inertial plane and the resisting, exploding reaction from the wave field anode spherical center.

This resistance is measured tonally and most dynamically, although it is an infinite regress of increasing resistance, at the locking points in the wave as +1, +2, +3 and +4. Cubes are created by the explosion from an inertial boundary point at the spherical anode center and the resisting, imploding reaction from the wave field cube boundary walls. This resistance is also measured tonally, and most dynamically although it is a continuum of increasing resistance, at the locking points in the wave as -4, -3, -2 and -1.

Thus spheres and cubes are created and destroyed out of mutual and inescapable interaction. What is shown are spheres and cubes within spheres and

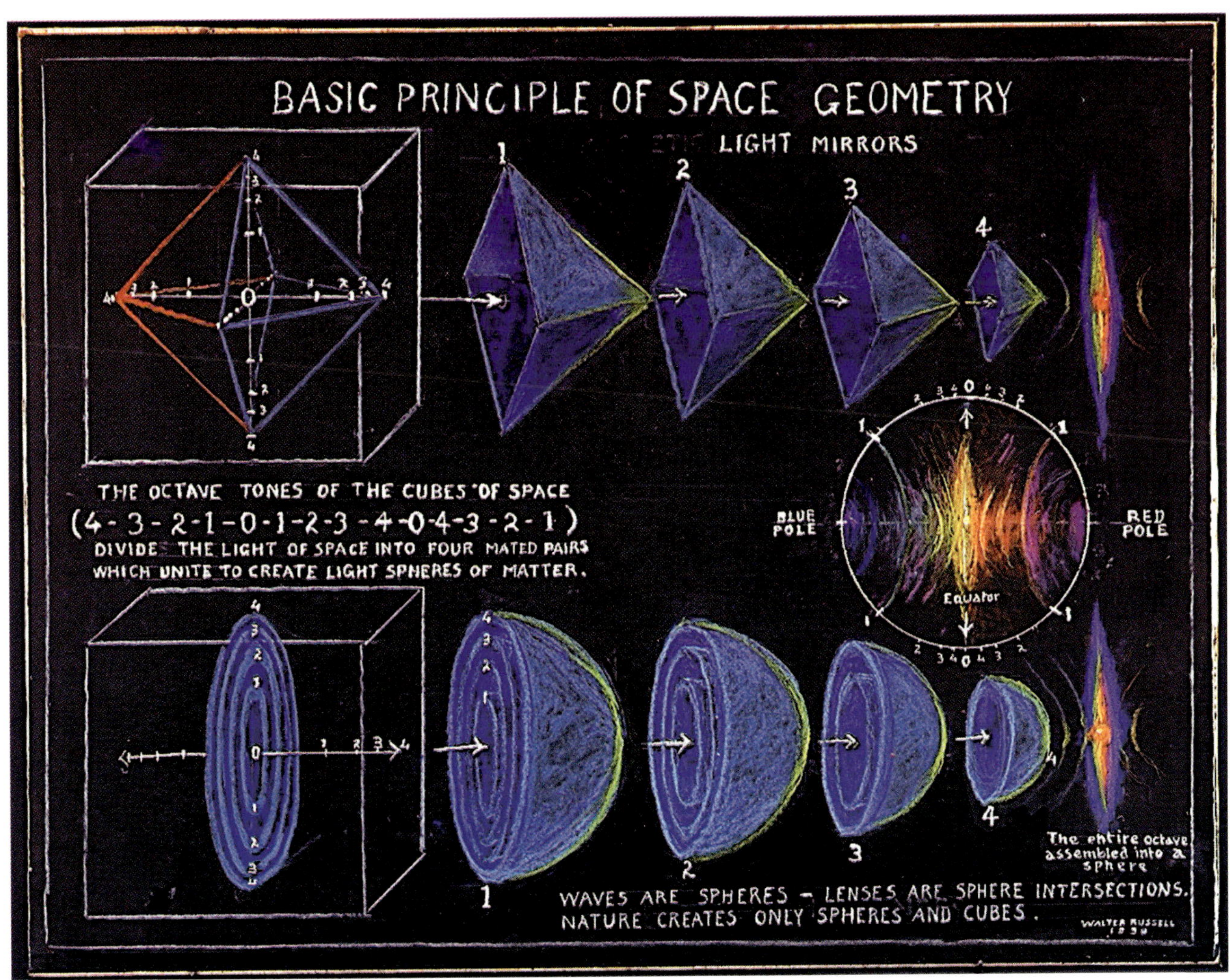

Figure 14

Completed in 1959 and not previously published.

cubes that have been extended for better visualization.

The figure on the upper left shows the cube wave field boundary planes which surround all wave systems and the anode center from which rings are re-projected into space toward the cube wave field boundaries. The lower left figure shows the now inertial cathode plane that was once an anode center that projects the rings in four successive efforts to another anode center.

Two-dimensional plane surfaces extend into three-dimensional cubes and tetrahedrons; two-dimensional flat rings extend and project into three-dimensional cones toward spheres. Motion to or away from the center of a system is expressed via the relation between these two geometrical patterns based on the cube-sphere archetype. Flat rings unfold into spheres, and spheres refold into cubes. These are the two simplest basic archetypes expressed geometrically.

The lenses formed by sphere intersections create the color spectrum and the elements. They are illustrated at the amplitude plus and minus four (±4) position of the wave as a fully formed sphere on the right side of the chart. This sphere shows the color spectrum of each tonal position in the wave. It also illustrates the male and female poles and their colors as elemental mates that unite in tonal balance at each step along the way to the amplitude plus and minus four (±4) position.

Sequential Reaction

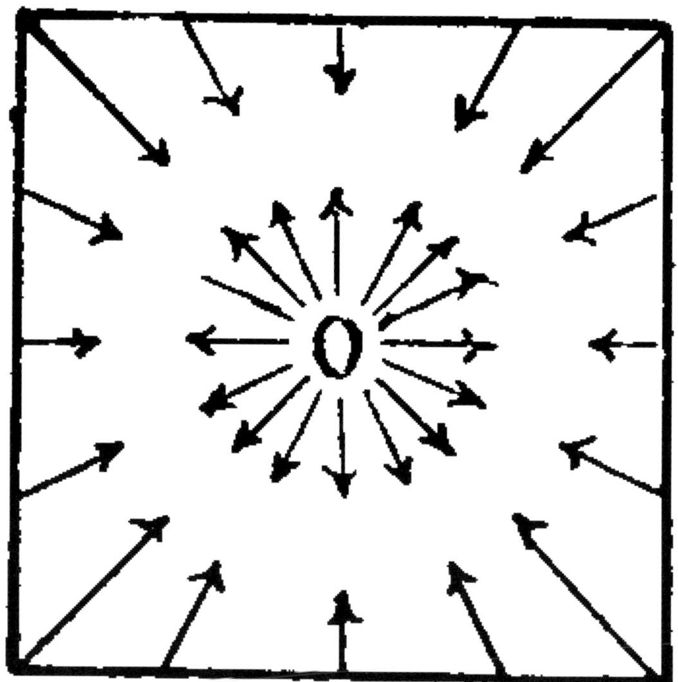

The Secret of Light, p. 221.

Figure 15: Untitled

This series of four wave paintings within one frame reveals the gyroscopic plane angles of rotation and the spectral colors associated with the male and female.

Figure 15

Undated. Not previously published.

The painting on the upper left shows a female centripetal charging vortex on the left coupled with a male centripetal charging vortex on the right.

The four locking point positions, which are the four archetypal gyroscopic plane angles of the Cosmic Clock, are placed three on each side of the centering fourth amplitude position. The male is denoted by the red spectral colors, the large + sign, and the small - sign, while the female bears the blue spectral colors, the large - and the small + signs. Each locking point in the wave is signified by the plane angle and a circular nodal center; the amplitude point is located at the largest nodal center.

The two lowest paintings and the painting on the upper right all reveal increasing detail in the spectral colors depicted in each locking-point position as well as an increasing size of the centering yellow within each locking point of the wave.

This appears to suggest that each succeeding octave in the entire nine-octave cycle has this increasing detail in each locking-point position and in each element in every succeeding octave. In other words, the increasing detail and centering yellow may simply signify a step in learning to see the spectral colorings of each locking point in the wave, or it may signify all of the above.

Figure 16: The Wave I

This wave painting is rich with meaning. The entire Russell Cosmogony is implied within it. It depicts a complete wave cycle which is a model for all action: everything that can possibly exist in the relative universe.

The upper half shows a male vortex on the right projected toward a female vortex on the left. Each vortex has four steps, or locking points, in its wave, with both sharing equally in the fourth, center, amplitude position of union.

Each position in these male/female vortexes is paired with its mate in octave progression, and each reveals its male or female polarity by a preponderance of red-orange or blue-green color.

The cathode, inertial plane boundary that projects the four rings is seen to project a male and female vortex from each of its sides: one going up, the other going down. The bottom surface of the male vortex inertial plane cone base is shown on the left-hand side and illustrates the inside of the vortex cone. The upper surface of the male vortex inertial plane cone base is shown on the right side and illustrates the outside of the vortex cone.

This painting is a model for everything in the universe and a symbol for the Creator's imaginings at work. The essence of all creation and change is here revealed for those who have the eyes to see and the understanding to know and interpret.

Figure 16

Undated. Published as cover of *The Fifth Kingdom Man*, 1991.

Figure 17: The Wave II

This painting shows many wave systems within wave systems, thus illustrating the infinite regress of the basic mechanism of creation. Two sets of large vortex whirls are clearly visible side by side with their cathode planes running horizontally through the center of the painting; these cathode base planes are oval concentric circular patterns colored blue. These cathodes are fulcrums from extend down from the centering cathode planes. The sexes can be distinguished by color: blue-green for the female and red for the male.

Locking points in the wave are revealed in the yellow anode points of gravitative preponderance. The spiral pattern of all movement is depicted in every stroke of this painting.

Figure 17 Undated. Published as a poster in 1989 and as frontispiece of *The Secret of Light* in 1947.

which lever systems are projected as pairs of cones with the cathodes as shared bases (the fulcrums) and the cone apexes toward the top and bottom of the painting (the ends of the lever extensions). Male vortexes extend up, and female vortexes While the painting is alive with movement, it also possesses the elements of serenity and stillness. The background blue color contrasts with the reds and yellows and contributes to the overall effect of soft, powerful, serene movement.

Figure 18. The Cube and the Sphere are the Sole Working Tools of Creation

The cube and the sphere are depicted with the tetrahedrons and cones that in turn are structures to be found within them. When all cones in the lower right figure meet and spin as a unit, they create a sphere at the apex in the form of a vortex whirl that sucks in and spews out motion/matter. inward toward a central focus to form spheres, and spheres project light outward that is dissipated at wave field boundaries to form cubes.

I believe it is important to realize that perfect cubes, tetrahedrons, spheres and cones do not

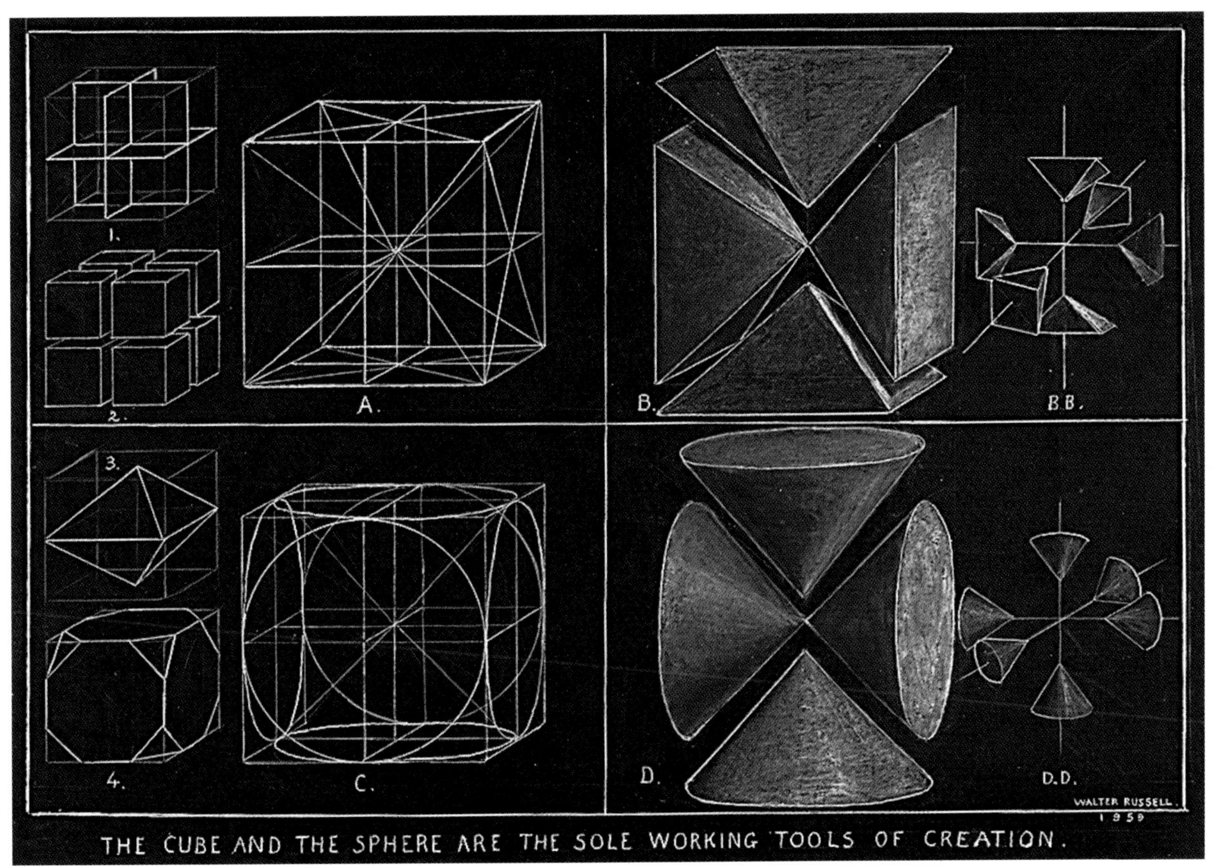

Figure 18 Completed in 1958. Published in *The Home Study Course* XI: 781.

Where all the tetrahedrons meet and demonstrate stillness, they create a cube that reflects inward to a central sun and then outward from the spheroid center to the adjoining wave fields. As the rotational motion of the spheres and cones is resisted and stopped, then cubes and tetrahedrons are formed.

When the cubes and tetrahedrons are directed toward the system center, spheres and cones are created. In other words, cubes reflect light exist in the relative universe except possibly for an instant in time; they only exist perfectly in the absolute universe. They are abstractions.

It is also important to realize, as Dr. Russell taught, that the relative universe of apparent stability, which is in reality in constant change, is ephemeral and illusory. Stability only exists in the One static Universe of God's still magnetic white light; there all that exists is eternal, omnipresent and omnipotent.

Figure 19. Untitled

Figure 19 Completed in 1958 and not previously published.

This painting shows the cube-tetrahedral wave field boundary planes in the upper half in octave progression from 1 to 4; in the lower half it reveals the point of union between two such pyramidal structures (vortexes) and the resulting spherical creation with its centrifugally projected equatorial rings from the center of this point of contact.

The center of the cube-sphere shows the carbon stage of matter's tetrahedral cube lens walls that direct the male and female vortexes of light-motion to collision. This form, the cube/sphere, is the prototype for all forms. The female and male polarities are represented by the blue and red sides of the carbon, diamond-shaped crystal

Figure 20. Geometry and Mathematics of Octave Waves

The geometry of the octave wave is illustrated by the centripetal spirals from the first to the fourth octave locking point positions; the fully formed sphere at the center of the fourth locking point position is diagrammed. The spheroids that accompany the first three octave locking point positions are not shown, and none of the cubes that surround these four spheroids are diagrammed. Figures 3, 4, 5, 14, 18, 45 and 46 partially illustrate this concept in detail.

The mathematics of the octave wave are illustrated in the multiplication of pressures diagrammed at the bottom of the chart. The ratio by which these pressures are multiplied appears to vary, and the significance of that remains a mystery. It may be that a mistake was made since the Russells speak in other writings of the pressures multiplying by a factor of eight with each octave. These ratios of pressures between octaves approximate this factor, but do not reflect it exactly.

This chart contains the following questionable statement by Dr. Russell:

> *tonal octaves are eight in number, but appear to be nine as the <u>first</u> half of the ninth octave is the <u>last</u> half of the first.*

I believe he reversed what he really meant to say and that it should read:

> but appear to be nine as the <u>last</u> half of the ninth octave is the <u>first</u> half of the first.

I believe that it could also be better stated as:

> the last half of the ninth octave and the first half of the first octave are identical — the same thing.

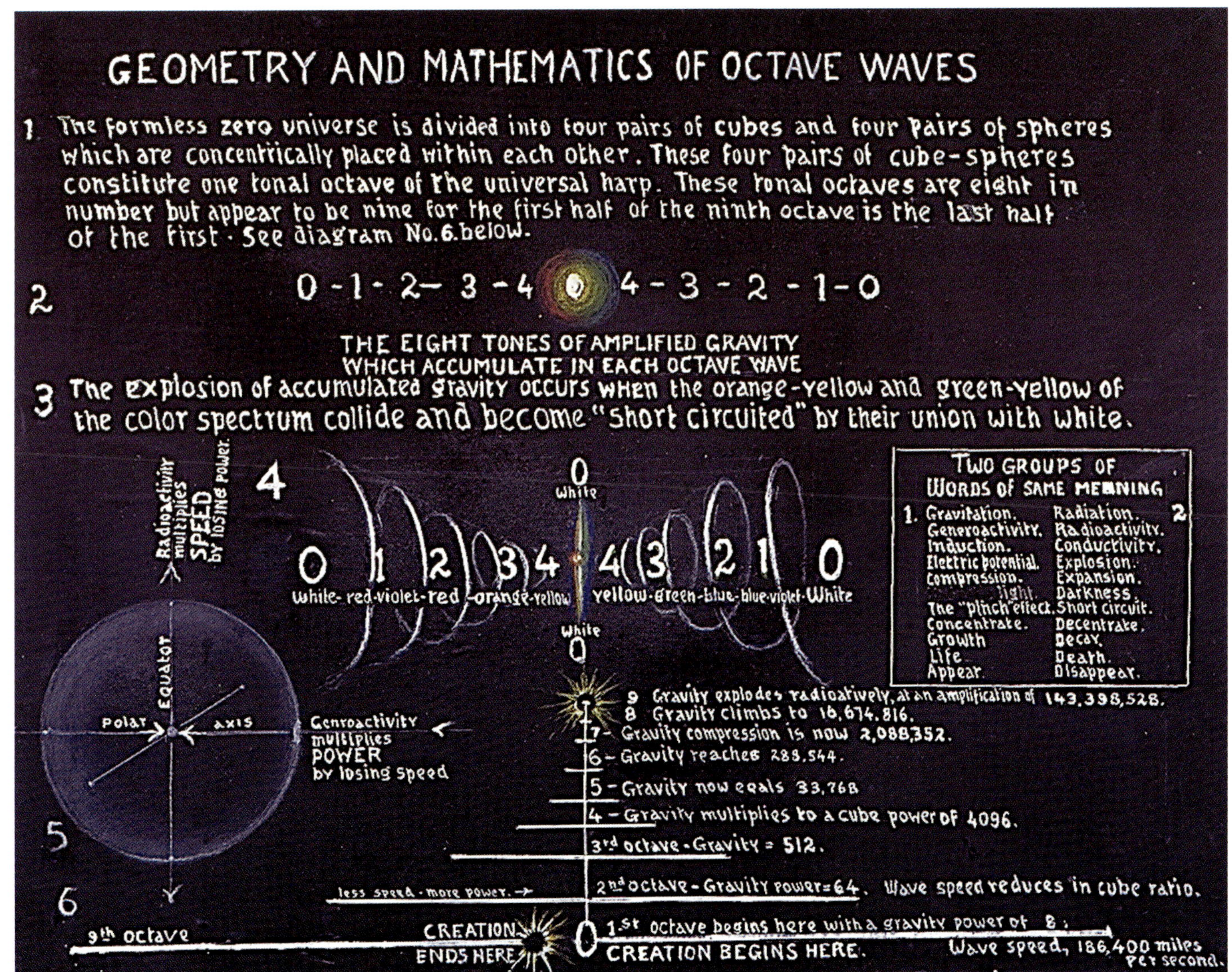

Figure 20

Undated. Not previously published.

If we remove one-half of the ninth octave and one-half of the first octave, we have removed a whole octave and indeed have eight octaves remaining.

In the small box on the right it says,

> *Two groups of Words of same meaning,*

This means that they have the same meaning because each word only has meaning in relation to its paired mate. Life only has meaning in relation to death; they are mirror images of each other. Each occurs simultaneously with the other, sequentially gaining preponderance over the other. This is true for all the words on the list. In terms of the language mechanics discussed earlier, these are Many words as opposed to words with no opposite which are One words or Words of God.

The spherical chart on the lower left demonstrates that generoactive movement toward the center of the system multiplies power by losing speed in the sense that a lower gear on a bicycle generates more power even though the rider moves slower and pedals faster. Radiative movement away from the center of the system divides power and multiplies speed just as does pedaling slower on the bicycle to go faster in a higher gear.

Centripetal motion toward the center increases revolution while slowing rotation, which, in turn, multiplies power at the expense of speed. For example, Mercury is a heavenly body with imperceptibly slow rotation on its own axis (virtually no change of day/night sides) and extremely fast — as we perceive it — revolution around the sun (very short years). The outer planets demonstrate the reverse of this with long years of slow revolution around the sun and very short days and nights as they spin fast on their own axes.

The Russell Cosmogony posits that the lower octave elements will correspond to Mercury in these power versus speed effects in their internal motions, and the higher octave elements will correspond to the outer planets.

Figure 21. The Wave Cycle

This chart depicts a complete wave cycle. Imagining a piston stroke while thinking of the wave action may help to clarify some of the details in this painting. As the cathode wave spirally compresses in a centripetal direction, the center of its spiral path defines the cube dynameter. This path is outlined in red and labeled A. At the same time as the piston compresses, the opposite anode wave spirally expands in a centrifugal direction. This expansion end of the piston path is rotated at 90 degrees to the dynameter, and the center of its path is outlined in blue and labeled B. This path defines the cube diagonals.

The dynameter is the result of all forces acting on a body. In this case, the dynameter is the result of all forces acting to create the wave/axis path. It appears from the chart that the anode and cathode wave paths both travel from the center point on the cube's side to the cube corner and that the dynameter and the diagonal are thus the same. The anode apex in time becomes a cathode base, and the cathode point in time becomes an anode apex. The word, dynameter, is used in place of diagonal simply to differentiate the function of centripetal compression, which carries the connotation of dynamic-dynamism, from centrifugal expansion, which carries the connotation of unwinding relaxing quiescence.

Dr. Russell's statement,

> *When cathode waves collide at maximum compression points at wave crests or troughs,*

means, among other things, that these points are where the anode poles exist at the cube corners, which is the center of a new cube system. I think this is an error in expression because the crest is where maximum compression occurs at wave amplitude, and the trough is where maximum expansion occurs at wave beginnings. This means that the maximum expansion point necessarily has to be at the wave axis or the cube side, which is where the cathode pole itself exists.

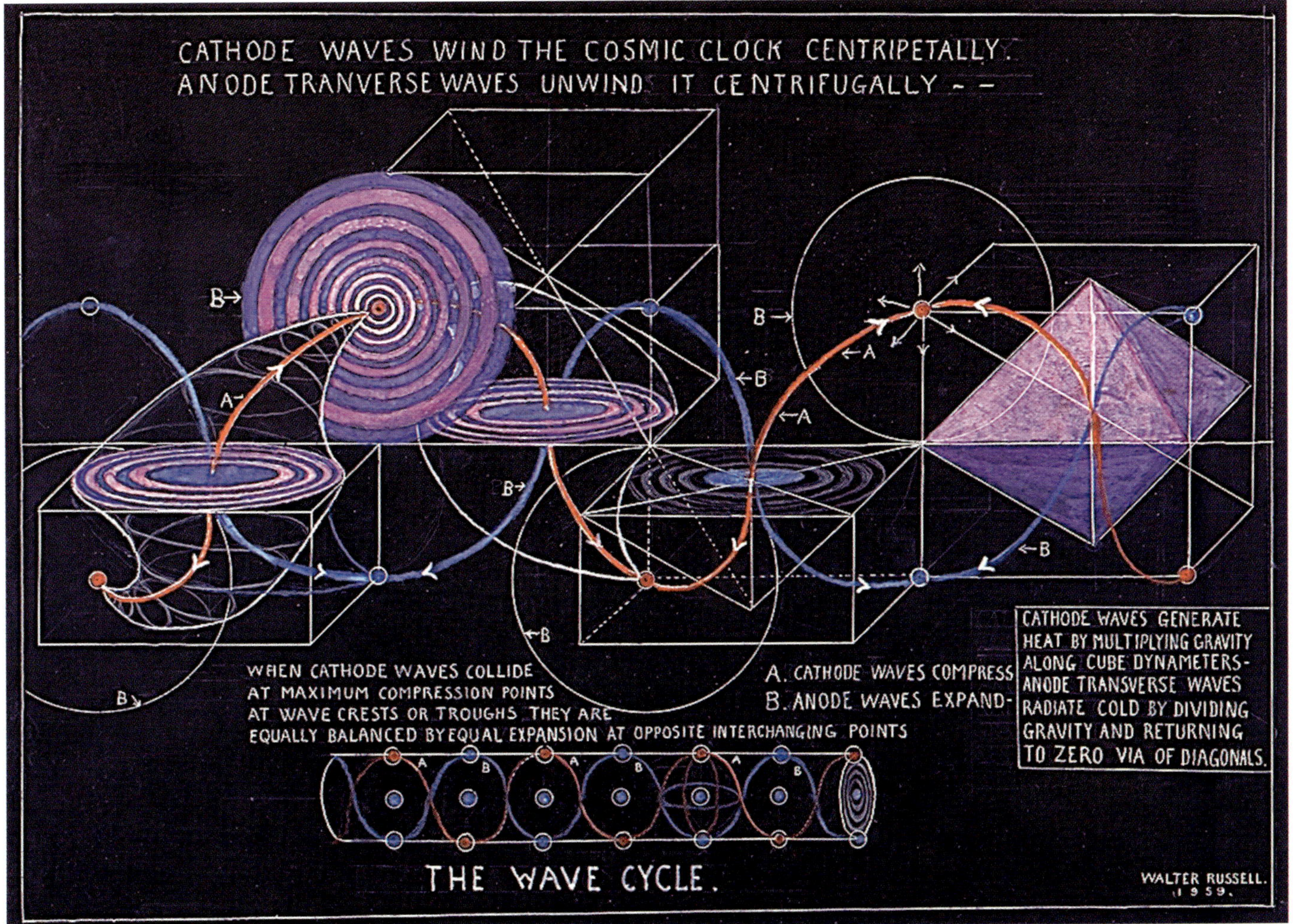

Figure 21

Completed in 1959 and not previously published.

By further stating,

> *They are equally balanced by equal expansion at opposite interchanging points,*

Dr. Russell implies that the anode and cathode poles sequentially change positions: the cube side becomes the cube corner and vice versa; furthermore, the expansion end occurs at cube boundary walls. This process of inside turning outside and then back inside is the nature of all change as is the birth to death to rebirth sequence of the mystics; everything in the universe exhibits this process of change.

This piston analogy is represented again in the lower chart and includes the red charging spirals and the blue discharging spirals to better visualize their relationships. Motion is transmitted from one wave field cube boundary plane to the next, creating crests at the end of centripetal compression and troughs at the end of centrifugal expansion. It is similar to an ocean wave, in that it compresses a wave to crest and trough.

The other aspect of the piston is the wave axis, and the wave motion is transmitted from one wave crest/trough to the next. There is no transfer of one wave to the other's place in the sense of a total displacement; it is simply a repetition of the motion along the wave axis. The wave axis centers both compression and expansion cycles.

Figure 22. Nature's Trinity Principle Wave Optics and Space Geometry Series, No. 1

This chart represents a male-female pairing, showing the lenses formed by the interference patterns created from colliding (interchanging) wave fronts. are three fully formed spheres as well as the two small anode spheres visible within the large cube that forms the painting borders.

Figure 22 Completed in 1959 and not previously published.

This painting illustrates the Trinity principle. It depicts the same three parts shown earlier in Diagram 1. The male and female parts form one part of the Trinity like the two extensions of the seesaw. The extensions are the polarized opposite male-female pairs and demonstrate the diversity or multiplicity within unity; these are the parts or Many aspect of the universe. The fulcrum, as the point of change, demonstrates relationship. The whole system, including the extensions and their centering fulcrum, is the One or the whole idea and, as such, demonstrates bottom-line unity.

It not only shows concentric circles within circles, but most conspicuously depicts the charging biconvex lenses arranged in octave wave progression from the initial cathode wave's first locking point through the fourth locking point position.

There are two fully formed anode spheres on each side in the center of their wave fields at the octave wave amplitude focal point position. There are also two fully formed pairs of generating octave wave lens systems, with the largest first lens for each of the two series in the center of the chart and the other separate lenses in each set at the left and right hand sides of the chart. In addition, there

In this chart, the two male and female pairs of lenses form one part of the Trinity, as do the two extensions of a seesaw. The lenses are sexed pairs, although their colors do not show their sex. The two fully formed spheres in the amplitude positions form a second part of the seesaw, analogous to the fulcrum, and the three together are the One. The fulcrum is represented by and appears not only in the amplitude point position in the wave, but also in the cube boundary walls. The cathode plane and the anode point both possess the element of stillness; they are the connecting/dividing points of polarity predominance reversal.

The significance of the colors is not totally clear other than that the cube wave field boundaries are in blue which represents the female expansive dominance. The pink-red at the small anode spheres signifies a mature compressed element at the center of the system under intense heat and pressure. The significance of the color of the two larger red spheres and the yellow spheres is unknown other than that they are still not at the point of aged centrifugal predominance where the hole bored from within changes to the color blue from the red of a younger, still prolating system. The color red symbolizes the male predominance, while yellow symbolizes the male-female balance.

Figure 23. Untitled Wave Optics and Space Geometry Series, No. 2

The cones, which are parts of spheres, and the tetrahedrons which are parts of cubes are illustrated in the small upper and lower charts. The tetrahedrons are also visible within Figure 23 itself on the left side. The inside-out, outside-in unity of these two fundamental structures is implied within this chart. The four steps to maturity and the four steps to old age are shown in geometric ratio.

These ratios for the sphere (circles and cones) and for the cube (squares and tetrahedrons) are shown geometrically and spatially. The progression of lengths from 0 to 4 is 1:2:4:8. Thus the distance from 1 to 2 is as the distance from 0 to 1 is as 0 to 1 is to the distance of 0 to the center apex point.

This chart is similar to the preceding chart in that both have similar cubes and spheres outlined. Figure 22 focuses on lenses, however, while this chart focuses on cones and tetrahedrons. The cones and tetrahedrons are archetypes for centripetal and centrifugal motions. Both point inward even though the direction of motion for cones is closing toward the center and that for tetrahedrons is opening toward the periphery. Thus, the function of the cone is integration or formation of matter, while the function of the tetrahedron is the disintegration of matter into tenuity.

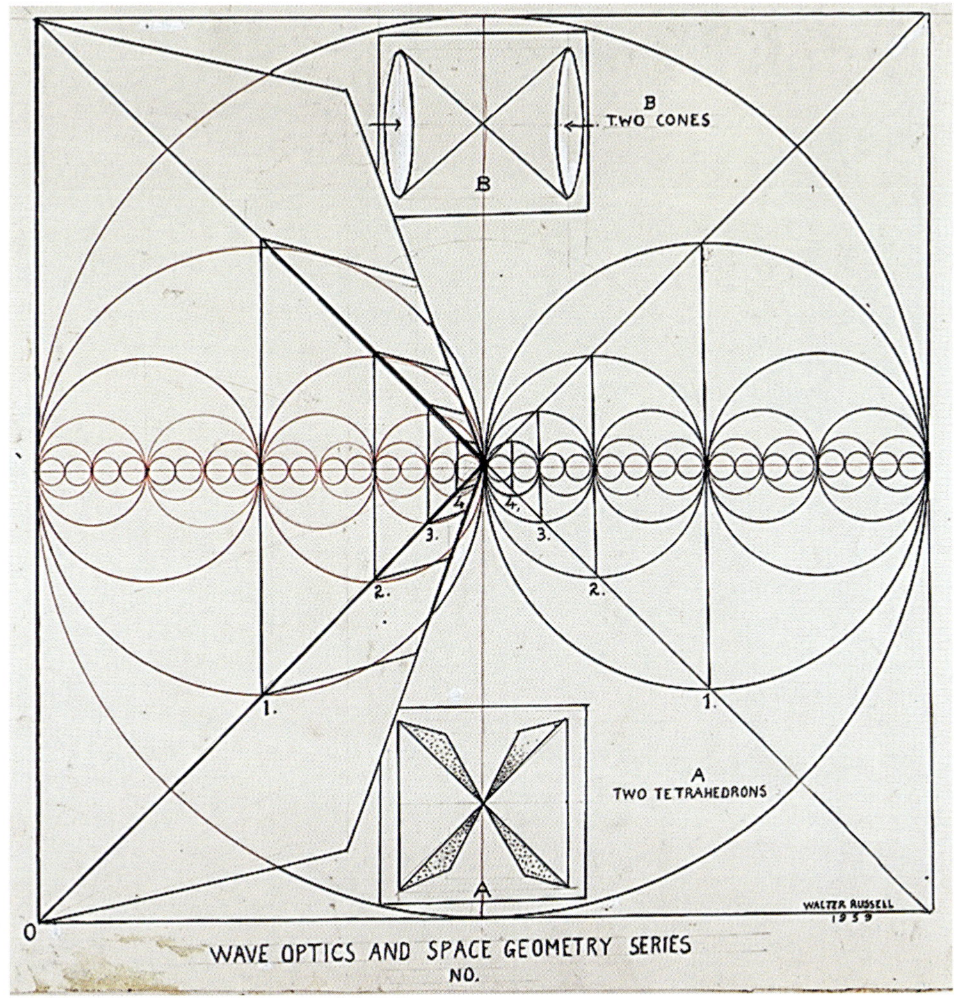

Figure 23 Completed in 1959 and not previously published.

Figure 24. Wave Geometry 1: The Secret of Creation Lies in the Wave

This diagrammatic painting details the wave, tracing the centripetal, compressive, piston stroke in four steps and implying the four centrifugal, expansive, vacuum strokes opposite them. The position of the fourth octave elements within the wave are shown in the lower center wave section. The four locking point potential positions are shown in their male red-orange and female blue-green colors on each side of the wave. Although an actual lens is not visible, its existence is implied by correspondence to the locking points.

The position of each mated element within the octave wave is illustrated geometrically, and each sex is identified by color. The gyroscopic plane angle of rotation for each potential position (plus for male or minus for female) at the first, second, third or fourth locking point within the wave is shown in the inner angle of the triangle made by the elements' potential-positional line with the wave midpoint and the cube side.

The static equator is shown by the horizontal wave axis line, and the dynamic equator is represented by the vertical amplitude element line at 90 degrees to the wave axis. The static equator is the domain of stillness and the dynamic that of maximum motion simulating stillness. Dr. Russell

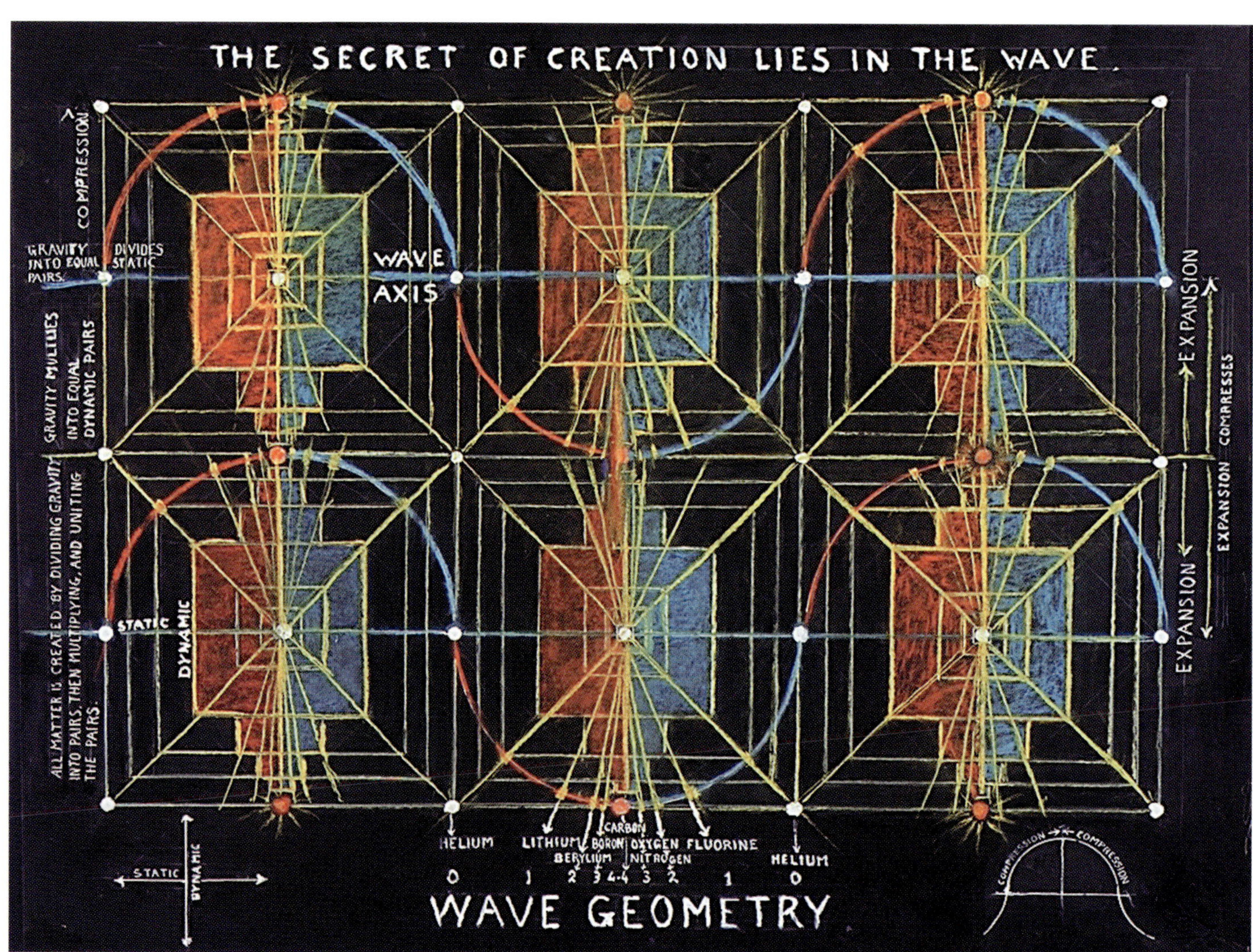

Figure 24 — Undated. Published in *The Home Study Course*, X:717.

depicts both static and dynamic directions in this chart. In a sphere, movement parallel to the static direction (right or left on any east-west equator) results in no change in potential, while movement parallel to the dynamic direction (up or down the north-south equator) results in maximum change in potential.

The points representing stillness are shown at the cube corners, cathode base cube boundary wall centers, and cube/sphere centers in white. The point of maximum motion and heat is shown in red at wave amplitude on a cube wall midpoint between the two sets of compressing lens systems representing an anode center.

The cubes that exist as partners to compressing series of centripetal cones are shown in their four potential locking-point positions with their relative sizes and are colored as male-female united pairs. The cubes that exist within an expanding series of centrifugal cones/tetrahedrons are similarly shown in black.

All matter is formed through the two-way effect of gravity which divides an equilibrium condition into compression/expansion conditions. Color is formed by the multiplying, electric, generative and compressive force of gravity into white hot light at system centers. Color disappears into the cold blackness of cube-bounded space by the dividing, electric, radiative, expansive force of gravity. Magnetic stillness controls gravity effects at the still point of system centers and wave field boundaries.

Figure 25. Wave Geometry 2

This chart is a close-up of one section of the preceding chart showing parts of the convex lenses formed through wave interferences. It reveals the interrelationships between the cube and the sphere (angles, lenses formed, cube and sphere areas) as well as the 1:3:9:27 cube ratio in cubes.

The small figure on the upper right reveals the radar reflector corners that guide all motion into and out of the center of any system; they ensure that there is no straight-line motion anywhere in the relative universe. They do this by resisting the outward movement at every point along the journey; the maximum resistance occurs along the cube wall center with the minimum resistance occurring along the cube diagonal toward the cube corner. This variation in resistance to outbound expansion directs the motion from the center outward toward the cube corner in a spiral movement.

The second of the three charts on the right side asserts that all motion is wave motion which is an interaction between cubes and spheres or between the cube boundary and the sphere center. The outward radial-directed spherical explosion is everywhere resisted by its cube wave field boundary, ensuring curvature everywhere.

The lowest of these smaller paintings relates the center of the large painting to the center of a tornado. The paired spirals to the side of this small painting reveal a below-ground, invisible, electric potential vortex as a mate to the visible tornado. Its existence is predicated on the premise that all vortexes come in pairs.

The male-female pairs are illustrated in their respective colors, the theme of this painting being to illustrate the compressive effects of both pairs in a multiplying direction to create united spherical wholes.

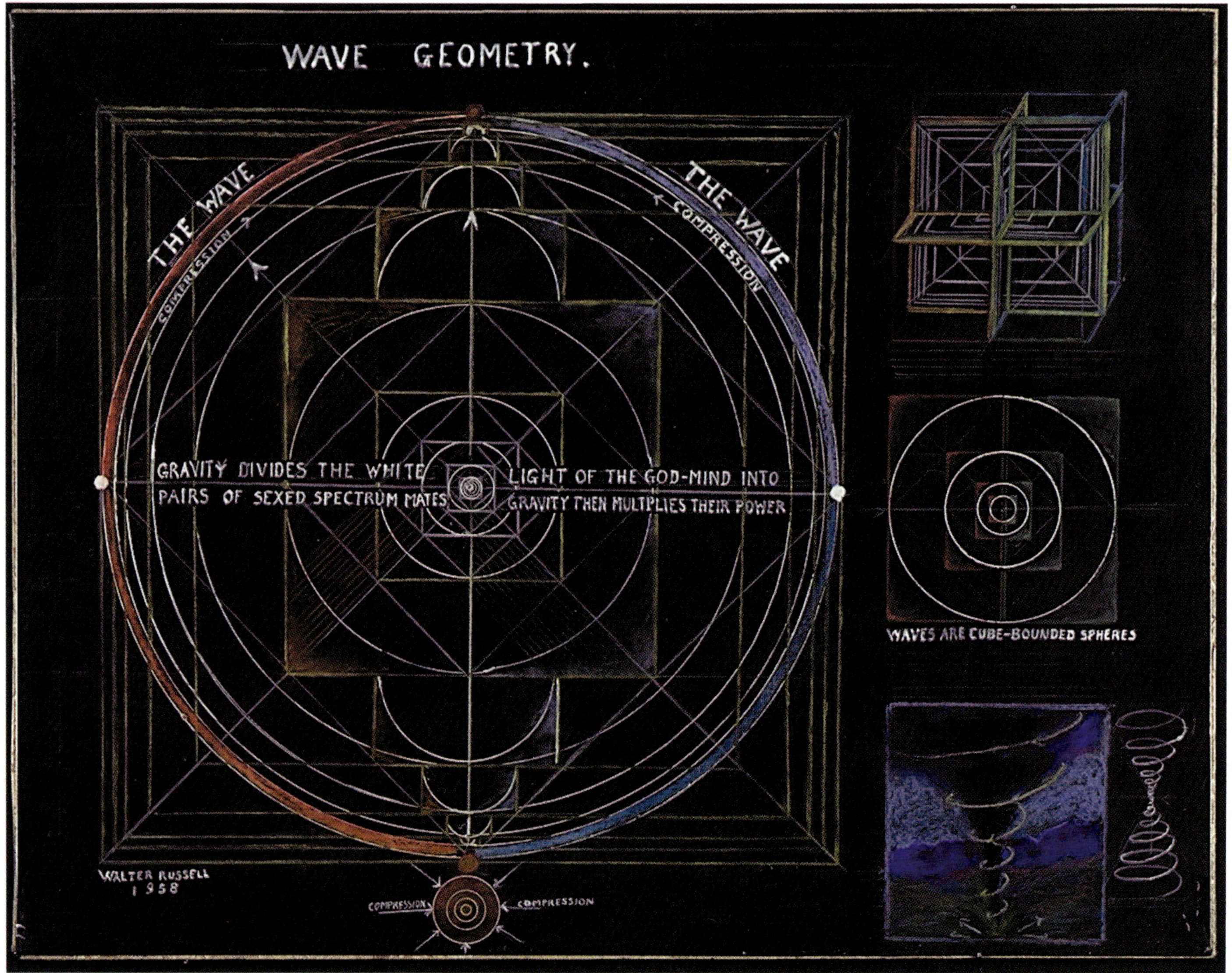

Figure 25

Completed in 1958 and not previously published.

Figure 26. Wave Intersections Are Forever Creating Radar-Divided Lenses within Lenses

Several convex lenses and at least one large concave lens are easily perceived. The red and black lenses are convex, and the large partially green and partially white lens in the center of the painting is concave. Concave lenses expand, and convex lenses compress. The convex lenses shown in this painting reveal the integrating half of the whole creation cycle. The disintegrating half, which is shown here as one large green and white lens, is born at right angles to the integrating series, although it is not shown as such in this two-dimensional representation.

The two tetrahedrons in the small diagram to the lower left with a thin lens or plane at their mutual apex show the expanding direction of motion that is created by concave lenses. The compressing direction could be symbolized by a pair of cones, apex to apex, with a sphere in between. That sphere at the center of the vortex ultimately becomes a boundary plane and then reverses direction of curvature (the inward motion becomes an outward motion) through concave expanding lenses. The tetrahedron represents the expansive direction from the anode center to the periphery via concave lenses.

The apexes marked as 'A's on both sides of the painting and in the small chart at the lower left appear to be drawing our attention to the fact that the compressing convex lenses are engineered by cones interacting with tetrahedrons which are only implied since they are triangles in the larger painting. The 'A' also appears to mean that this is the anode center of the system even though the tetrahedrons draw our attention to the outward directed motion away from the anode center.

The lenses created by wave intersections interfacing with other waves in an integrating direction create the cones that direct the motion to the center of the vortex. The concave lenses at right angles to the convex lenses create the tetrahedrons that direct the motion to the peripheral cube boundary wall where motion then reverses potential and direction to again compress inward.

Radar-divided lenses mean, among other things, that lenses are always formed in balancing pairs. Wave intersections are created by pairs of expanding wave fronts that reverse direction at their meeting to become compressing wave crests at wave field boundaries.

This painting is a two-dimensional representation of a three-dimensional process. Spherical wave interference produces three-dimensional circular lenses in sex-divided pairs of compressing and expanding convex and concave lenses.

The two opposed tetrahedrons represent the cube wave field boundary reaction to the outward expanding radial force. Cones and tetrahedrons work together to create the lenses that radar back the motion in an inward compressing spiral direction to an anode center.

The locking point potential position of each lens is depicted. Red lenses represent the compressing convex male, and the green lens represents the expanding concave female opposite.

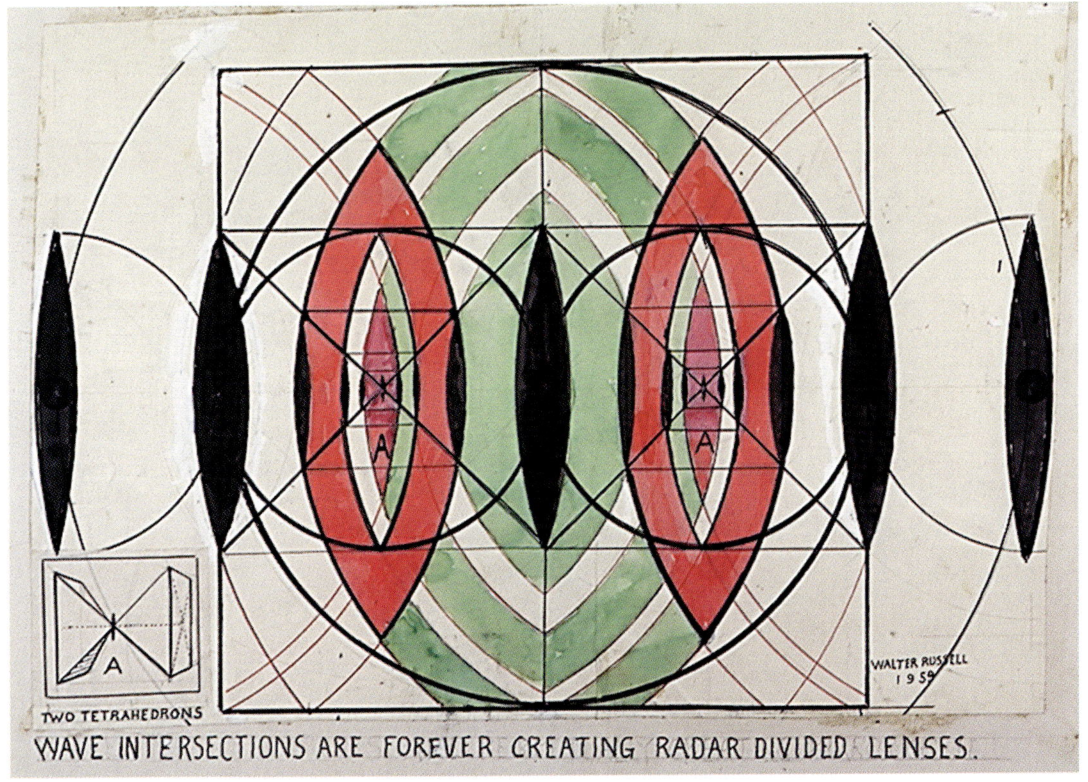

Figure 26

Completed in 1959 and not previously published.

Figure 27. Exemplifying Nature's Disintegrating Process

Two of the convex lenses of the four sets in the octave wave that focus to form the amplitude balanced, perfect sphere position are illustrated along with the four disintegrating concave lenses that oblate spheres; they are depicted with their respective blue-green female and red-orange male colors to differentiate sex. The lower set of spheres show an oblated sphere undergoing further oblation from left to right. This represents the disintegration process.

The oblation process can perhaps be better visualized by turning the book 90 degrees so that the blue compressing, interpenetrating cones are at the top and bottom of the picture. Oblate spheres are flattened at the poles and extended at the equator, while prolated spheres are extended at the poles and flattened at the equator. We usually envision these forms with the poles at the top and the equatorial plane extending horizontally rather than as Dr. Russell has placed them in this painting — exactly 90 degrees opposite.

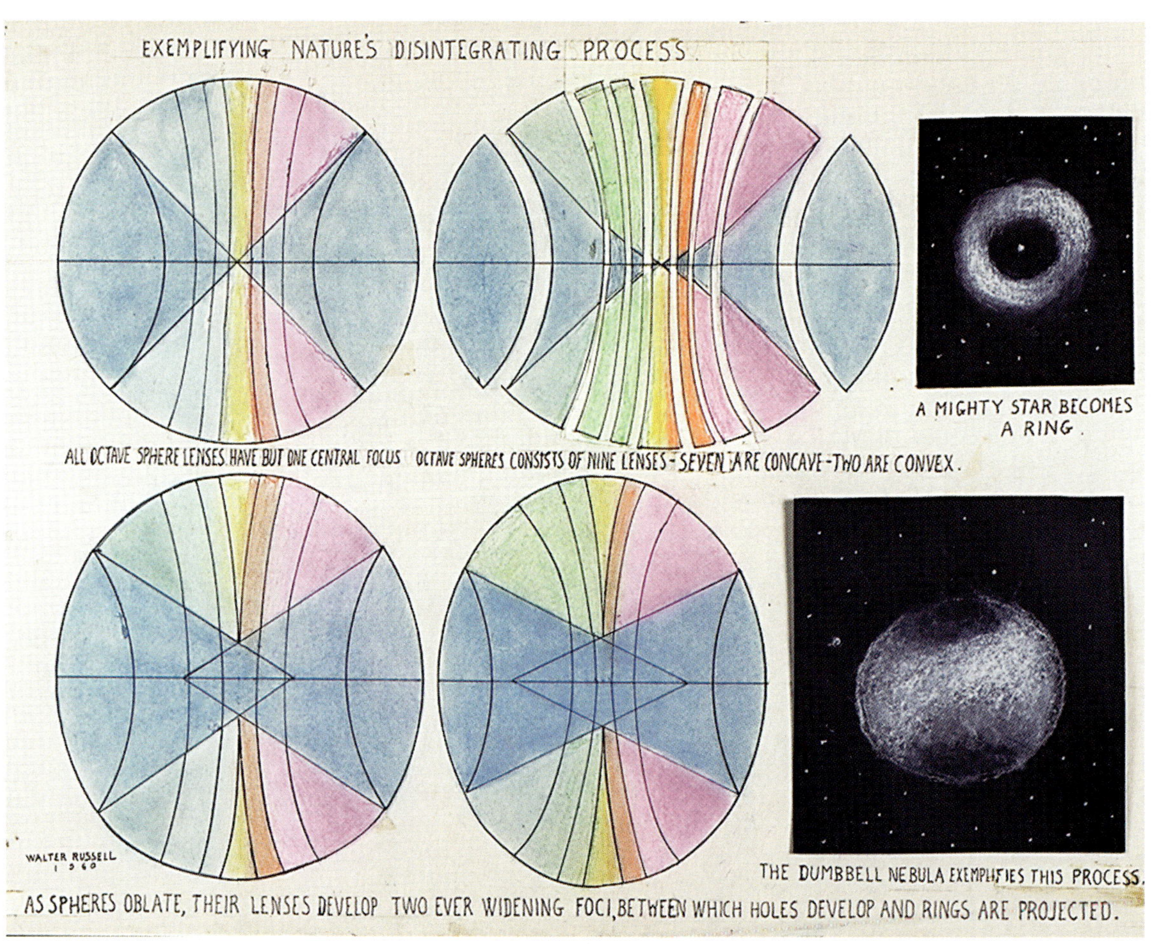

Figure 27 Completed in 1960 and not previously published.

The picture of the dumbbell nebula is already positioned with the compressing vortex motion on the top and bottom and expanding vortex motion on the sides.

These oblate spheres demonstrate the widening equatorial ecliptic plane that develops as they oblate further. The widening separating foci of the centripetal polar spiral vortical apexes create a thinner convex lens at the polar cone base, with more concavity to the other seven concave lenses.

The separating foci represent and form the hole that is bored through the center of disintegrating systems and through the equatorial area from which rings are projected centrifugally at 90 degrees to the compressing rings.

The celestial pictures show this effect with the lower one of the pair in a similar position as the oblate spheroids to its left, except that it is rotated 90 degrees from the oblate spheroids and is shown in a horizontal equatorial plane view. The upper picture is the same structure as the lower one, but seen from a viewpoint rotated upward 90 degrees to look down on the poles and to view the horizontal ring in end or plane view. In other words, the lower picture is seen on a side or edge view, and the upper is seen from a top or bottom view.

Figure 28. All Radar Mirrors Manifest the Love Principle upon Which This Universe is Founded

This chart may at first appear confusing. These lenses appear as oblate spheres if they are seen as in the preceding chart with the charging centripetally directed north-south poles coming in horizontally. The lens in the third diagram from the left on the second row can be considered as an oblate sphere when viewed as though its charging centripetally directed poles are on a line with the foci drawn on the right and left sides of the lens. This lens would be a prolated sphere if you were to consider its two foci to be on the equatorial centrifugally directed horizontal plane of discharge or rotated 90 degrees from where they are now. Dr. Russell, however, considers the convex charging lens to be formed by the north-south charging poles whether he shows the poles horizontally or vertically. Therefore this lens is an oblate spheroid seen with the charging poles placed horizontally.

Waves and wave systems pass through each other relatively unchanged and unobstructed by each other when they are structures of different orders.

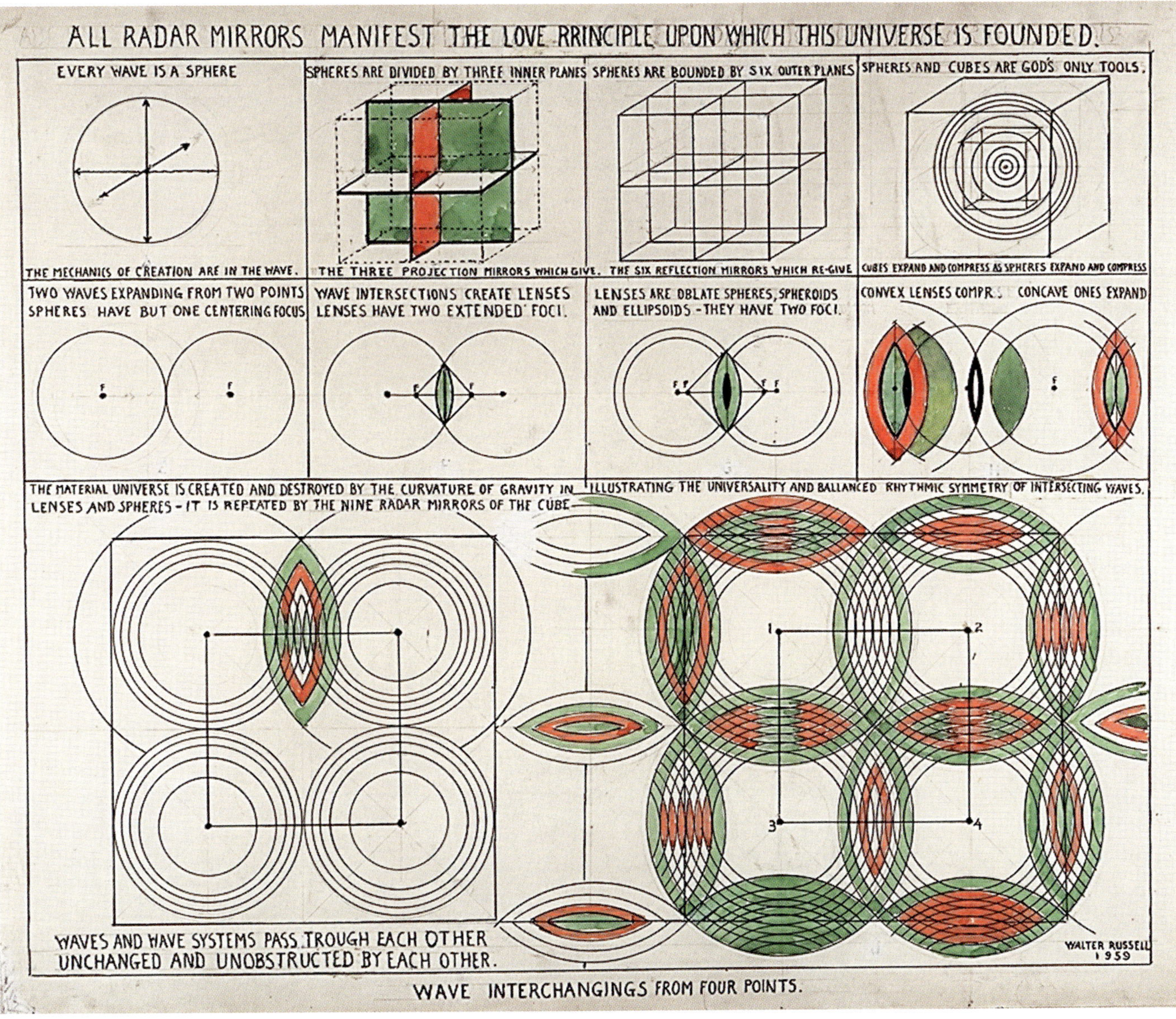

Figure 28

Completed in 1959 and not previously published.

Walter Russell sculpting F.D.R.

Waves of the same order can cancel or reinforce each other, synchronize or clash, or multiply or divide each other depending on their frequency and direction. For example, radio waves pass through us and our homes relatively unobstructed and unchanged since they are different order structures. But radio waves can be jammed, obstructed or amplified by other radio waves since they are structures of the same order, just as we can walk into each other's paths and obstruct, reinforce or otherwise change them.

Likewise, x-rays and cosmic rays pass through us unsensed and unnoticed even though they do affect us at the molecular level since they are structures of similar order. Thus these x-rays and cosmic rays affect structures within us that are of the same order and frequency as themselves.

Note that the small f in the center of the circle represents the focal starting point of the wave: the two foci that extend from or to the lens are also marked as small f's. These are on the same line and are both related to the intersection and lens formation of the wave fronts, yet represent different aspects of the interaction of waves.

Working together, projection planes and reflection planes cause cubes and spheres to exist only in relation to each other. Their reciprocal workings cause both cubes and spheres simultaneously, and yet sequentially in predominance, to either expand and/or compress. As spheres compress, there is a balancing cube expanding around them, or vice versa depending on the age of the entire system. A sphere compresses into form with an expanding cube surrounding it; then the sphere develops a hole within itself as mass disintegrates and this hole expands. Thus motion/mass returns toward the cube wave field boundary at ever decreasing speed, there to again collapse into the vacuum suction of the hole left from the disappearance of another anodal spherical mass, and finally to rebirth a resurrected spherical form.

The copper orange and green colors, while they could be used to symbolize male-female pairings in lens systems or planes, do not appear to be used in this way in this chart. The colors seem to only differentiate one lens within another or one plane from another.

The inner mirror planes that project outward toward the periphery could be considered as female, representing the expanding centrifugal direction, with the outer mirror planes that project inward toward the center representing the male contracting centripetal direction. Convex lenses that compress light into form can be considered male, with concave lenses that expand light into darkness symbolizing the female essence.

Figure 29. Untitled

A spherical wave form is shown in three dimensions with alternately expanding dark and white layers — in direct square ratio when going in and in inverse square ratio when going out. The square ratios are shown in the upper left sphere.

The other three double spherical wave intersections show lenses demonstrating different degrees of focal strength depending on the degree of wave interference and sphere interpenetration.

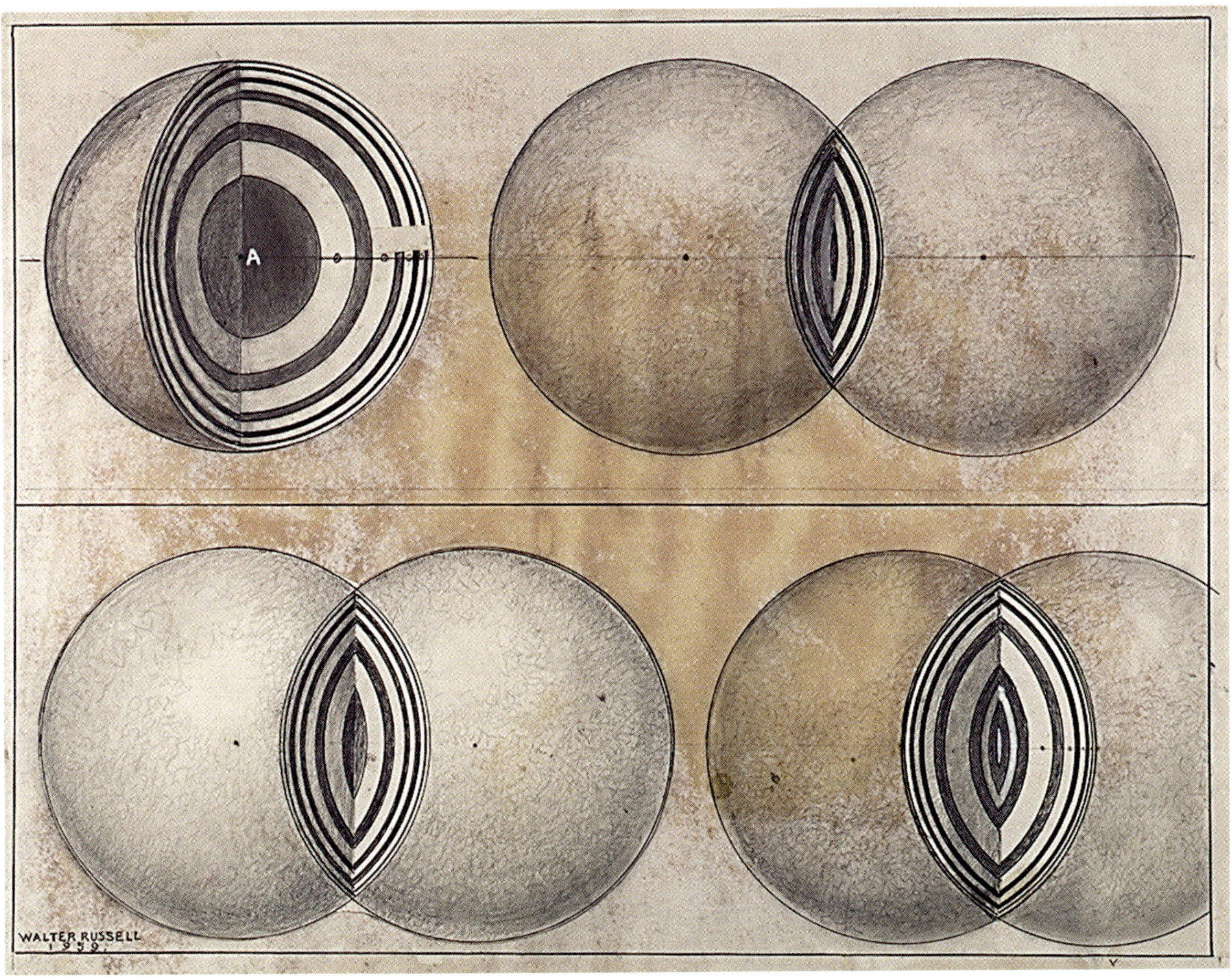

Figure 29

Completed in 1959 and not previously published.

The dark/light rings signify crests and troughs in the wave. The wave rings are but crests of waves expanding outward or inward. The small black dots in the white portions of the upper left sphere delineate the direct square ratio of the compressing spherical rings. These dots correspond to the locking points in the wave, with each wave centered around that locking point position.

The A in the upper left sphere appears to label the sphere's center and the anode point.

As the sphere/waves interpenetrate more deeply, the lens formed intensifies in light wave (gravity) bending potential, and its compressing power of centripetally directed magnification increases.

FOURTH SERIES. Thermodynamic Series

Figure 30. The Genero-Radiative Energy Cycle

The charts on the left illustrate the generating and radiating polarization process which is the birth and death of all energy. These charts depict the right predominately female polarity and the left predominately male polarity; the four octave focal point steps to maximum energy multiplication through gravity's compression are pictured from left and right into the center of the painting. The four octave focal point steps to maximum energy division through gravity's radiation or distribution are shown from the center to the top and bottom of the painting.

The paintings on the right illustrate the same idea with the equatorial plane again shown from top to bottom rather than from a horizontal side-to-side view. The four rings are being projected inward to close the hole in the center. As the center is yet blue, this represents a young element. Once the hole closes in a yellow white blazing color, it reaches maturity; as it ages, it progresses from red through blue to black. (I deduce that the hole is closing in a contracting system because the rings are becoming denser and thicker toward the center.) The black on the outside is what we can see

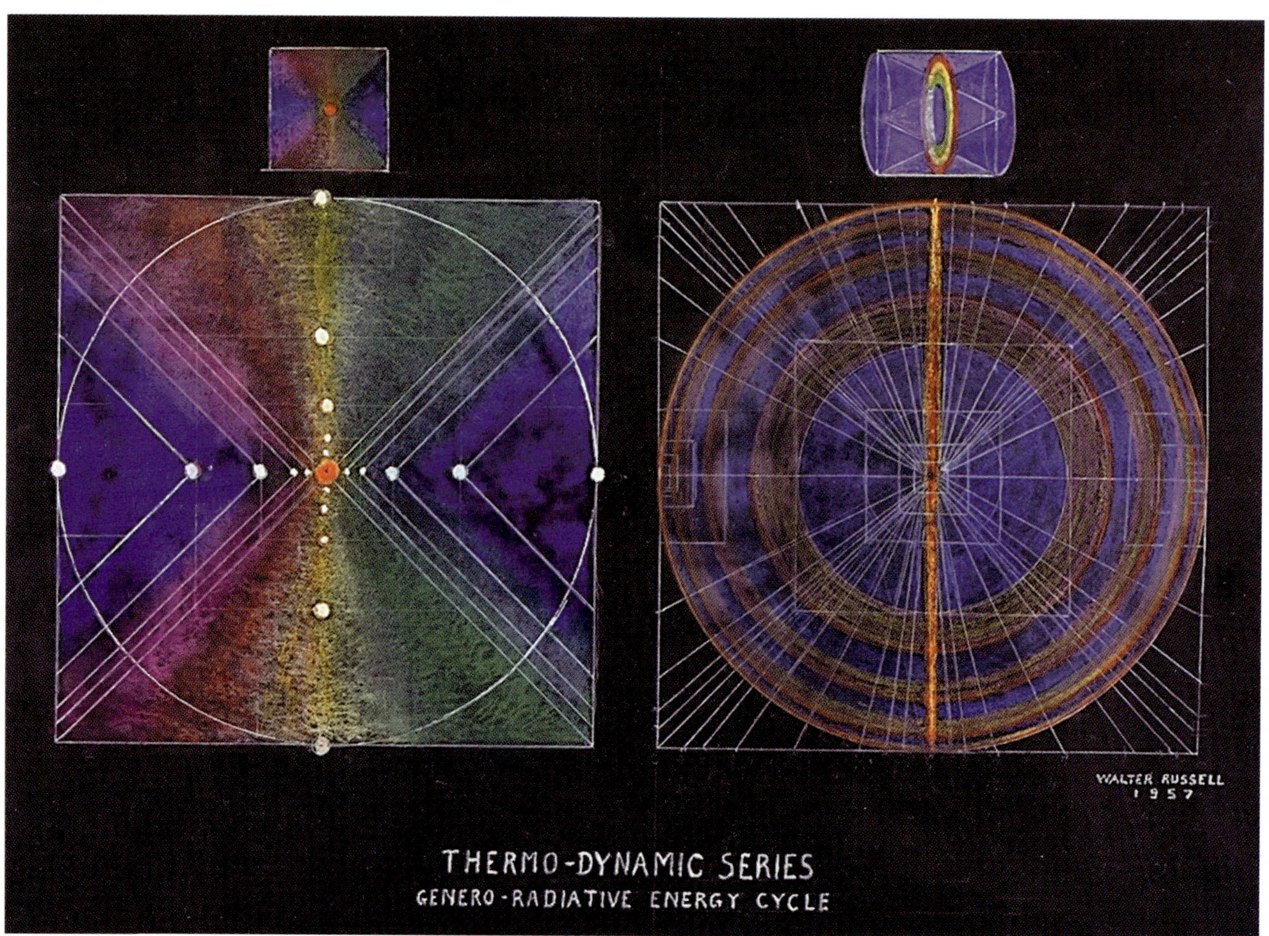

Figure 30

Completed in 1957 and not previously published.

of the surrounding cold that balances the development of this heat structure.

The small picture on the upper left shows the same pattern as the larger one beneath it minus the focal point steps in the wave. The small picture in the upper right appears to rotate the thin equatorial plane to show it more from a plane view rather than a thin side edge view in order to demonstrate the hot outside and cool inside of a younger structure.

The interchange between the sphere and the cube is suggested in both larger paintings by the spheres within cubes and the cubes within spheres. This interchange is the essence of all motion and energy expression. All energy is expressed through this polarization process: the interchange between gravity's compression/implosion/generation and gravity's expansion/ explosion/radiation. The wave cycle simultaneously runs up to a crest on one side of the piston stroke and runs down to a trough on the other side.

Walter Russell with the last bust he sculpted and several of his last paintings.

Figure 31. Untitled

This beautiful painting of a comet returning to the sun in the form of a human figure serves to remind us that Clausius was right for one-half of the cycle; energy does eventually run downhill after it has been birthed and returns to its source for eventual rebirth, as do we all. This eventual rebirth, the running up of energy, is the other first half of the cycle that Clausius did not recognize in his revised second law of thermodynamics.

The Russellian Seven Laws of Thermodynamics describe the complete cycle and can be summarized as:

> Cold causes compression, contraction and generation which cause heating
>
> Heating causes expansion, extension and radiation which cause cooling again to repeat the cycle. See Figure 32 for more on thermodynamics.

The feminine figure is appropriate as a traditional symbol for the disintegrating half of the creative cycle and is colored with an outer green hue to represent the feminine polarity.

The sun appears to be setting as the colors in the entire painting are predominately those of the feminine polarity which represent the last half of the cycle with its approaching darkness. The comet figure underscores that, at this point, the energy/motion is predominately returning to the sun center. It is twilight time.

Figure 31 Undated. Published as cover of *The Electric Nature of the Universe*, 1991.

Figure 32 Direction of Force in the Gravity Cycle

This chart could be titled "The Other Side of the Coin" in relation to classic thermodynamics. It illustrates the continuous, cyclic and simultaneous running up and running down of all polarization/energy/phenomena in the universe.

Note that as division multiplies, multiplication divides (something and/or everything), and as discharge charges, charging discharges.

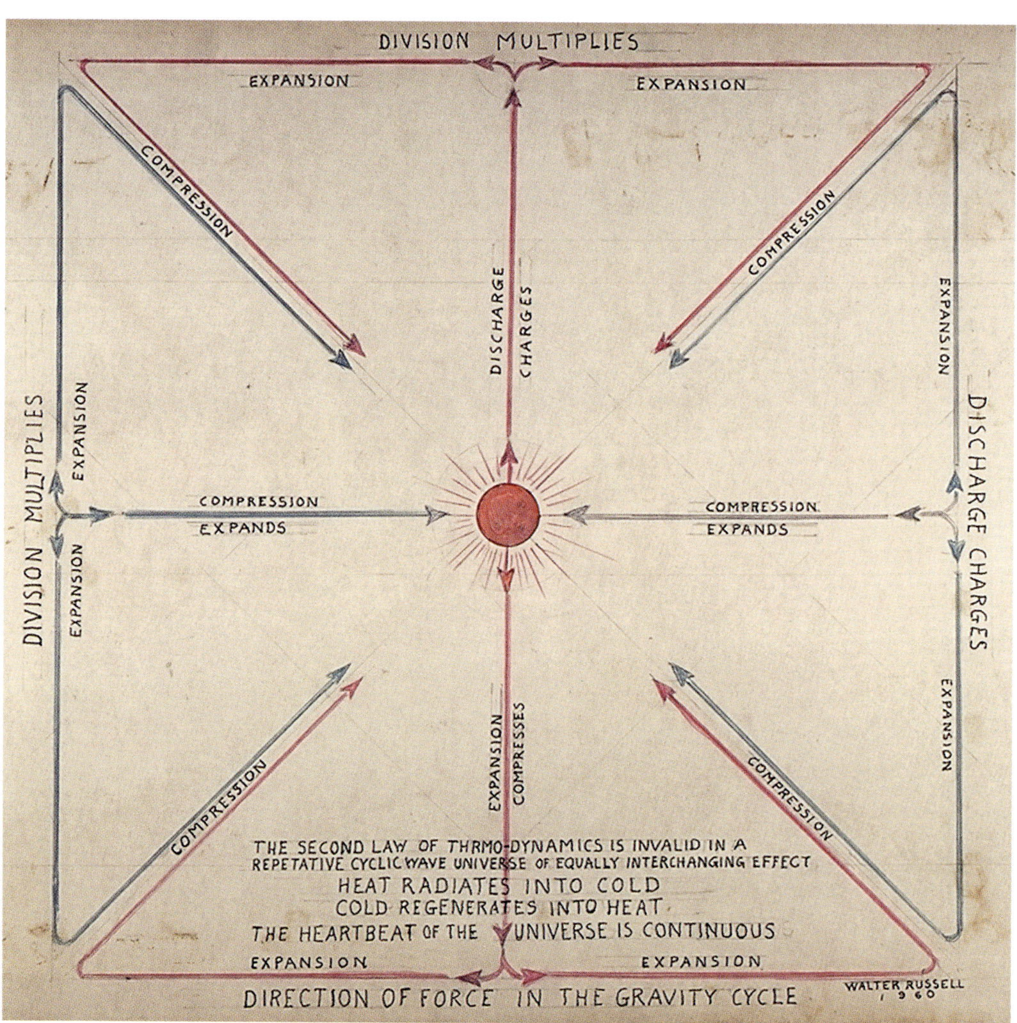

Figure 32

Completed in 1960. Not previously published.

Compression is shown with both male and female polarity colors, underscoring the fact that both polarities do charge. The discharge is colored red, emphasizing that this process of heat radiation ultimately and simultaneously charges. The charging is colored blue which suggests that this process of cooling generation ultimately and simultaneously discharges.

The simultaneous occurrence of both complementary/antagonistic/opposite forces and directions is literally and figuratively illustrated in this chart that summarizes the essence of the entire two-way expression of the gravity cycle. This reveals that Walter Russell's concept of gravity as a whole cycle is always simultaneously an imploding, sucking, pulling, and an exploding, blowing, pushing, two-way force.

Figure 33. Cathode Light-Multiplying Compression Rings

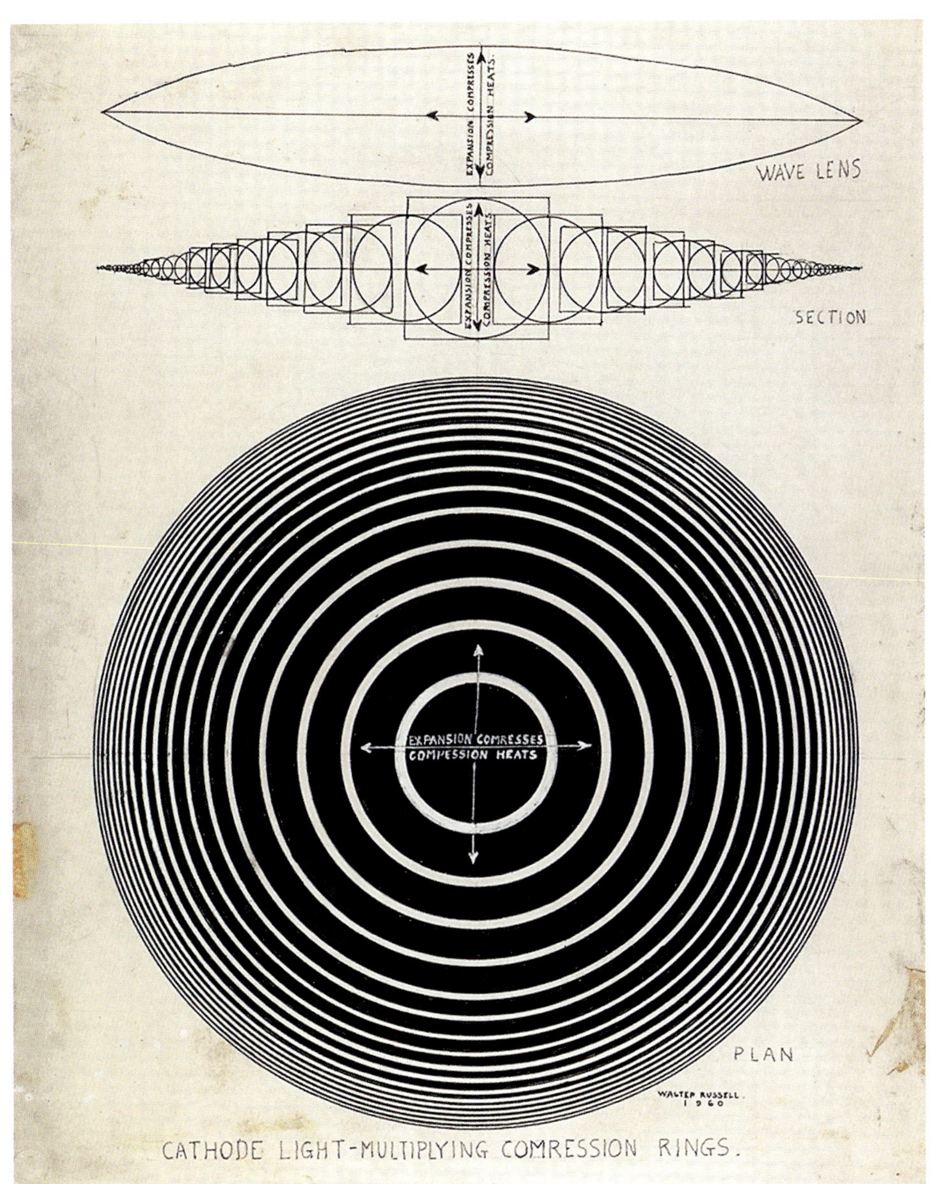

Figure 33 Completed in 1960 and published in *The Home Study Course* XI: 795.

The cathode end of the wave is a series of convex lenses that multiply expansion to greater compression by a centripetal spiral focusing motion of light toward the apex or anode end of the wave.

The top figure diagrams a single convex or light multiplying lens. The middle figure represents this lens in section and a series of such lenses. The lower spherical figure is a plane or end view of such a series.

This illustrates the principle of infinite regress just as a bar magnet is a series of bar magnets.

The white rings represent the convex compression lenses and the dark rings the space between them or vice versa. The white rings could also be considered as crests and the dark as troughs in the wave as that is what compressed and expanded conditions represent. Intense dense system centers are surrounded by vast space that separates them from other intense dense system centers that are surrounded by their vast separating spaces.

Any outward explosion/expansion is resisted by its wave field boundary cube walls, and the resistance to this outward movement is registered as compression, heating and increased density. The explosion is replaced in time by a vacuum at the explosion center and a pressure or compression condition around it. The vacuum or implosion is a reversal of condition that manifests as and/or through the convex series of lenses. These are also represented by a series of compressing rings.

The end view figure suggests this increasing compression toward the anode center of the imploding vortex by increasingly dense, more closely-packed spherical rings as the rings are compressed inward. As motion converges to the vortex center, density and temperature increase and 16 other dimensions change simultaneously toward the amplitude position of the fourth locking point in the wave. All inward implosions tend toward more perfect spheres as centripetal movement voids friction through synchronization approaching radial inward-direction voiding curvature, and more perfect spheres evolve from prolated forms.

All outward explosions will be ever more imperfect spheres tending to more cubic form as resistance to the outward radial movement is simultaneous to the outward movement and immediately curves the straight line radial direction to ultimately flatten against the wave field cube boundary wall. All lens systems in nature operate with an equal balancing mate.

Figure 34. Anode Light-Dividing Expansion Rings

The anode end of the wave is a series of concave lenses that divide compression toward greater expansion in a centrifugal, spiral, relaxing motion of light toward the cone base cathode end of the wave.

The top figure diagrams a single concave light-dividing lens that again implies the infinite regress of detail. The middle figure represents this lens in section and a series of such lenses. The lower figure is a planar or end view of such a series.

The white rings represent the concave expansion lenses and the dark rings the space in between or vice versa. The white rings could also be considered as crests and the dark as troughs in the wave as that is what compressed and expanded conditions represent. System peripheries are vast spaces near the vast spaces of other system peripheries. Any inward implosion/compression eventually desires the release of its confining tensions. The resistance to this inward movement is registered as expansion, cooling and decreased density or increased tenuity. The implosion toward a

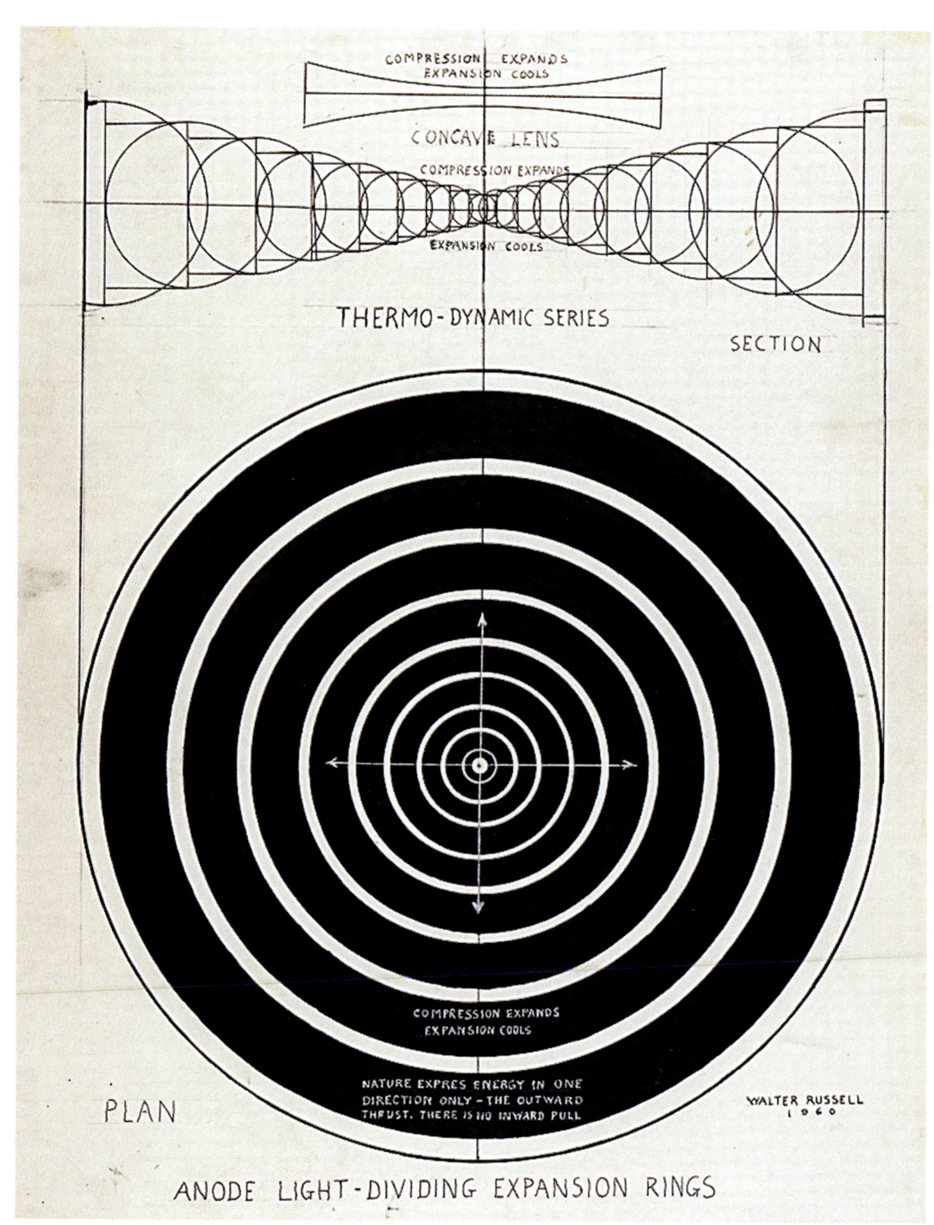

Figure 34 Completed in 1960 and published in *The Home Study Course XI*: 796.

center is replaced in time by a pressure condition at the implosion center and a vacuum or suction around it. The resulting pressure at the center of potential explosion is a reversal of condition that releases in time through the concave series of lenses.

The end view figure suggests this increasing expansion/decreasing density by less dense/more tenuous, less closely packed/more separate spherical rings as they expand outward. As motion diverges to the periphery of the vortex, density and temperature decrease and 16 other dimensions change simultaneously toward the last unlocking point in the wave which corresponds to the first locking point position. As the rings are projected inward toward the center of the centripetal spiral, they are compressed into ever smaller, ever more dense structures.

All outward explosions will tend to create more perfect cubes and more imperfect spheres as they progress outward since centrifugal movement voids synchronization through increasing friction, and motion approaches more tangential curved lines in the outward direction (this increases curvature). Thus more perfect cube forms evolve from oblate spherical forms.

All inward implosions will be imperfect cube/spheres tending toward more spherical form as resistance to the inward movement is voided by synchronization and curved lines seek more straight line radial direction which ultimately becomes a sphere at the center of the vortex point of maximum motion. Simultaneous to this inward, compressive, increasing, straight line movement, there is an outward explosion in a radial direction that is ever more curved by the equal resistance from cube wave field boundary walls to this outward movement. No lens system in nature functions without an equivalent balancing mate.

Figure 35. Nature's Power Multiplication Principle

This principle is hidden in a gravity recorder bar (commonly called a bar magnet). This chart illustrates the principle and reveals many unknown aspects about a gravity bar.

The small diagram at the upper right illustrates at least one, if not the main, meaning of Dr. Russell's statement that a gravity bar (and all vortex spirals) has four poles instead of two and that both male and female poles charge. There is a pole maximum on each end of the bar, the charging north and south poles. There are also two discharging east-west poles extended perpendicular to the north-south charging poles.

One possible alternative way to consider these two east-west cathode poles would be that they are in the center of the bar and extend out as one pole instead of two. As the cathode pole is One, so is the east-west pole One. The anode poles are two. The center of the bar, the midpoint of the wave, is where the fourth positional tone in the wave is created from the two united charging male and female tones; here they simulate stillness. This is the point where polarity is voided to become One. The anode poles, the north-south charging poles, form the anode between themselves. The anode eventually and sequentially discharges and ultimately becomes the cathode. The cathode poles, the east-west discharging poles, sequentially and eventually charge and ultimately become the anode.

The cathode extends its pole out in greatest centrifugal intensity from the center of the bar at 90-degree angles to the bar's wave axis, but it fans out at all other angles, even to minus one, in progressively lesser intensity. The direction of the cathode pole is circular or around an arc of 360 degrees, so that anywhere you travel on this east-west pole is the same. A point moving continually east eventually is located in the west, and, if it continues in the same direction, it eventually is again located in the east. Direction on the cathode pole is arbitrary in the sense that the degree of pole strength does not vary as it does in moving toward or away from the bar center on the north-south poles.

Each of these considerations are reasons for saying that the east-west cathode pole is One, whereas the north-south anode poles are two. The east-west cathode pole is One because it is an equilibrium condition at and extending from the center of the bar axis. The north-south poles are two because they are constantly varying, pressure conditions extending to and away from the center of the bar axis.

Direction in the anode poles is relative in the sense that the degree of pole strength constantly varies when moving toward or away from the center of north-south pole union. This movement is a spiral, centripetal motion toward the center; its strength varies logarithmically toward or away from the center. On the anode poles as you move toward or away from the anode pole center, polarity increases or decreases. This is implied by the lower gravity bar chart with both poles shown with "+," the charge sign as detailed in Lesson 42 of *The Home Study Course*.

The primary diagram of this chart reveals the lens structure in cube ratio that centripetally multiplies pressures as motion is spiraled through each mate to the opposite end of the gravity bar through the still center point of voidance of polarity. The largest middle lens occupying the zero tone in the wave demonstrates lack of polarity at its center (the cathode pole). The cathode pole is formed from the merging of two male-female halves (opposite sexed poles) united as one at the center which was previously an anode point. (See Diagrams 12 and 13). It reveals no polarity at any place on the midline.

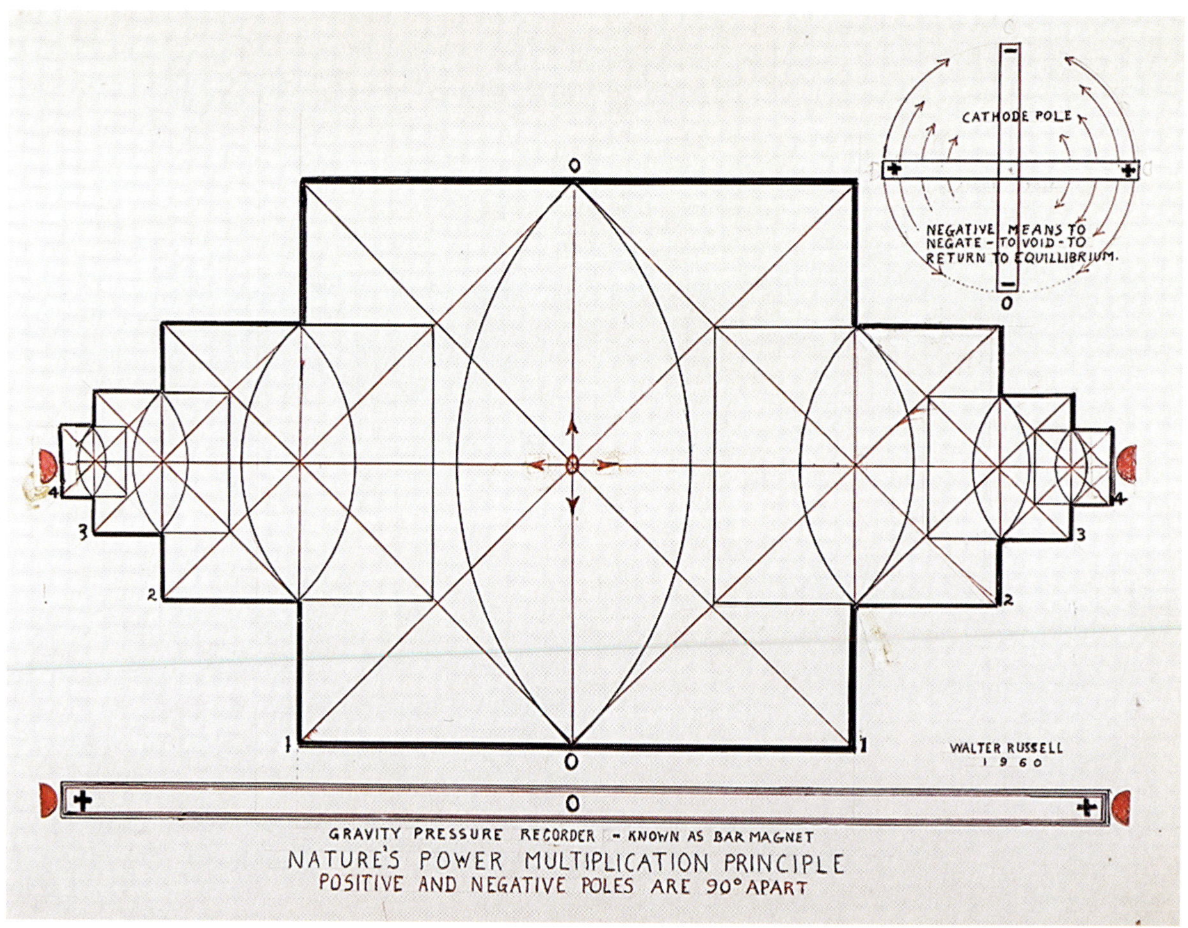

Figure 35

Completed in 1960 and published in *The Home Study Course* XI: 810.

Figure 36. Untitled

This chart is fraught with possibilities. It implies so much that it would require a volume to discuss all the possibilities. The essence of all creation is revealed herein. The mechanics of creation starting the omnipresent and omnipotent implosion/explosion! This first division immediately radar extends itself into another equal and opposite division of the two first equal opposite divisions. This is

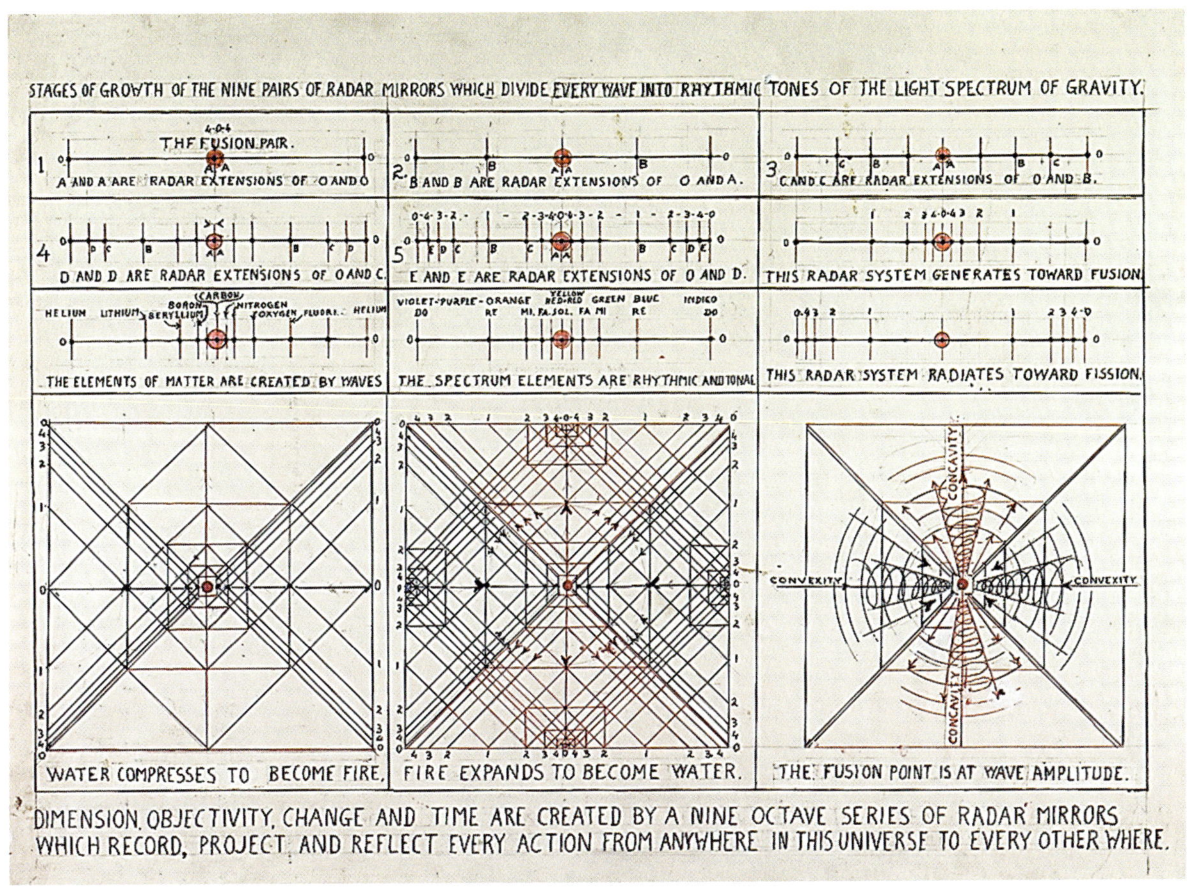

Figure 36

Undated. Not previously published.

with the basic polarization process are shown in the first small chart. The progression of this first splitting of the One into the Many by means of the universally constant octave wave is sequentially outlined.

The first division of the One into the Many radars its need for equal mates which is shown as the fusion pair. The division of a line into two equal parts symbolizes the first motion and thus creation: shown progressively in a series of such radar divisions that manifests the entire octave wave of seven divisions with a balancing beginning/ending keynote and balancing midpoint amplitude position to complete the nine octave wave steps.

The middle chart on the far right side of the nine small upper charts (follows Chart 5) is a multiplying series rather than a dividing series. The chart directly below it is a dividing series. The difference between them is that in the multiplying chart the movement occurs or is extended from the keynote (left to right) and is, so to speak, stopped at the first locking point when it meets its equal mate there.

This same progression occurs in a logarithmically increasingly compressing ratio until full union is manifested at the amplitude fourth locking point middle-of-the-line position of the wave. The dividing series then continues from this amplitude middle-of-the-line position in reverse direction to the keynote, baseline, no locking point position in the octave wave. The amplitude is the carbon line position, and the keynote is the inert gas position.

The mechanics of the creation and dissolution of matter, or fusion and fission, are symbolized in their respective radar mirror systems in the lower three charts with the blue triangular vortexes symbolizing the fusion/compression cycle and the red triangular vortexes symbolizing the fission/expansion cycle.

The lower three charts speak in almost alchemical language: the basic polarization process is simply described in terms of fire and water. The unity of these two apparent opposites is revealed. Their interchange and dance is the basis of creation: both birth/fusion in the centripetal vortexes and death/fission in the centrifugal vortexes are symbolized in the chart on the lower right.

The parallel lines in the lower three charts portray the same concept that the upper nine charts symbolized about the radar system that is created from the first division or multiplication of the One into the Many. First a pair is created; from this seven pairs are simultaneously created including both an amplitude polar united pair that is the mature point of the wave and a baseline polarless pair that is the beginning and the ending of every octave wave. These lines reveal the radar multiplication/division cycle of every octave wave in triangular vortex form.

The lower right-hand chart's blue charging vortexes are both clockwise, charging, centripetal vortexes when viewed from their respective bases. The red discharging vortexes are both counterclockwise, discharging, centrifugal vortexes when viewed from their respective apexes. The apex of each vortex has the greatest revolution and the least rotation (considering the vortex itself as having both revolution and rotation). The base of each vortex is exactly the opposite, having the least revolution and the greatest rotation. This last statement is not specifically depicted in the chart, but it is implied by the Russell Cosmogony.

Figure 37. Fusion. The Anode

This painting shows the fusion ring patterns projected from the cathode to the anode. The anode is represented by the red center of the painting. The essence of the cathode can be symbolized by the black space surrounding the fusion rings.

The colored series of rings run from the outer red-violet ring to red to orange to yellow rings symbolizing the male spectrum. This is paired with a female color spectrum coming to meet it from the inside as blue-violet rings to blue to green to yellow rings meeting the male pair as a yellow blending.

This painting has five clearly visible and distinguishable male-female spectrum pairs, with two or three more nearing the fusion center which are barely distinguishable. The red anode appears to have a barely distinguishable yellow ring; immediately next to this is a blue ring.

The male-female color spectrums representing the fusion compressing rings illustrate that all things are created from male-female pairings. As this is a compression series of rings, Dr. Russell has chosen to color the anode red on the inside and blue on the outside, the sign of a generating system. Red is the symbolic spectrum color for male preponderance. The red anode ring has just a hint of blue in its center that represents the hole that is progressively being closed through compression from the outside inward; this again shows a generating system closing the hole in the center. The cathode surrounding it is black, the symbolic spectrum color for female preponderance.

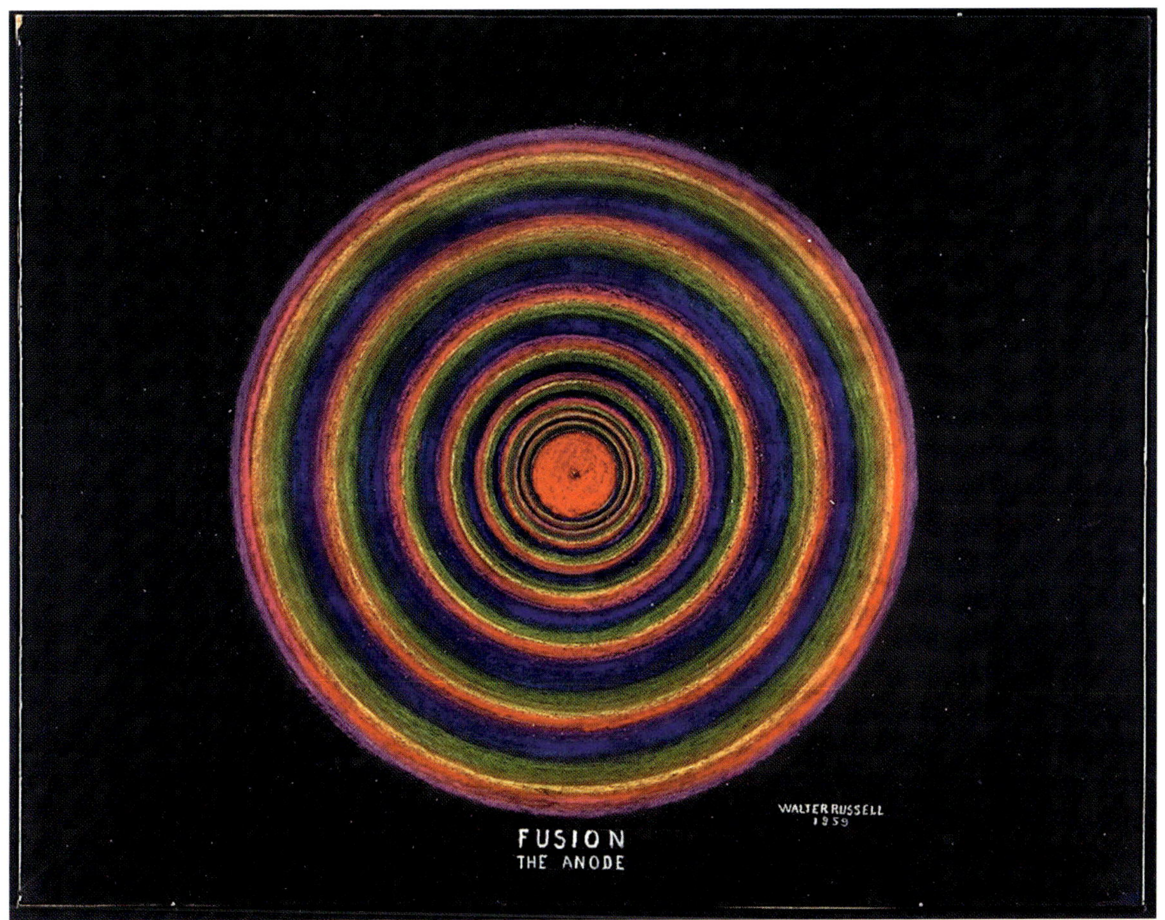

Figure 37

Completed in 1959 and not previously published.

We do not have a painting titled *Fission: The Cathode* for comparison, but we can envision what it would illustrate from our knowledge of the cosmogony, this painting and the other charts. Figure 33 is a fusion series of lenses similar to this chart. Figure 34 is a fission series of lenses that would correspond to the projected fission chart mentioned above as the opposite of this fusion chart.

The opposite mate to this fusion chart would have a thicker, more dense lens series around the center of the chart that would become thinner and less dense as the periphery is approached. Its center would be a blue hole in the process of being opened rather than being closed. The first centrifugal ring closest to the spherical center would be a yellow ring as in this fusion chart and then proceed outward in reverse color order to this fusion chart. Accordingly, the ring next to the yellow would be a red-violet ring followed by a red, then an orange, and finally a yellow ring blending with the female yellow ring. The succeeding feminine rings from green to blue to blue-violet would follow as the rings expand outward.

The color of the border depends on the view presented, either from the center looking out or the periphery looking inward. In this painting where the border is black, the view is from the periphery and represents the cold, dark, tenuous, formless beginnings of the cathode end. When viewed from the center looking outward along the journey from the hot, compressed, anode center, the border would be white or yellow to correspond to the intense coronal centrifugal discharge. I am unaware of any evidence in nature or in spectrum color science to support my ideas on the color reversal. We can feel the difference between a sunrise and a sunset. What exactly is the difference? Do the spectral colors differ? Refer to page 275 in *The Secret of Light* for more information on the color spectrum and the wave.

FIFTH SERIES. Diffraction Rings – Wave Patterns Series

Figure 38. Diffraction Wave Pattern on Equator of Lens

This chart is patterned on the equator of the wave sphere, a lens itself. There are also an infinite series of such lenses around the sphere, more or less off the equator of the wave-sphere lens, that illustrate the nature of the infinite regress of basic pattern in the Universe and the holographic nature of this basic pattern; they are not illustrated, but can be understood to exist as stated.

The harmonic periodicity of the universe is illustrated in the octave wave itself and the four locking points in the wave (four to maturity and four to dissolution); these are illustrated in the center of the large wave sphere. The large lens series shows two sets of nine compressing lenses on each side of a wave sphere.

Figure 38 illustrates all of these ideas in the integrating direction of life because every lens, lens series and wave sphere is shown in this chart as compressing, centripetally directed, winding up, convex, charging bodies and/or systems. The other half of the universal cycle, the dissolution or death series, is left for us to envision.

Insert A is a smaller version of the large wave sphere forming the background of the chart without the smaller spheres and lens detail. Insert B illustrates that the larger lens series is in effect the same as a single, convex, compression lens and that a single lens is made up of a series of such lenses. This visually illustrates the infinite regress of detail, the harmonic periodicity, and the holographic nature of the light wave universe for which Dr. Russell was the harbinger.

The significance of the red color for the convex lens series and smaller single lens may be to symbolize the generating, male, heating aspect of the lenses. This is an argument for deducing that he meant the lenses to be integrating even though he placed them on the equator where the disintegrating lenses are usually placed.

The barely visible small print in the upper left corner of the chart contains the following explanation by Dr. Russell:

> *Diffraction rings are wave spheres in action. They have an orderly rhythmic, mathematical and geometrical relation to the sphere, the cube and whatever lenses occur when light waves intersect. This diagram gives that mathematical relation. Insert A indicates a miniature of the large diagram within which a lens is drawn as shown in Insert B on small scale. The exact width of each white and dark space is thus determinable with mathematical precision. See Figure 7 for further detail of the law which determines diffraction ring dimensions.*

There is no certain record as to the identity of Figure 7, but I assume that he was referring to Figure 39, *Polarization and Fusion Foci. Diffraction Wave Pattern on Axis of Lens,* which I have placed next in this series.

This chart appears to refer to the pattern on the polar axis of the wave/lens/vortex, although Walter Russell says it is on the equator and not the polar axis. Perhaps he is considering that the pattern appears on the equator although the cathode light multiplying lenses constitute the polar axis of the wave after the equatorial expansion reverses to become the cathode axial compression.

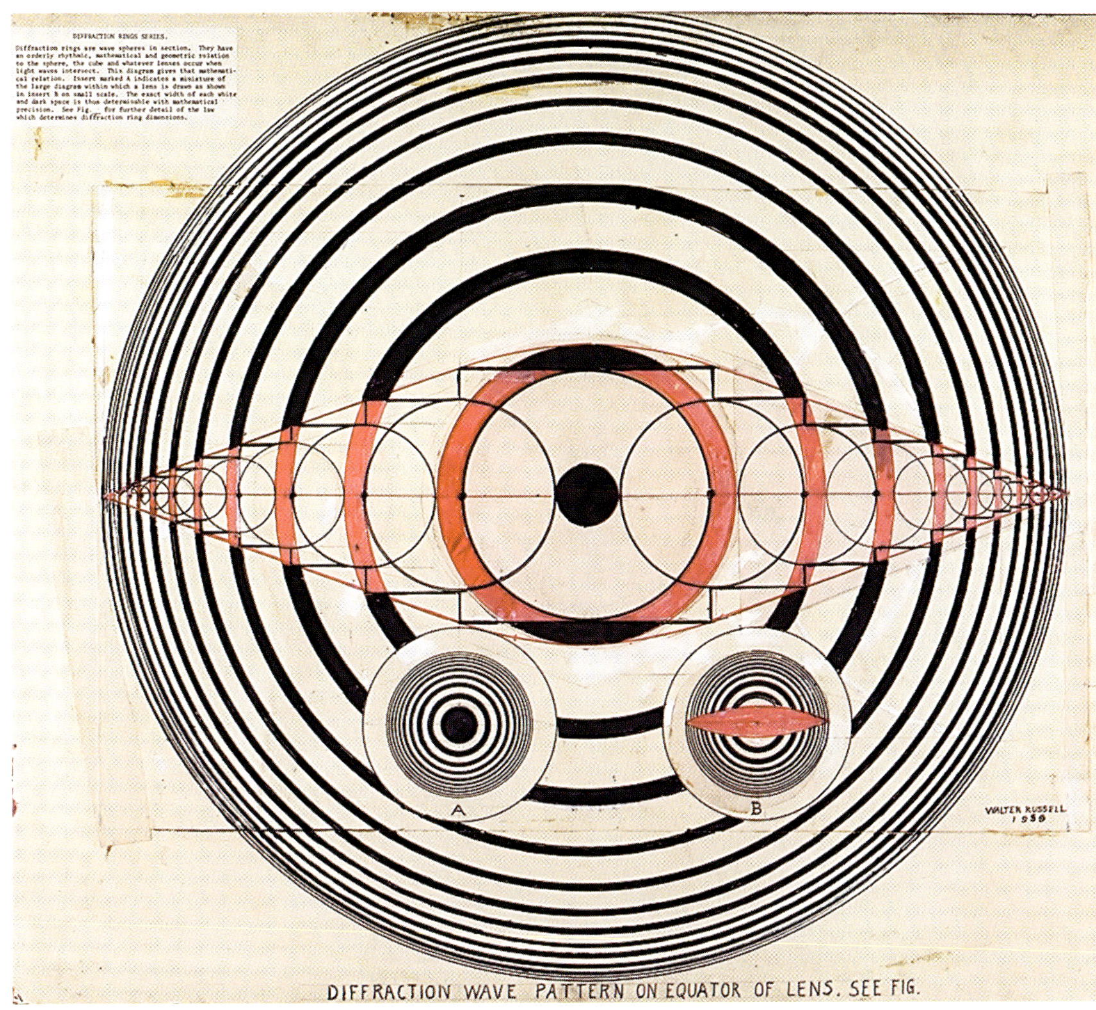

Figure 38

Completed in 1959 and not previously published.

Walter Russell refers to Figure 39 which follows as the "pattern on the axis of the lens" of the wave/ lens/vortex, which I understand to be the cathode light multiplying compression rings depicted in Figure 33. I believe these to be the same as the pattern on the axis in Figure 38. In either case, both Figures 38 and 39 are referring to the same whole-cycle gravity process in different parts of the wave. Thus it is likely that his reference to Figure 7 refers to Figure 39 in this book.

In Figure 39 it is clear that Dr. Russell has painted two sets of lenses compressing to meet at a fusion anode center. These are similar to Figure 33 except that the lenses are arranged so that they focus from two different cathodes and face each other toward a common center. In Figure 33, the lenses face away from each other and do not share a common focus at gravity maximum. Yet Figure 39 is similar to Figure 34 in the placement of lenses across the spheres. By expanding toward the periphery, the black and white rings in Figure 39 suggest expansion predominance.

Therefore I think there may be the possibility of confusion in this chart in that the lenses are labeled as on the equator, yet they are arranged as compressing lenses in Figure 33. The concentric circles appear as in the compressing series, so how can they be said to be on the equator when the multiplying lenses focus along the polar axis?

Perhaps the answer to this question is that Dr. Russell arranged the lenses on the equator only to show the mathematical ratio. If so, then he was not concerned with the relation of the lens pattern axis to the polar vortex axis. Since the wave is spherical, and assuming symmetry, the lens axis pattern can be rotated around any axis and still give an accurate view of the mathematical ratios. When interpreted in this way, Figure 35 also correlates well with Figures 37 and 42.

In this interpretation, this chart reveals spheres, with their cube wave field boundaries surrounding them, as wave systems that intersect and form lenses. In this case the lenses appear to be either an expansion or a compression series, although the insert marked B shows a convex compressing lens rather than a concave expansion lens. The width of each white and black space in the large circle and the smaller wave spheres does follow a mathematical formula related to the size of each cube/sphere and the lens angle. This formula is not specified; Dr. Russell simply noted that it must exist. I think the formula may be hidden within the lens pattern shown in this chart.

Figure 39. Polarization and Fusion Foci Diffraction Wave Pattern on Axis of Lens

These foci are at the center of each lens and at the center of the chart along the axial center around which all the lenses are focused. The diffraction wave patterns that form along the axis of the lens are illustrated as wave sphere circles with their field cube boundary walls. There are nine such convex lenses, cubes and spheres arranged in the centripetal, wind up, direction of multiplying compression and placed in collision juxtaposition to create a mature spherical lens wave sphere at the focal center of the chart.

It is noteworthy that Dr. Russell chose to illustrate these ideas in this chart as well as Figure 33, 34 and 38 with a nine-series lens system rather than the four series he used in Figure 35 which is how he usually spoke of the octave wave in relation to lenses. He usually stated that there are four steps coming in from each polarized male-female pair that unite at the amplitude position to make nine, yet here he used two sets of nine-steps lenses.

One possible explanation is that he chose to use nine polarized pairs to illustrate the infinite regress of pattern or the literal fact of infinite lenses within and without lenses that constitute this light wave universe of seeming motion. But if so, why nine? Nine is the number of divisions he gave to the universal octave wave which is thus the universal harmonic periodicity number for the most pronounced recognition of pattern reoccurence. Nine would thus be a good choice to illustrate the infinite regress of the basic harmonic pattern.

These series of lenses are arranged on the lens axis as stated by Dr. Russell; the lens axis is the center of the centripetal spiral to the center of focus where fusion is consummated. In the thermodynamic series, the lenses in both Figures 33 and 34 show an excess of four pairs of lenses. The only reason they might exceed four is again to suggest the infinite regress of wave pattern interferences. In other words, there is a literally an infinite regress of lenses within everything, although the biggest changes within the cycle and within any and all octaves still occurs in nine steps: four from birth to maturity, four from maturity to death, with the polarities sharing the central fourth step together.

There is a difference between the lens systems shown in Figures 33 and 34 and the one in this chart. Here the center lens series is arranged and shaped like the anode, light-dividing lens shown in Figure 34; yet it is titled *Polarization and Fusion Foci*, and the lenses are clearly convex, light-multiplying lenses. The light direction through this series of lenses is from outside both sides into the center of the sphere at the red center marked 9. The lens system in Figure 34 defocuses or divides light from the inside center to the outside of the chart through concave lenses.

The direction of light into a center or out from a center and the lens shape (convex or concave) is chart are clearly visible and even colored to emphasize them. Furthermore, Dr. Russell illustrated the convex series of lenses in Figure 33 as the two halves of the one large lens of Figure 39 placed pointing away from each other, cone base to cone base, rather than as in Figure 39 with the two halves placed pointing toward each other, cone apex to apex.

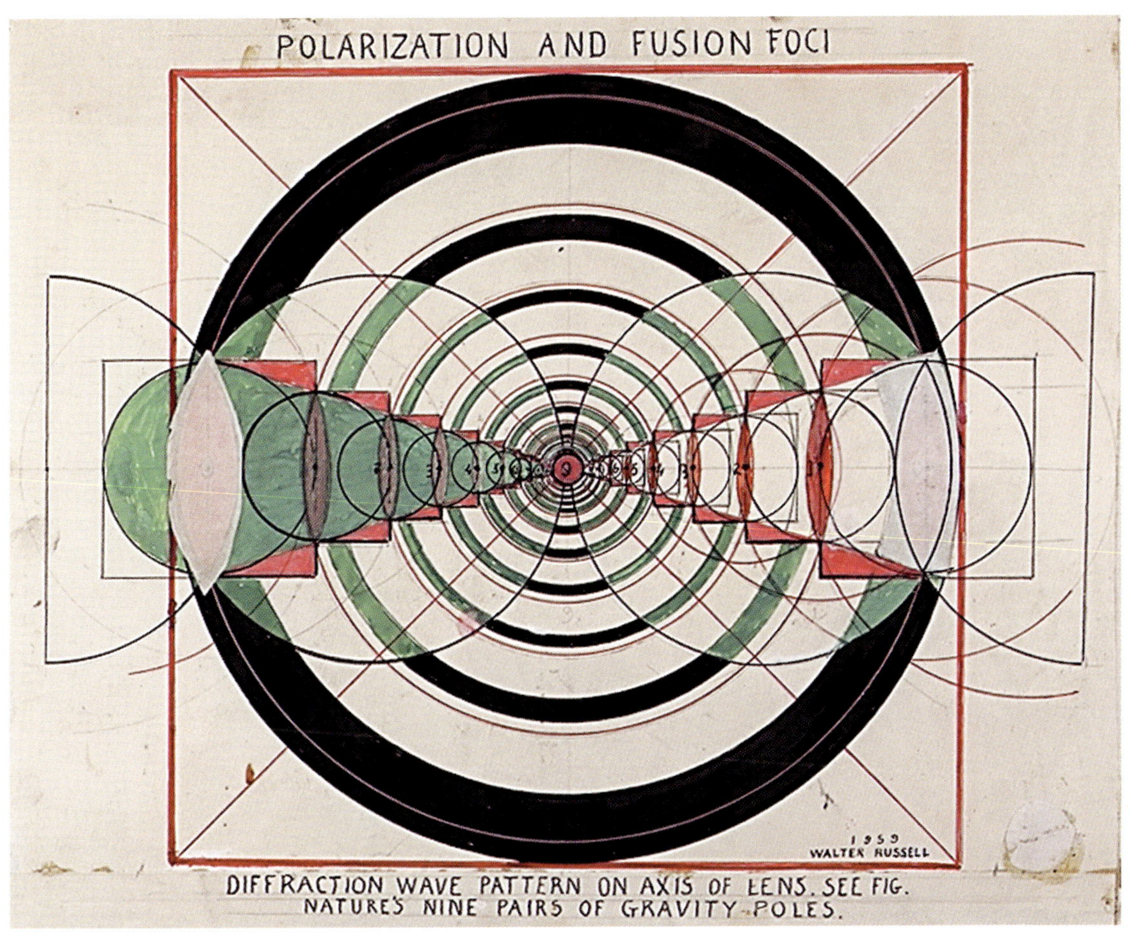

Figure 39

Undated. Not previously published.

crucial to understanding the lens' function and thus the meaning of these charts. The concave lenses within Figure 34 are not easily, clearly and uniformly visible within the one large concave lens across the chart center; although both are present, the concave predominates so they are only implied as imperfect concave lenses. This is further complicated by the fact that convex lenses within the one large concave lens across this center of the

The blessing in all of this is perhaps, as mentioned above, to see the infinite regress of detailed pattern and harmonic periodicity in all things in the Universe.

SIXTH SERIES. Solar Energy Series

Figure 40. Solar Energy Series, No. 1

This painting has four series of black convex lenses focusing from top and bottom and both sides to the center of the painting in centripetal cathode to anode multiplying systems. Although all cubes have six tetrahedrons, only four are visible in two-dimensional renditions. These four are distinguishable as triangles with their bases as the sides of the large cube. The other two tetrahedrons can be visualized by seeing the area of the cube these four form as the base of each of the other two tetrahedrons; the center of the painting is their apex. (Refer to Figure 18.)

The significance and symbolism of the colors in this chart elude my complete understanding other than Dr. Russell's typical usage of red or red-orange to signify the male spectral side and green the female. Black signifies the cathode with its formless, tenuous, beginning life stages, and the violet surrounding the central orange-red solid sphere signifies the female spectral color. There is a male to female alternating sequence from the outside to the center except that the last female green pattern is followed by another female violet pattern. The convex multiplying lens system illus-

Figure 40

Undated. Not previously published.

trated in the chart is black. Perhaps the color choice was simply artistic license.

Dr. Russell named this chart, *Solar Energy Series, No. 1*. Therefore, he must have felt that this figure had some significance in relation to his ideas on solar power production: arranging banks of convex lenses in direct square ratio and focusing them on a common point to superheat water to power steam turbines. I also see partially complete concave lenses between the convex lenses.

This chart suggests an arrangement where the banks of lenses are placed to correspond to the six tetrahedrons that unite their focus as One at the center of the system. This would be the most all-encompassing and powerful geometric placement possible to focus maximum light and heat to a central point whether the source were omnipresent — coming from all directions at once — or even intermittent, and granting that it was not possible or desirable to turn the lens bank to align with the source.

The question as to how any lens system can do more than focus the existing light and heat from any source to a focal point remains unanswered, although the Russells implied that it could and did do more. A convex lens simply focuses the light and heat from any source to a tighter focal point, so a series of lenses would appear to do no more. Or is there some other explanation not yet seen that would explain how such a series could multiply the total amount above the original source? Presently I see none.

Figure 41. The Earth's Gravity Field: Nature's Sex Principle

This painting of the earth and its gravity field shows the polar sex opposites with their respective color spectrums: blue-green female on the top and orange-red male on the bottom.

What is both curious and amazing about this painting is the way Dr. Russell has depicted the charging and discharging poles in relation to the rest of the field. This is the only instance where he used this type of illustration for the earth's gravity field. In every other case, both charging poles enter from opposite sides as head-on centripetal spirals directed toward each other with the discharging centrifugal spiral field exiting at planes of 90 degrees or less to the axis of the charging poles as it fans out to form the ecliptic plane. In this case he has a charging pole (here singular, where in all other instances there are two) on the red-orange male side and the discharging pole on the blue-green female side. See the following painting of the sun, Figure 42, as an example of his usual illustration of the male charge and the female discharge.

This painting emphasizes the polarity predominance of the male as charging or centripetally directed toward the center of the system and the female predominance as discharging or centrifugally directed toward the periphery of the system. It is much like his earlier descriptions in *The Universal One* where he identified female with discharge and male with charge more as pure types.

The painting is titled *The Earth's Gravity Field* and *Nature's Sex Principle*. As the title indicates, this painting symbolizes the essence of male and female as pure abstract types. In other words, this painting is unlike his other charts and paintings where the earth's field is accurately depicted with the two charging poles at the north and south polar caps and the discharging east-west poles at the equatorial expansion rim.

The Russell Cosmogony verifies that both charging and discharging poles have their opposite within them in varying degrees. The north and south poles have maximum charge and a minimum of discharge at the polar axis, while the equatorial rim east-west pole has maximum discharge and a minimum of charge. The incidence of the opposite force increases in proportion to the distance from the polar axis or equatorial rim.

In this illustration of abstract male and abstract female as pure types, Dr. Russell revealed the secret for a new transportation device or an

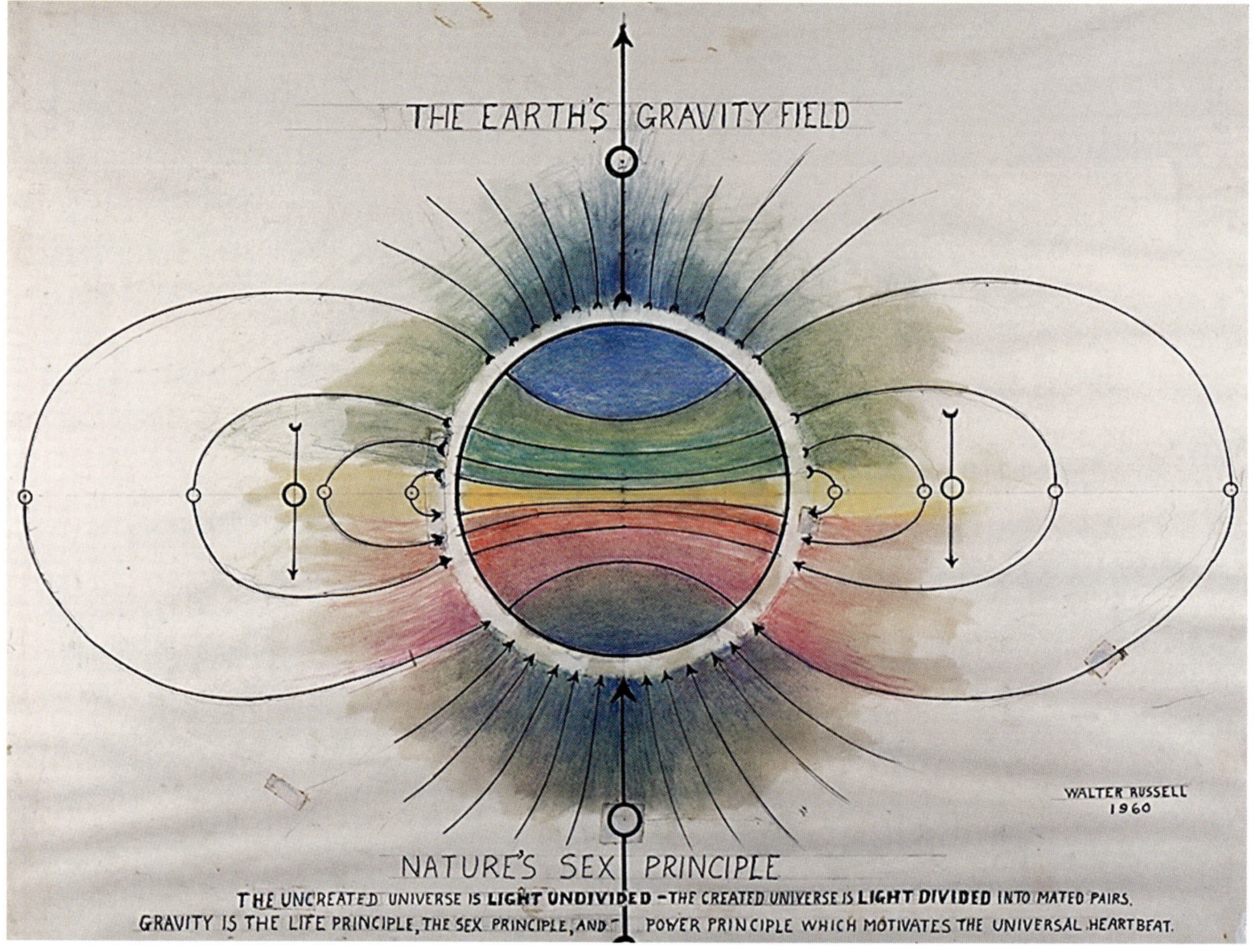

Figure 41 Undated. Not previously published.

engine. The net effect of polarizing the field of the earth or any body as shown is to move it through its surrounding medium in the direction of the arrows pointing to the top of the painting. This direction would be as close to linear as possible in a universe where there is no linear motion. The surrounding medium (water, air, even ether) moves in the direction of the downward pointing arrows. Acceleration in this abstraction approaches infinity.

In *The Secret of Light* Dr. Russell said,

> *The uncreated universe is light undivided.*

which could be symbolized by either a uniformly black or white canvas. Furthermore he said,

> *The created universe is light divided into mated pairs.*

This further draws our attention to the fact that he is symbolizing the "light divided into mated pairs" as pure abstract types.

His statement,

> *Gravity is the life principle, the sex principle, and the power principle which motivates the universal heartbeat.*

should alert us that Figure 41 is an abstract model for all engines and all transportation devices as well as the model for all motion. It is in essence a lever, albeit a continuous lever, in motion.

Walter Russell sculpts the figure of John Philip Sousa.
His busts of Mark Twain and Gabrilowitsch are on pedestals behind him.

Figure 42. Untitled

Figure 42 Undated. Not previously published.

In this painting, a sun, with its equatorial plane golden colored centrifugal coronal discharge fanning out from the equatorial rim and the dark blue polar caps centripetal polar charge converging inward toward the sun's golden boundary, vividly suggests the possibilities of new energy sources through understanding nature's winding and unwinding process. This painting corresponds more to an actual body and its field, be it atomic particle, earth or sun, whereas the preceding Figure 41 is an abstract symbolic painting illustrating the pure female and pure male polarities that exist in all physical bodies.

I find the simple beauty of this painting useful as an object of meditation first with eyes open and then later closed to concentrate the attention on the essence of the universal engine and its maker.

Figure 43. Untitled

Figure 43 illustrates a solar system or simply a sun viewed on edge. It shows the geometric and spectral color relationships between the two charging male and female poles and the discharging equatorial plane. The black space around the painting represents the vacuous state that balances the increasing compression toward the center of the colored portion of the painting with the maximum compression at the bright yellow colored center. The purple-violet color at the center of the expanding equatorial plane's centrifugal spiral represents the feminine characteristic of expansive preponderance beginnings.

The charging poles come into the solar center horizontally as the black vortexes. The discharge spirals out on each side of the center and reverses direction to reenter the system revealing predominately male or female preponderance by the spectral colors of red-violet for male and blue-violet to green for the female. The more vacuous blue is blended with the black surrounding both predominately male or female poles to demonstrate the tenuous cold beginnings of the journey toward greater compression, color and heat. The discharging equator is on edge and vertical with the male charging pole on the right and the female on the left.

Viewed as presented here or rotated 90 degrees, this painting resembles a UFO or flying saucer! Our solar system is such a flying machine as well.

Figure 43

Undated. Not previously published.

Figure 44. The Octave Spectrum Pairs of Sex-Divided Light

Figure 44 is similar to Figure 27 without the lenses explicitly drawn in. These are illustrated with different shades and tones merging into each other, although they still reveal their sex polarity unmistakably. The left side reveals feminine preponderance and the right male preponderance. The right male side has blue at its first octave position as well as infrared to red showing by the blue that this is the beginning stages of compression from the vacuous black of tenuous space toward the red-orange to yellow of compressed dense matter. The left feminine side has a hint of red-violet-yellow in its first octave position, illustrating that the female predominance has a bit of male in it and vice versa for the hint of blue on the side with male predominance.

The gyroscopic plane angle of rotation of the spectral colors, which is also the gyroscopic plane angle of rotation, and the elements within each of the nine octaves are illustrated. Each color is paired with its mate. These mates can easily be identified by the chart as the left and right numbers: their colors are corresponding mates. This chart can predict the color of any element by knowing its gyroscopic plane angle; likewise the plane angle can be predicted by knowing its color.

The significance of the small red circle in the upper left corner is unclear. It may simply represent the compressed hot anode surrounded by the black cathode of space. The small diagram on the upper right reiterates the four gyroscopic plane angles of rotation in male or female polarity in four steps on each side of the centering amplitude male-female balanced position.

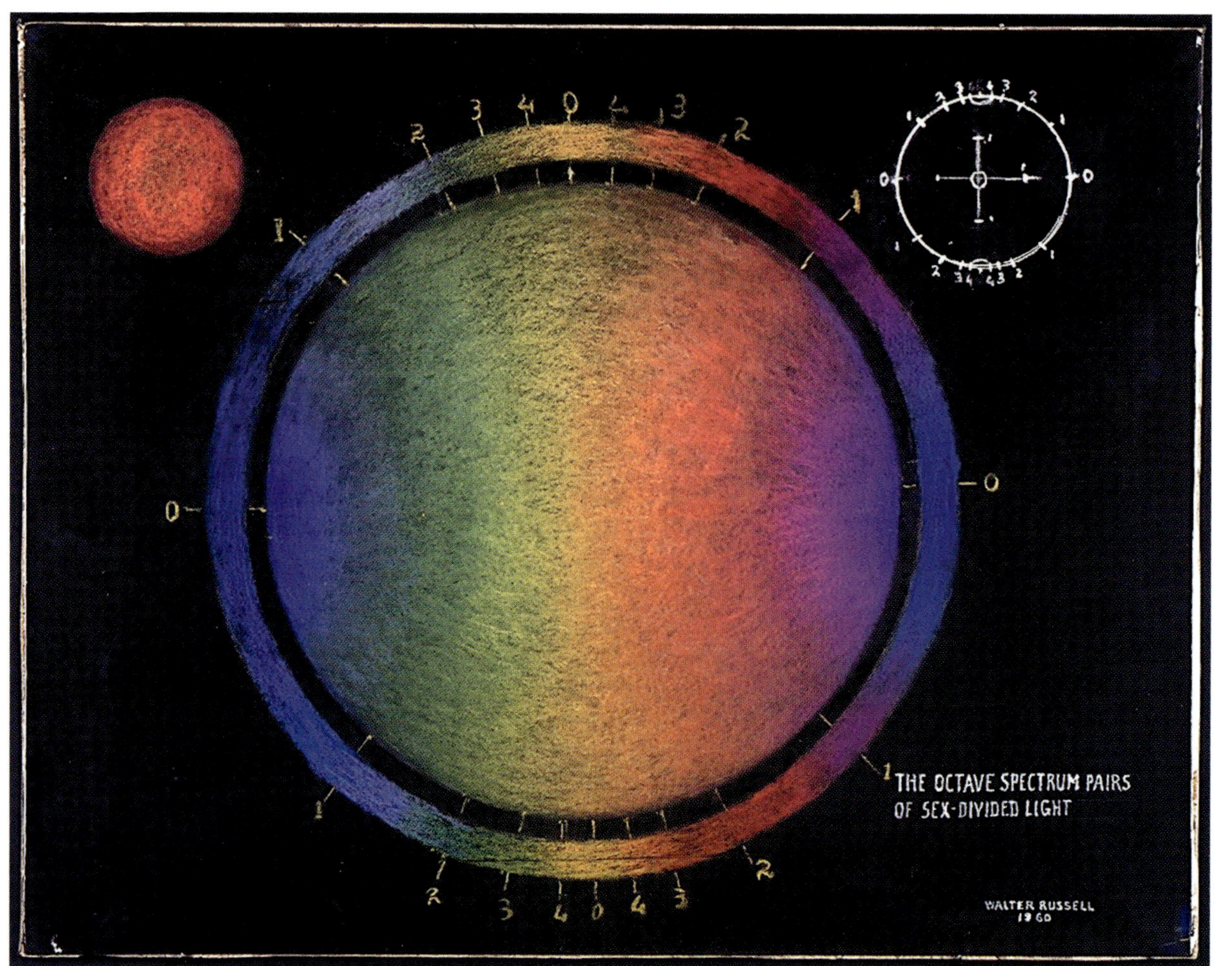

Figure 44

Completed in 1960 and not previously published.

Figure 45. Untitled

It is important to note the location of the gravitational center of the sun. We usually think of the sun existing separately from its wave field. Obviously the gravitational center is the sun center itself, and the sun in these paintings is found at the anode collision point between the two male-female wave systems. It is the small orange sphere on each side of the lower painting and in a similar position in the upper paintings. The blue-green cathode beginning represents the cathode as well as the vast blue emptiness surrounding the gravitational sun center of the system which is blue. Thus the cathode is one of the wave field cube boundary planes.

These painted charts reveal the spectrum lines in an octave wave (sun) system in their four-step tonal locking point positions in direct or inverse square ratio depending on whether the steps are toward the spherical compression anode center or toward the cubic expansion cathode boundary. The male spectrum the two wave systems are marked by vertical strokes. The cathode poles crossing the center line of the spherical wave pattern in the painting are at the cube wall boundary around the central anode sphere of a system; these walls are only shown as cathode pole lines colored light blue-green.

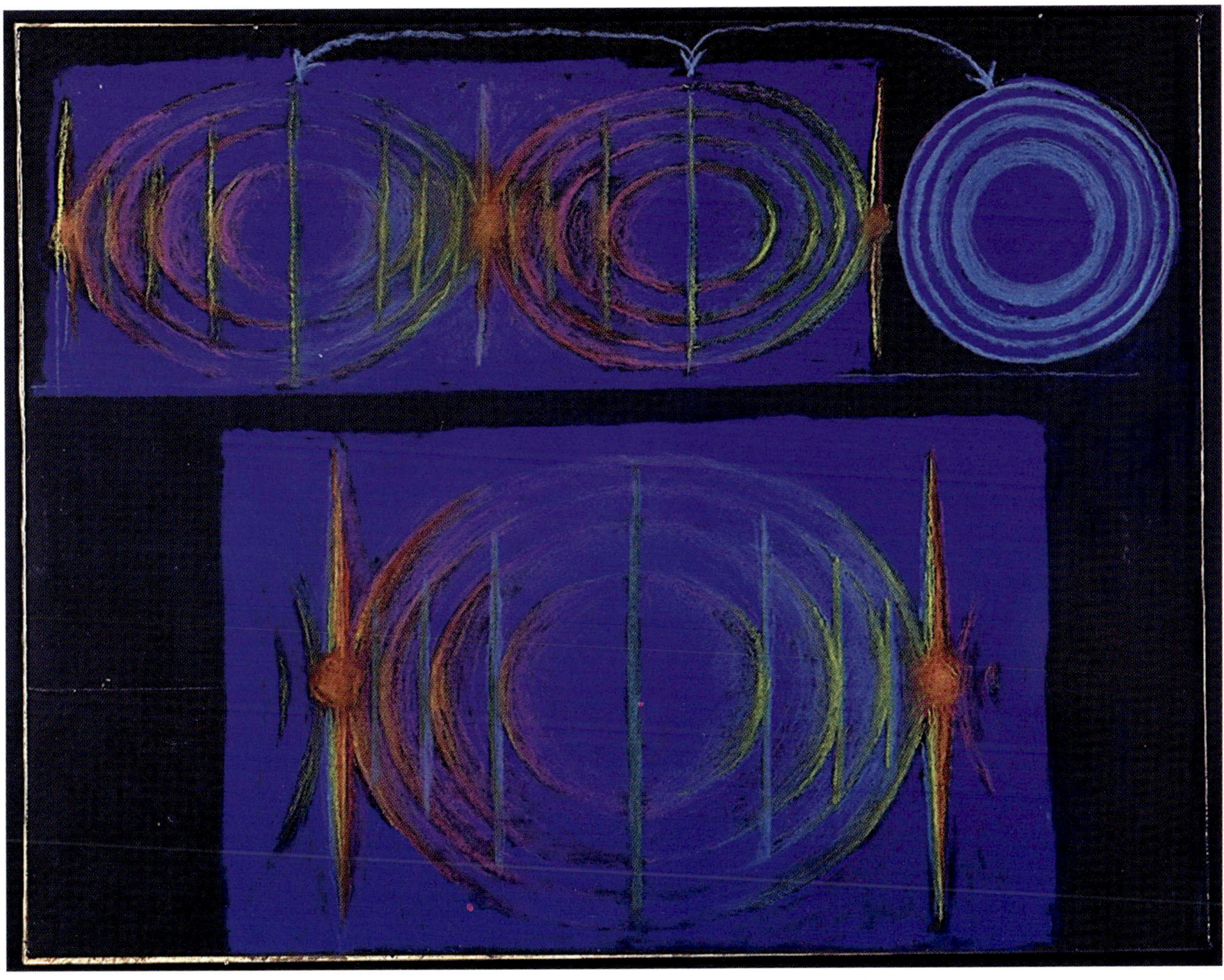

Figure 45

Undated. Not previously published.

appears on the left side of the spheres and the female on the right side.

Considered as such sexed pairs, the steps are only toward the compressed anode center and are in a direct square ratio. The four steps to union from the cathode poles in the center of the spheres to the anode pole point of collision at the field interface between

Viewed on end, the upper right spherical figure reveals the electric current flow and the wave cycle beginning from the cathode base compression cone. The arrows connecting it to the cathode bases (shown on edge) of the other two male-female spheres identify it as such. The lower large painting shows a single wave system which is the same as either of the two upper connected wave systems.

SEVENTH SERIES. The Life (Life and Death) Principle Series

Figure 46. Mechanics of the Universal Heartbeat. The Cathode. The Anode.

The cathode and anode ends of the octave wave are illustrated as four centripetal inward and four centrifugal outward projecting rings symbolizing the four octave wave locking point positions and associated elements and isotopes. The plane surface wave field cube boundary walls surrounding each element/system and inner cube dividing walls forming radar reflectors are also shown.

The cathode rings shown in the left painting contract and compress inward in ever increasing thickness and density toward the center with decreasing circumference. Space, as symbolized by circumference, is squeezed out of the ring and into the blue space surrounding the white rings.

The anode rings in the right painting are expanding outward in ever increasing thickness and circumference and less density. They symbolize space being sucked or pushed back into the ring and more space appearing in the space between the rings. Space decreases in the direction of compression and increases in the direction of expansion. Density increases in the direction of compression and decreases in the direction of expansion.

Figure 46 Undated. Not previously published.

Blue vacuous centers, as illustrated by the blue center of the left cathode chart, implode as matter is pushed into them from the outside or pulled in by the vacuum from the inside which is the same thing from a different point of view. Red-orange anodes, as illustrated in the right chart, explode as matter is pushed out of them from the inside by the relative pressure there, or sucked out of them from the outside by the relative vacuum there — again the exact same process by a different name and viewpoint.

The cathode is centered by space (a hole) and colored blue to symbolize its female preponderance that gravity in its inward-bound, centripetally-directed compressing phase is in the process of closing through compressing the rings into a tightly bound, hot, dense white (orange-red in this case) sphere that desires to escape its boundary by exploding to express formlessness. The anode is centered by this now well-matured hot sphere colored orange-red to symbolize its male compressive preponderance. Gravity in its outward-bound, centrifugally-directed expansive phase is in the process of opening up a hole from within this sphere by throwing off and expanding rings from the equatorial rim. Thus is the cycle again repeated of hole formation in solid spheres, a concomitant vacuum and the desire to again implode to express form.

While we see both of these as separate on a plane side view, Dr. Russell usually shows these as they exist in eternal embrace together at 90-degree angles to each other within the same whole compressing-expanding system eternally exchanging polarity and condition and, in so doing, becoming the other.

This chart reveals the essence of the Life Principle which includes both a coming-into-form phase, which we usually call life, and a going-into-formlessness phase, which we usually call death. In expressing this concept as *The Life Principle*, he called our attention to the fact that he used the word, "life", as a word with no opposite; that effectively makes it another word for God, a One word and a word of God.

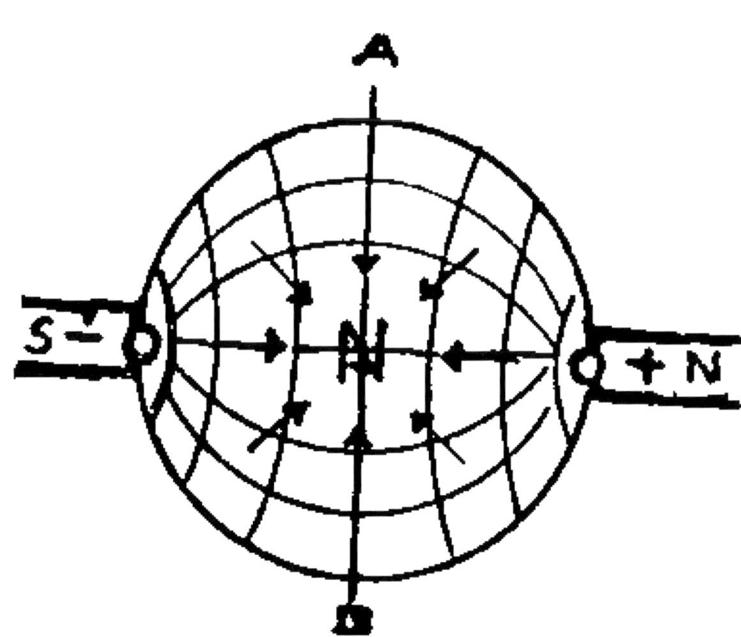

Figure 47. Untitled

This painting of a planet — perhaps earth and its moon with the beautiful blue and other octave wave spectral colors in the planet's wave field — reveals the spectrum colors of waves within waves in their octave tonal positions. The planet itself occupies the center anode collision point of the wave. This center point is the position of maximum density, heat and pressure. This center has the most yellow color, while the wave fields farther out have increasing blue color preponderance symbolizing the cold tenuous vacuity of space. Each step in the wave itself shows all the spectrum colors revealing waves within waves.

The small moon also reveals that it has its own octave wave of spectrum colors surrounding it in a barely visible similar fashion. The color progression is from the outside to inside, female to male.

Figure 47 Undated. Published as the cover of *The Immortality of Man*, 1991.

Figure 48. Untitled

In a cosmic sense, this painting illustrates the application of the Russell Cosmogony to biological systems and, since all systems are essentially the same, to biological, astronomical and atomic systems as well. In the upper scene the female seed on the left and the male seed on the right are mutually attracted toward union. The lower scene depicts the union of the two which will result in further division and then reunion and the growth of a biological system.

The spectrum colors identifying the sex are obvious: blue-green for the female and orange-red for the male. The center of both polarities is golden yellow. This reveals the intense hot compressed center of ning of life or the beginning of compression into form. In its beginning stages, any system or element is cold at the center, represented by a blue spectral color. This hole is the initial vacuum condition of birth toward which mass gravitates, thus creating the phenomenon of growth. Likewise, the hot periphery is colored golden yellow. It will be hot at the periphery or golden yellow fading to red and then green at the center. As

Figure 48

Undated. Not previously published.

their individual systems. That color with their other male or female spectral colors identifies their sex. Each system is the union of the male and female polarities into a unit and centered by yellow with a female or male preponderance signified by the other spectral female or male colors.

It is important to note that the blue center of the unit that is created out of their union represents the beginning

the system ages and closes the hole at the center, it becomes golden yellow at the center fading to red and green, and finally blue at the periphery. As it further ages, another hole is bored through the center, and the color spectrum, density and pressures reverse again. Aging produces a hole or rot at the center just as an old tree may rot in the center.

Figure 49. Nature's Method of Creating Power

The creation of power through octave wave compression is symbolized here. This chart illustrates the ever progressing density of matter throughout the entire nine-octave wave of creation of elements of matter from the first to the ninth octave. It also illustrates the

The reason for the yellow, red, blue, orange-red, orange, light blue or green, to orange colors is unclear. The colors seem to bear no symbolic meaning as Dr. Russell was accustomed to using them; here they seem to be used only to differentiate one cube from

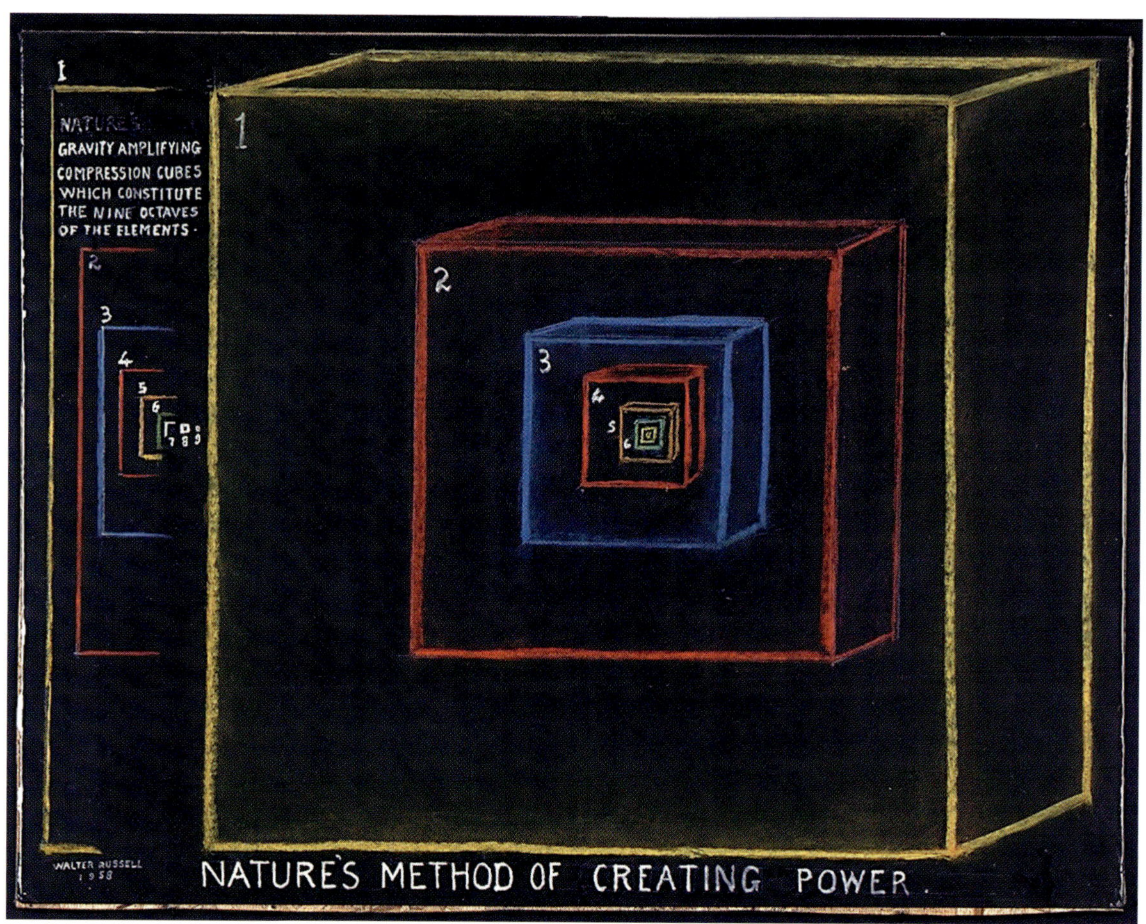

Figure 49 Completed in 1958 and previously published in *The Home Study Course* XI: 825.

wave field cube boundaries that keep the ever more densely compressed matter/motion in form.

The logarithmic ratio of ever increasing compression in ever smaller cubes in octave wave progression is illustrated in this figure. The length ratios are approximately 4:2:1:($\frac{1}{2}$):($\frac{1}{4}$): or a factor of 2. The volume ratios are 64:8:1:($\frac{1}{8}$):($\frac{1}{64}$) or a factor of 8. The pressure in each cube wave field/sphere is inversely related to the volume; the smaller the volume the greater the pressure and vice versa.

another or for the love of color. Comparing them to his usual symbolic meaning for the colors, they would suggest that the first octave step is one of overall sex balance, the second preponderantly male, then female, to male, to male, to female, to male, to male; the white on the left for the eighth and ninth octaves would then suggest overall balance. Since this analysis of color symbolism is not congruent with his cosmogony, I can only conclude it was artistic license and not a deliberate choice to illustrate a symbolic cosmological concept.

Figure 50. Untitled

This painting demonstrates the tornado or cyclone principle of winding light waves through a progressively compressing vortex into intense pressure at the apex. This is nature's method of creating power as detailed in the following chart.

It also demonstrates the creation of life and substance in biological systems as in the preceding chart. Living tissue is created in the same fashion as elements and tornadoes. As a physician I cannot help but notice the resemblance of this painting to the female uterus — the womb — and the beginnings of life.

In the womb the egg begins its descent from the fallopian tubes which are represented in this painting as the darkest blue tubes coming in from each side of the top to meet in the center. Then the egg descends down into the womb itself which is represented by the darkest blue tube down the center of the painting. The bottom end area around this lowest end of the tube could represent the cervix.

As a tornado or cyclone, the painting shows us a section through the funnel's structure revealing different pressure zones as represented by the coloring and size. Each side of the funnel section consists of male and female couplings as revealed by the colors: the blue-green on the inside being female and the red-orange being male. Their union is in the yellow area which is the area of greatest activity and pressure.

Since all things are created from such a union, this demonstrates very well the soft blood-filled inner tissues of the womb as feminine polarity and the more dense muscular outer structure of the womb as male polarity.

As a tornado or cyclone, the most intense activity is experienced in the yellow high pressure zone while the deepest blue center is a point approaching stillness.

The space around the outside of the tornado on the bottom part is a low-pressure zone represented by blues fading into green and yellow; these latter colors show a gradually increasing feminine pressure. The bottom border is ultraviolet which, by proximity to the yellow-green, suggests female polarity beginnings. The space on the top of the painting is ultraviolet with a hint of red suggesting male polarity beginnings.

This painting might aptly be titled *The Womb, The Cyclone, or The Origins Of Life.*

Figure 50 Undated. Not previously published.

Figure 51. Untitled

This painting symbolizes the ultimate expression of the death principle in the form of an atomic bomb explosion and might well be titled *Humanity at the Crossroads?* It reveals the unseen paired expansive counterpart to the familiar mushroom cloud issuing from the intense hot explosive center of expansion. This paired expansive counterpart is also visible in the crater left by the explosion.

Centripetal poles at the sides coming into the center are suggested in infant form by a dark blue color. The expansive centrifugal spiral poles are suggested by the dual mushroom clouds spiraling out from the explosive center of expansion. As the explosion progresses, the infant centripetal spirals gain strength as a vacuum replaces the intense outward radiative discharge.

The overall color of the painting is blue with violet suggesting the ultimate end of the expansion effect of the explosion, while the golden yellow and white illustrate the released heat from the radiative center.

Figure 51

Undated. Not previously published.

EIGHTH SERIES: The Enigma Series

Figures 52 and 53. Untitled

These two paintings and a penciled chart were left untitled by Dr. Russell. Figure 53 had the penciled drawing attached to it. I think that in Dr. Russell's mind there was some connection between these charts and the lenses that were part of the new solar optico dynamo generator he was working on at the end of his life.

The penciled drawing shows lenses arranged in four octave wave compression steps to the collision of union at the 4-0-4 position.

One important note in this drawing is that Dr. Russell appeared to have each lens focusing its apex in the center of the next lens, whereas in other instances it appeared that he may have had them all arranged to focus at the anode position.

Since at the time in his life when he did most of these painted charts he was also making his last efforts to demonstrate new energy sources, I think these charts should be studied for the possibility that they might reveal his thinking in this area. Accordingly, the four wave spheres may relate to the four poles and/or to the four-pole position of the electromagnetic fields for transmutation that Dr. Russell wrote about in *A New Concept of the Universe* and in *The Home Study Course.* On the other hand, if they relate to the solar optico dynamo generator, they might suggest an interpenetrating arrangement of a series of four such lenses.

The painting suggests four poles and/or four spheres or octave waves interfacing in a specific position. It reveals the wave interfaces within interfaces that result from this spatial arrangement. Some of these wave spheres show compression series of rings, as the four larger red spheres do in Figure 52, and some of them show expansion ring series, as do the smaller blue spheres within the red spheres. The large blue sphere encompassing all others in Figure 52 shows an expanding series from the center and a compressing series from the periphery.

There are cubes within cubes and spheres, and spheres

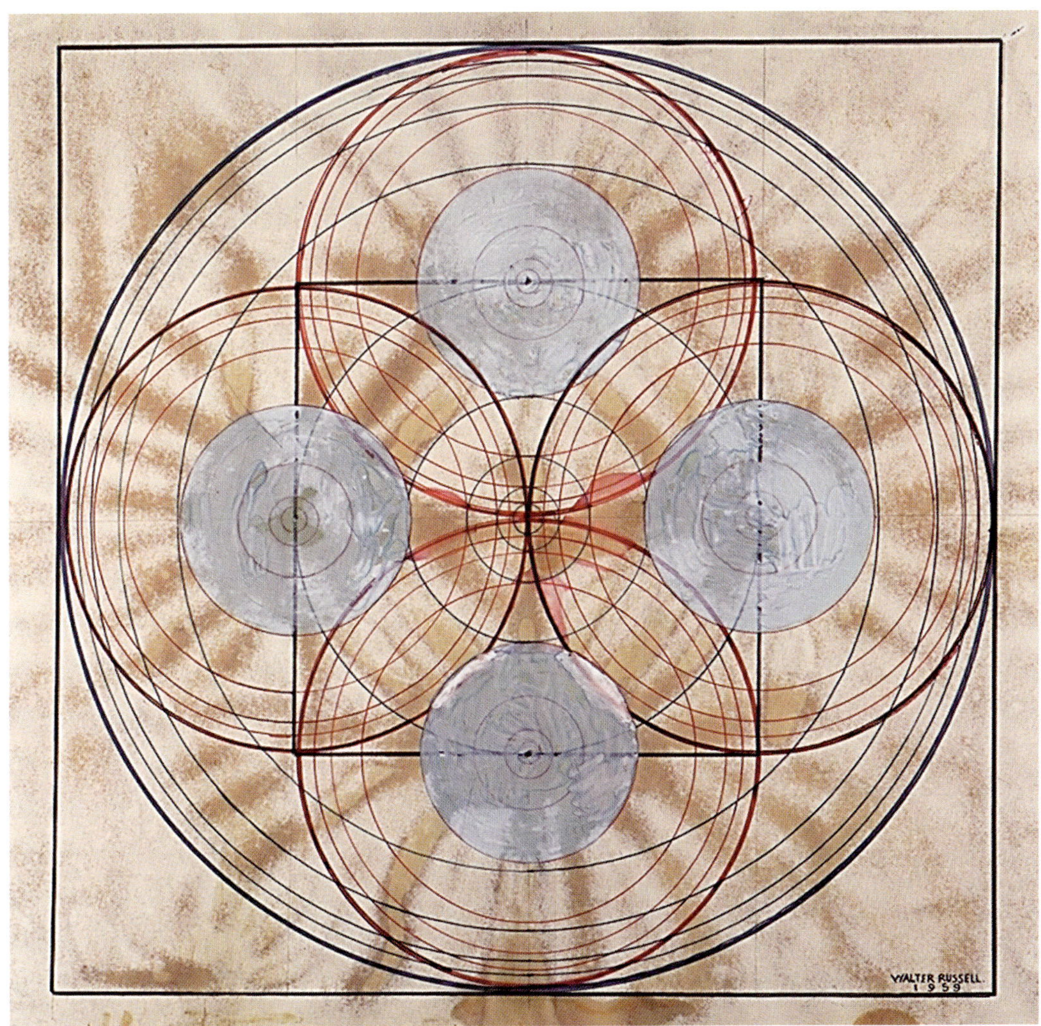

Figure 52

Completed in 1959. Not previously published.

within spheres and cubes. There are convex and concave lenses formed by the wave field interference patterns of the wave spheres.

Figure 52 has four convex lenses and two large concave lenses with a sphere in the center, all outlined in the four pole/sphere/wave field arrangement. The four small convex lenses are formed between the four blue spheres by the larger four red spheres interpenetration and interference pattern, while the two large concave lenses are found within the inner cube and formed by the interpenetration of the four red spheres.

The larger cube has a smaller cube within it. Its sides are formed by the lines passing through the centers of the four spheres. In the center of this smaller cube are smaller wave spheres. There are compression and expansion rings within the entire large sphere, within the four smaller spheres, and within their wave fields.

The second of the two charts, Figure 53, has two large convex lenses outlined in relation to the spheres and a cube bounding the entire painting as well as a cube at the center. Smaller convex lenses are suggested in the painting, some of them more heavily outlined within the small cube at the center of the painting.

The red, blue and black color choices appear to have the following symbolism: The small blue spheres are expanding lenses with the blue signifying the feminine expansive spectral color. The larger red spheres are compressive spheres which signify the male spectral color and function. The larger blue sphere, by virtue of its expanded form, correlates with the blue feminine spectral polarity even though it reveals both expansion and compression rings. The black lines for cube wave field boundary relate to the feminine principle.

These paintings bear a strong resemblance to various eastern and western mystical mandalas that have been used for meditation to accomplish specific ends. They are indeed mystifying, although I hope that perhaps some of their enigma has been clarified by virtue of being included in this volume of scientific charts and paintings and my attempt to fathom and describe some of their meaning.

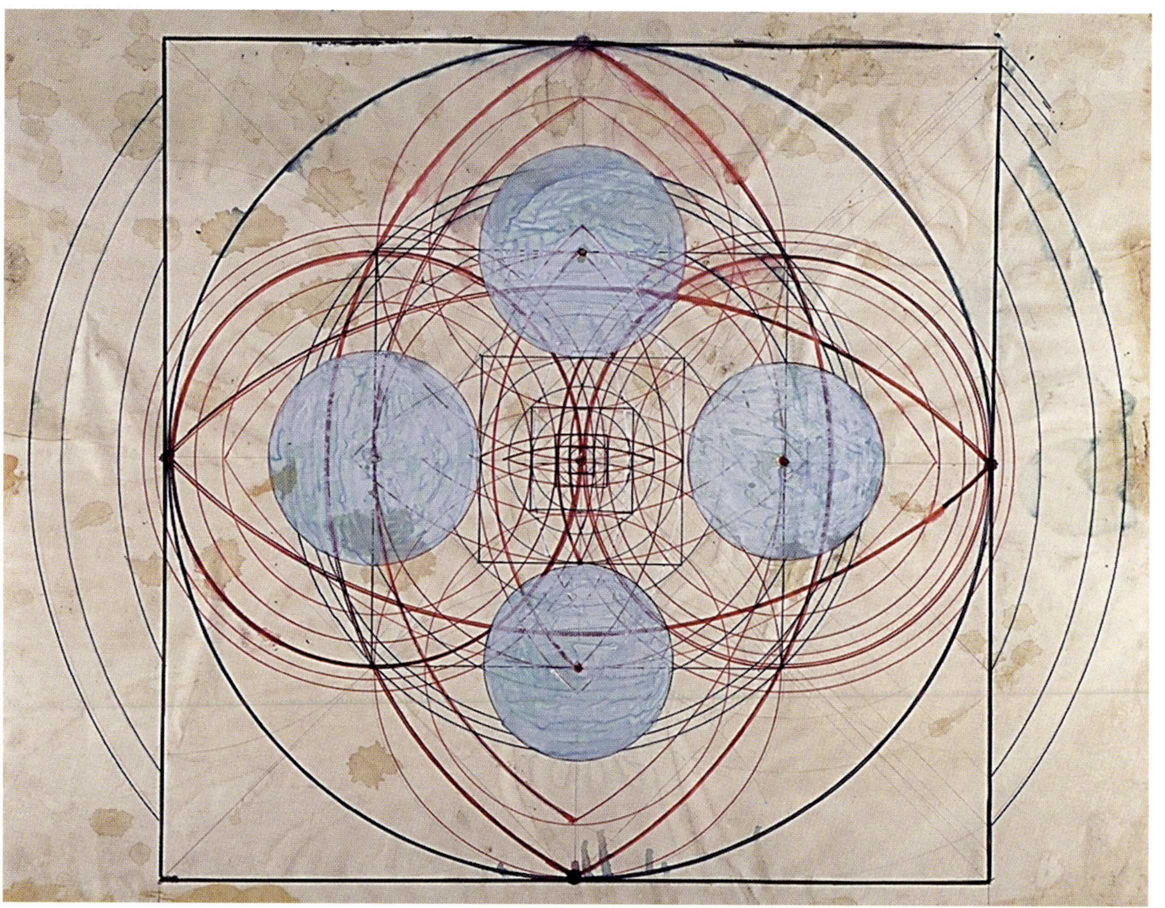

Figure 53

Completed in 1959 and not previously published.

These remain enigmatic paintings for me in that the ultimate significance and meaning that Dr. Russell conveyed through them escapes me. The mystery that they represent is sharpened by my conviction that they were meant to convey at least some of the secret of power multiplication production via the octave wave in the form of the solar optico dynamo generator for humanity's success.

NINTH SERIES: The Last Scientific Painting of Walter Russell

This pastel was discovered in the back of Dr. Russell's studio tacked up on an easel. It is a pastel of a vortex whirl as a model of the universe or of a solar, galactic or atomic system. It illustrates the two archetypal male and female polarities that result from the division of the One into the Many.

male principle. These two north and south poles are the charging poles of the vortex whirl system. The yellow-white equatorial ring shades into the respective color-identified sexed spectrums top and bottom. This ring symbolizes the discharging centrifugal spiral of both the male and female poles and is the position of the east-west pole.

Figures 54. Untitled

Figure 54 Undated. Not previously published.

The upper blue-green pole symbolizes the female principle; the lower red-violet pole symbolizes the At the center of union of the north and south poles and the focal center of the east-west pole is the anode center of the whirl. This is the place of intense activity simulating stillness, intense heat, light and pressure. This can symbolize the present in time. The spherical anode is colored half male and half female colors symbolizing their mutual and inescapable participation in the creation of anything from an atom, cell, animal, human being, planet, solar system, galaxy or the universe. God is both male and female.

The black border merging into purple-blue symbolizes the vacuous cold cathode of space that is the necessary opposite to the compressed anode material center. This is the region of the formless beginnings of all things, be they elements, plants, animals, or celestial systems.

Together these two north and south poles with their common east-west pole create the vortex whirl which is the ultimate model for the Universe in the Russell Cosmogony. All phenomena can be understood and explained through an understanding of this symbol.

Through this pastel painting, Dr. Russell reveals his vision of the Universe where the beginning and the ending are one and the same. This pastel summarizes the vision as: first the One, divided into the two, and the two divided into 10,000 things, *ad infinitum* then muliplied back into the One. The mechanism is hereby revealed.

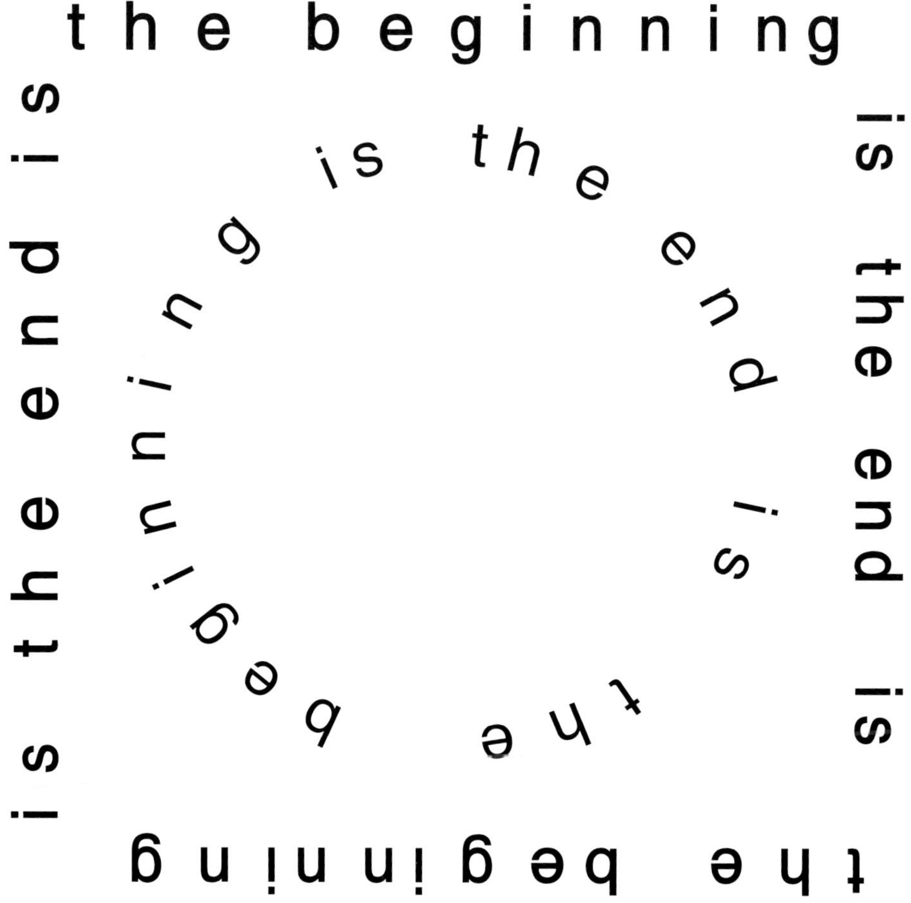

INDEX